ENGLISH DECLARATIONS OF INDULGENCE 1687 AND 1688

by

RICHARD E. BOYER

1968

MOUTON

THE HAGUE · PARIS

Printed in The Netherlands by Mouton & Co., Printers, The Hague.

FOR SHIRLEY

PREFACE

The history of religious controversy during the reigns of Charles II and James II is fascinating as well as important. The story of James' short reign and the subsequent Revolution has been told by several authors yet not one has focussed attention upon the most important immediate causes of the Revolution, namely, James' Declarations of Indulgence in 1687 and 1688.

Because in the twentieth century liberty of conscience is taken for granted it is hard to get excited over the right to worship as one pleases. The story was quite different in seventeenth century England. To most Englishmen the idea of liberty of conscience was unfamiliar. Anglicans, Nonconformists, and Roman Catholics alike denied the rights of conscience and the first two enforced conformity by political disabilities and legal penalties. The persecution of the Anglican clergy prior to 1660 must be taken into account before any judgment can be made concerning the Church's future policies. On both sides during the century men raised voices in favor of toleration, but that policy was discredited by its association with militarism, and by constant recourse to military force to establish and maintain it. It is rather paradoxical that the Stuarts, who lost a throne in 1649 partly because of religious intolerance, lost it later on through an attempt to introduce toleration.

The idea of all sections of Protestant Englishmen as to the lawfulness of coercion in matters of religion had been shaped by the habit of persecuting the Catholics, as the years of the "Popish Plot" bear out. The "Plot" while largely suppositious did contain many elements of fact.[1] The fear of Popery was very real to the Englishmen of 1680. There was, perhaps, nowhere in Europe during the last quarter of the

---

[1] Perhaps the best work on the Popish Plot is John Pollock's *The Popish Plot* (London; Duckworth and Co., 1903). While dated in some respects this work still covers the topic very thoroughly.

seventeenth century a group of people comparable, for boundless credulity, to the London populace. The political duplicity which had
boomed the fantastic imposture of Oates was at work again, and the
people who had so readily swallowed the line of Oates believed without hesitation that King James intended to bring over French troops
to convert his countrymen by force to popery. Among people naturally
credulous, who had been taught for generations that papists were
always ready to commit every sort of atrocity, it was easy to raise a
panic. The massacres in Ireland and the persecutions on the continent
afforded first hand proof to the Englishmen that their fears were
justified.

   The Declarations of Indulgence were the natural outcome of the
consistent policy of James to secure a toleration for Roman Catholics
and Dissenters. The confusion and contradiction which surround the
history of James II are largely owing to the rapid growth and almost
universal acceptance of a tradition hostile to James in order to justify
the expulsion of the Stuarts and fortify English loyalty to the Han-
overians. The most obvious reason for the success of this group was
its appeal to the prevailing prejudices against popery. Belief in the
wickedness of James would not have been so readily accepted without
proof by most Englishmen in the nineteenth century, had he not
been a papist. Macaulay was able to convince the Victorians that
King James was a "bloodthirsty tyrant." [2] Hazlitt wrote that "the people
of England lived in bodily fear of being executed as rebels or burnt
as heretics." [3] And even at the present day, distinguished writers
repeat the Whig doctrine that King James was conspiring against the
liberties of Englishmen and that he was cruel and intolerant by
nature.[4] The Whig tradition maintains that the attempt made by
James to secure, and to sanction by law, freedom of conscience for
all his subjects, was merely a decision to obtain relief for the Catholics;
and that his real objective was to destroy the Church of England. It
further maintains that fortunately, by the intervention of a man of real
honesty, a genuine upholder of liberty, and a man whose word could

[2]   Thomas Babington Macaulay, *The History of England From the Accession of
James II*, 2 Vols. (New York, Harper and Brothers, 1849).
[3]   P. P. Howe (ed.), *The Complete Works of William Hazlitt in Twenty One
Volumes*, XVI (London, J. M. Dent and Sons, Ltd., 1932).
[4]   David Ogg, *William III* (London, Collins, 1956); Winston S. Churchill, *Marl-
borough His Life and Times*, I (New York, Charles Scribner's Sons, 1950); Tresham
Lever, *Godolphin His Life and Times* (London, John Murray, 1952); Thomas C.
Nicholson, and S. A. Turberville, *Charles Talbot, Duke of Schrewsbury* (London,
Cambridge At The University Press, 1930).

be trusted, England was saved. The Whig hero, of course, is William
of Orange.

It would be tedious but instructive to make a complete list of the
writers, in England and in Scotland, who have helped to foster the
growth of the fictions first spread by Gilbert Burnet.[5] No one who
knew James well ever had any doubts about his early sincerity. Some
believed, many pretended to believe, that Popery and freedom of
conscience were incompatible. Burnet thought that the King had been
corrupted by Popery. Never did James cease in public and in private
to proclaim his adherence to the principle that conscience should be
free; he persecuted no man in Scotland or in England on account of
religion. The only charge which could be laid against him is one of
intention, a charge easier made than proved. The Whigs who say he
was not to be trusted, or that he was pretending in his religious
views, cannot explain why, at the most critical moment of his life,
when a gesture of duplicity might have avoided so much trouble, he
refused to make it against his conscience. The idea that a man, merely
for a principle would give up the throne, did not enter their minds.
The story of the supposititious Prince of Wales, while nearly failing
in its initial purpose, was probably the most flagrant example of the
early attempts to discredit James. After the arrival of William in England the pretext of the fraudulent birth was at once dropped.

What follows is not a history of the Revolution of 1688. Needless to
say, the problem of the Indulgences cannot be considered in a vacuum,
and in the course of any study concerning the period prior to 1688,
one has to take into account all the forces which influence the Revolution itself. Since it is my contention that the two Declarations were
primary causes of the Revolution, it will naturally follow that events
leading up as well as those subsequent to the Revolution must receive
proper emphasis. What follows also is not the history of James II.
Nevertheless King James as the creator of the Declarations must be
studied in some detail in order to ascertain his reasons for issuing
them. Moreover the very spirited contest between Catholic and
Protestant leading up to the issuance of the first Declaration of Indulgence requires attention; the story has been based upon contemporary pamphlets. To prove the evil of all "Popery", the truth or

[5] Gilbert Burnet, *Bishop Burnet's History of His Own Times,* III (Oxford,
Clarendon Press, 1832). Burnet, one of Charles II's most avid supporters, differed
with James over his pro-toleration policy and became the most famous of the
exiles at The Hague and outspoken critic of James.

falseness of transubstantiation or the Eucharist, and the pro's and
con's of an English or Latin mass, all assumed an important political
aspect in these years. To see a writer like John Dryden, a relative
novice in ecclesiastical controversy, try to match wits with Edward
Stillingfleet, a man whose entire life had been devoted to religious
argumentation, is fascinating. The Anglican side of the literary battle
had many experienced authors; but at times the Roman Catholics
seemed to win the majority of the ecclesiastical arguments.

In the pamphlets quoted the original spelling, punctuation, and
capitals have been followed; but the long s has been eliminated, j has
been used in place of i; w in place of uu; and v for u. All pamphlets
are published in London except where noted. Pamphleteering could
only flourish when printing, legal or illegal, was fairly easy. Probably
a slight flavor of illegality promoted the pamphlet. It will be seen
that many pamphlets are anonymous or were printed abroad and then
smuggled into England. This was normal in the seventeenth century
when most governments were both oppressive and inefficient. No one
in power would allow his adversaries a fair hearing but in a day of
inadequate police illegal literature circulated freely.

The Revolution of 1688 completed what the Civil War began: the
battle against prerogative was fought and won. The issue of sovereignity seemed to have been settled once and for all. With it disappeared the quarrel over finance which had vitalized politics since
1603. Kingship was appreciably changed when the king became the
state's best paid servant. The conception of the rights and duties of
the state for which Lord Strafford, adviser to Charles I, and many
before him had given their lives disappeared. The establishment of a
workable system of government and of essential political freedom,
was the supreme English achievement of the seventeenth century;
perhaps the most important in all English history.

TABLE OF CONTENTS

CHAPTER I

EARLY ATTEMPTS AT TOLERATION

Of the many problems which faced the restored monarchy in 1660 none was more complex, difficult, or pressing, than the settlement of the religious question. Every monarch since the Reformation had found that this question not only demanded deliberation and tact, but keen insight. Toleration was dismissed as not only unsafe but morally wrong; not even foreign Protestants located in England were allowed to worship in peace. But if the religious difficulty was at least a hundred years old, it had never been so pressing as at the Restoration. All sects then hoped, and with good grounds, for toleration. Yet, although men were weary of bitter strife, and fanaticism was generally distrusted, many Anglicans, who had suffered with and for Charles I, looked to his more fortunate son to make up for their sufferings. They had returned with memories of hardships endured in exile, and with deep seated prejudices. Presbyterians seemed ready to forego their own liberty rather than extend the same freedom to others.

Charles II, the man to whom all looked, was singularly ill-fitted for the task imposed upon him. Easygoing, he would certainly take the line of least resistance. On the whole, he disliked Presbyterianism owing to his experiences in Scotland, but was attracted to Roman Catholicism, and was not unwilling to redeem promises made to Roman Catholics. Of no religion, a so-called deist, he was, perhaps, genuinely desirous of seeing religious toleration granted to Protestant dissenters. He was certainly convinced that God would not damn a man for taking a little pleasure.

Charles' first expression on religious affairs appeared in his declaration issued at Breda on April 4, 1660.

Because the Passion and Uncharitableness of the Times have produced several Opinions in Religion by which men are engaged in Parties and Animosities against each other, which, when they shall hereafter unite in a Freedom of Conversation, will be composed, or better understood; we do declare a liberty to tender Consciences; and that no man shall be disquieted or called in question, for Differences of Opinion in Matters of Religion which do not disturb the Peace of the Kingdom; and that we shall be ready to consent to such an Act of Parliament, as, upon mature deliberation, shall be offered to us, for the full granting that Indulgence.[1]

The Declaration impressed all outside the Church as a distinct promise that all should enjoy complete religious liberty as far as the King could enforce it. Meanwhile Parliament had not been idle. On May 26, 1661, William Prynne, Presbyterian pamphleteer and member of Parliament reported an order "touching quieting Possessions of Ministers, Schoolmasters and other Ecclesiastical Persons in sequestered Livings until they are legally evicted". It was read and referred to a committee, which reported two days later, that "No person or Persons, Ecclesiastical or Temporal, should presume, indirectly or forcibly, to enter upon or disturb the said Possessions, or any other till the Parliament take Order therein or an Eviction be had by due Course of Law." [2]

With the aid and advice of Lord Clarendon, his Lord Chancellor, Charles promised the ministers that he would exercise his influence on their behalf. True to his promise, he informed the Council, probably on the following day, that he intended if it were at all feasible, to issue a declaration of indulgence, to all Protestant dissenters from the Church of England.[3] The scheme was opposed by Gilbert Sheldon, Bishop of London, who, with all the bishops in town, had been called to this meeting of the Council, although he was not yet a member. In bitter opposition to the King's proposal, he declared that if it were carried his position would be rendered intolerable, for he had not only turned out the non-subscribers, but had already filled their places. He had even affronted some noblemen by over-riding the rights of patrons. Sheldon carried his point; the Council refused to abandon this policy.[4]

If the Council would not give its consent, then Charles would ignore the Council. With the help of his immediate circle of friends, primarily advised by Clarendon and Henry Bennet, Secretary of State, Charles prepared a declaration of indulgence. Clarendon, confined to his room by the gout at Worcester House, read the declaration once or twice, suggested alterations, and approved of it, though he warned

[1] Charles II, *Declaration of Breda* (London, 1660), 2.
[2] *Journal of the House of Commons*, VIII (London, Printed by the Order of the House of Commons), 47.
[3] *Ibid.*, 49.
[4] *Great Britain, Public Record Office, Calendar of State Papers Domestic, 1663-1664* (London, His Majesty's Stationary Office, 1906), 65.

Bennet that by the time he had written as many declarations as Clarendon himself had done, he would find that they were a very "ticklish commodity".[5]

Charles now brought forward his intended declaration. Clarendon sent a copy to three dissenting divines, Edmund Calamy, Edward Reynolds, and Richard Baxter, on September 4th, "With Liberty to give notice what they liked not." They presented their exceptions which were chiefly the work of Baxter, and at Worcester House on October 22nd Charles met with his council and representatives of Anglicans and Presbyterians to consider its final form.[6] After reading a petition from the Independents and Anabaptists pleading for freedom of worship, Clarendon suggested the addition to the declaration of a clause to the effect "that others also be permitted to meet for religious worship, so be it they not do it at the disturbance of the Peace."[7] All saw too clearly the studied vagueness of "others": they read the King's intentions to secure freedom of worship for Roman Catholics. This document which is called, rather misleadingly, the first Declaration of Indulgence, was drafted by Clarendon, and made public on December 26, 1662.[8]

Once again the King promised to move Parliament to grant religious freedom, this time not to Protestant Nonconformists alone, but to Roman Catholics as well. The Declaration was not intended as a permanent settlement; it was to hold good only until a synod of divines could be called. In it the King only declared that his residence abroad enabled him to testify to the approval by foreign divines of the Church of England. The purpose of the Declaration as one finds it stated therein, was to reassure "His Majesty's loving and dutiful subjects" on four points. First, he determined to uphold the Act of Indemnity, an act passed by the Convention Parliament in 1660 which offered pardon and indemnity to all political offenders — the Regicides excepted — for acts committed between 1642 and 1660. Secondly, he abhorred rule by military force. Thirdly, he intended, now that the uniformity of the Church had been established by his care, to carry out the Declaration of Breda in the point of relief to tender consciences.

[5] T. H. Lister, *Life and Administration of Edward, first Earl of Clarendon*, III (London, Longman, Orme, Brown, Green and Longmans, 1838), 233.
[6] *Life of Reverend Richard Baxter* (New York, American Tract Society, n.d.), 62-63.
[7] Lister, *Clarendon*, III, 110.
[8] Charles II, *His Majesty's Declaration to All His Loving Subjects* (London, 1662).

We shall make it our special care so far forth as in us lies, without in-
vading the Freedom of Parliament, to incline their Wisdom at this next
approaching Sessions, to concur with Us in the making some such Act
that purpose, as may enable us to exercise with a more universal satisfaction, that Power of Dispensing which We conceive to be inherent in Us.
Nor can we doubt of their cheerful cooperating with Us in a thing wherein
We do conceive Ourselves so far engaged, both in Honour, and in what
We owe to the Peace of Our Dominions . . .[9]

Lastly, while denying all charges of his inclinations toward popery,
and professing approval of laws intended to hinder the spread of that
doctrine, he admitted his dislike of the sanguinary laws against
Catholics, and avowed:

We shall with as much freedom profess unto the world, that it is not in
Our intention to allude Our Roman Catholic Subjects . . . from all share
in the benefit of such an Act, as in pursuance of Our Promises, the wisdom of Our Parliament shall think fit to offer unto Us for the ease of
tender Conscience.[10]

From all quarters there arose a cry of No Popery! No Popery! Nonconformists themselves were half inclined to add their voices to the
clamor. Charles, suspecting that an open attempt to indulge Roman
Catholics would have this effect, tried to conciliate the leading Nonconformist divines. Bishop Sheldon, who had previously disapproved
of any declaration, now begged the King to "take into your consideration, what the Act is, next what the Consequences may be. By your
Act you labour to set up that most damnable and heretical Doctrine of
the Church of Rome, whore of Babylon." [11]

The fate of the Declaration lay, by its own admission, in the hands
of Parliament, which reconvened on February 18, 1663. The Court
had made great efforts to secure a favorable majority in the Commons,
calling on all members upon whom it could rely, to attend, and flattering the men to whom the house was most willing to listen.[12] The
speech from the throne referred confidently to the Declaration and
explained that its purpose was not to grant a toleration to Catholics,
nor to enable them to hold office.

If the dissenters will demean themselves peaceably and modestly under
the Government, I could heartily wish I had such power of indulgence,

[9]   *Ibid.*, 8.
[10]   *Ibid.*, 10.
[11]   Gilbert Sheldon, *Fair Warning or XXV Reasons Against Toleration and Indulgence of Property* (London, 1663).
[12]   Frank Bate, *The Declaration of Indulgence 1672* (London, University of
Liverpool Press, 1908), 38.

to use upon occasions, as might not needlessly force them out of the Kingdom, or staying here, give them cause to conspire against the peace of it.[13]

Both dissenters and Catholics wondered how their status was affected by this announcement. Clearly Bennet had not departed from the opinion he had previously expressed to the King, that mitigation of the act was not safely within the scope of the prerogative.[14] On the other hand, the King asserted that the power of dispensing lay inherent in him, but to exercise it he must be enabled by an act of Parliament. Until Parliament should meet, therefore, the Act of Uniformity remained intact. Clarendon's plan, as opposed to Bennet's, was more direct and immediate; he would have the King suspend the Act of Uniformity prior to its execution date. Why, then, was the Declaration put forth at all? Why did not Charles wait until he could address both Houses in a speech from the throne? Ostensibly of course, to smooth the present unrest by promising a remedy, but really to make that promise so overt that Parliament must feel engaged to fulfil it, unless the Houses were prepared to hazard a quarrel with the King.

In the House of Lords, the Duke of York introduced a bill to give the effect of law to the late Declaration by enabling the King to dispense with the Act of Uniformity.[15] Read for the first time, February 23, it passed various stages, and was committed to a committee of the whole two days later. Not content with throwing out the bill, the Commons remonstrated against the policy set forth both in the declaration and in the speech from the throne, protesting "that it was in no sort advisable that there be any indulgence to such persons who presume to dissent from the Act of Uniformity by and from the religion established".[16] The Commons believed that the Court would not have used so much ingenuity in any but a very bad cause. If the King wished to relieve the Catholics as a reward for their fidelity, why did he not say so openly? What dark purpose of betraying England to popery might not underlie the subtlety of this proceeding? In their vote of thanks the Commons accepted that portion of the King's speech which dealt with the Declaration; then they drew up an address

[13] *Journal of the House of Lords, Beginning Anno Primo Jacobi Secundi*, XIV (London, 1685), 478.
[14] Violet Barbour, *Henry Bennet, Earl of Arlington* (Washington, American Historical Association, 1914), 60.
[15] *Historical Manuscripts Commission*, 8th Report (London, George Eyre and William Spottiswoode, 1881), 167.
[16] *Journal of the House of Commons*, VIII, 443.

wherein it was pointed out that the sovereign had not the right to invalidate a law to which he had signified his assent, and that the indulgence which he wished to exercise would establish schism by law, and destroy the public peace.[17]

An address, following up this remonstrance, prayed the King to lay aside that extreme indulgence which had brought into England so many Romish priests and Jesuits, and recommended that all such persons quit the Kingdom within a certain brief time.[18] An exception, introduced by the consent of Parliament itself, in favor of the priests attached to the service of the two queens and of the ambassadors from Catholic powers, neutralized the whole measure for a host of English priests remained under shelter of this exception.[19]

Though the action of Parliament voided the King's Declaration, the knowledge that Charles was himself averse to persecution had some effect. Generally speaking, there was less suffering during the succeeding year, except in the metropolis, where Sir John Robinson had succeeded to the mayorality in October 1662. No one should conclude, however, that because Charles released a few Quakers from prison, and because some justices refused to convict, that persecutions ceased. Certain bishops and justices carried on a relentless crusade against nonconformity of every kind. Mobs spoiled and carried away goods, and broke many windows.[20] Nonconformists abstaining from attendance at church were fined 12d a Sunday.[21]

It was clear why the expected vote of supply by Parliament was delayed and would continue to be delayed as long as Charles stuck by his Declaration. Few if any of the pamphleteers thoroughly understood the absolute dependence of Charles for money grants upon Parliament, or the bigoted episcopalian spirit of the Commons. By March 5th the Queen Mother, Bristol and others of the Roman Catholic party decided that further efforts in behalf of legal indulgence would be futile and result in persecution for their friends. Charles saw also that he must yield, and so, on the 16th of March made answer to the address that though he found what he had said not well understood, he would not continue the argument.[22]

17 *Ibid.*
18 *Ibid.*, 444.
19 *Ibid.*, 445.
20 *Calendar State Papers Domestic, 1663-1664,* 10, 31, 50.
21 *Ibid.*, 337.
22 William Cobbett, *Parliamentary History of England from the Norman Conquest in 1066 to the Year 1803,* IV (London, 1806), 260-263.

Even while these paper settlements were being made and solutions offered, Parliament was debating a measure against conventicles beyond all moderation. By the series of acts erroneously known as the Clarendon Code, commencing in 1661 and ending in 1665, nonconformity, hitherto unrecognized by law, became a political and constitutional fact. The first Act, the Corporation Act (1661) required all persons holding municipal office to renounce the Covenant — a test which excluded many of the Presbyterians; to take an oath of non-resistance — a test which excluded Republicans; and to take the sacrament according to the rites of the Church of England — a test which excluded Roman Catholics.[23] Thus the effect of the Act was to limit municipal office to Royalist Anglicans. The second Act, the Act of Uniformity (1662) called for mandatory assent and consent to the Book of Common Prayer.[24] The third Act, the Conventicle Act (1664), was intended to prevent the dissenters from preaching to unauthorized congregations of their own.[25] Thus matters stood when, in March, 1665, England entered upon a war against Holland. Now, if at any time, the Commons might have been expected to see the advisability of granting some measure of toleration in order to secure a united front against a powerful foe. Unfortunately many of the sterner Nonconformists were more than suspected of sympathy with the Dutch, and of hopes that Holland would give them help in altering the form of government either to a Republic or to a Protectorate. These hopes were fostered too by those English refugees living in Holland who still kept up communication with their party at home. Consequently, the war led not to amelioration, but to the adoption of further precautionary measures to check the spirit of disaffection which was widely diffused, especially in the West of England. The final act, the Five Mile Act (1665), forbade ejected clergy to "come within five miles of any city, borough, or corporate town, or of any parish or place where they had preached in a conventicle or had had regular care of souls." [26]

From 1665 through 1670 persecution declined appreciably, perhaps

[23] 13 Car II, c. 1, Reprinted in Grant Robertson (ed.), *Select Statutes Cases and Documents* (London, Metheun and Co., 1909), 54-57.
[24] 14 Car II, c. 4, Reprinted in Grant Robertson (ed.), *Select Statutes Cases and Documents*, 37-53.
[25] 16 Car II, c. 4, Reprinted in Grant Robertson (ed.), *Select Statutes Cases and Documents*, 70.
[26] 17 Car II, c. 2, Reprinted in Grant Robertson (ed.), *Select Statutes Cases and Documents*, 67-70.

increasing again a little as a result of the terror and suspicion connected with the terrible plague of 1665, and with the London Fire.
The fire, regarded by fanatics as another example of God's heavy
wrath and indignation against a godless city, was in reality a blessing
in disguise, sweeping away those germs of disease which still clung
to the city. Nonconformists, Papists, and foreigners, all fell under
suspicion. Few Englishmen were sensible enough to see that the
fire was mere accident. Generally speaking, during the decade
following the failure of the 1662 Indulgence, Nonconformists were
generally unmolested as long as Parliament was not sitting. Whenever
conventiclers appeared before the Council to answer for their mis-
deeds, they often escaped with no more than a reprimand or fine.[27]
Nonconformists must have recognized that they would not be allowed
to escape for any length of time, however, as the question of supply
was always pressing. Parliament had the upperhand; it controlled the
purse. Consequently, from May, 1670 to April, 1671, that is to say,
while Parliament sat, dissenters in England suffered as perhaps they
had never suffered before. Trained bands and the military were called
out to break up meetings; in London, at least, blood was shed.[28] A
good example of this persecution was the trial of William Penn and
William Mead in 1670, on a charge of conspiracy to address a tumul-
tous assembly.[29] The case needs no comment, other than to say that
it was one of the most disgraceful exhibitions of injustice ever known
in an English court. The jury was fined for not bringing in the verdict
desired by the Judge, but despite the bitterness of the persecution,
the end was not achieved.

Early in 1671, rumors circulated that proposals for liberty of worship were being again discussed. No such proposal had been made,
but many about the court were urging the King to grant toleration by
the exercise of his prerogative. Through his secret Treaty of Dover
with France in 1670, Charles had sufficient money to enable him to
dispense with Parliamentary aid.[30] He would now ignore Parliament
and gain his end by proclamation. By December those close to the

[27] Edward M. Thompson (ed.), *Correspondence of the Family of Hatton,* I (London, Camden Society, Nichols and Sons, 1878), 58.
[28] *Ibid.*
[29] *Great Britain, Public Record Office, Calendar State Papers Domestic, 1670*
(London, His Majesty's Stationary Office, 1908), 440; Bayly T. Howell, *State
Trials,* XII (London, T. C. Hansard, 1810), 951-999.
[30] Charles Bastide, *The Anglo-French Entente in the Seventeenth Century*
(London, John Lane, n.d.), 67-73.

King took for granted that a declaration of indulgence was imminent. Sir Joseph Williamson, Charles' secretary, was so convinced on this point that he proceeded to lay down the principles that must govern its construction. He wrote that, "as to all consolidation let the rule be as wide as may be, and then a provision for liberty to all Dissenters under certain incapacities. ... This is to be first framed by the King with all secrecy, upon feeling of the pulses of all parties."[31] The secrecy was well maintained. The Kings Gracious Declaration of Indulgence was issued on March 15, 1672. Seemingly the work of a few days, the Declaration was based upon the experiences of almost a decade.

The Declaration itself was liberal and politic in its provisions. In being free from compulsory oaths, it was much more liberal than dissenters had either hoped for or expected. The Declaration is important enough to quote from at some length. It was primarily concerned with three issues. The first one concerned the Church of England:

And in the first place, we declare our express Resolution, Meaning and Intention to be, that the Church of England be preserved, and remain Entire in its Doctrine, Discipline and Government, as now it stands Established by law: and that this be taken to be, as it is, the basis, Rule, and Standard of the General and Public Worship of God, and that the Orthodox Conformable clergy to Receive and enjoy the Revenues belonging thereunto.[32]

Perhaps the most important provision pertained to the Nonconformists. Charles states thus:

We do in the next place Declare Our Will and Pleasure to be, That the execution of all, and all manner of Penal Laws in matters Ecclesiastical against whatsoever sort of Nonconformists or Recusants; be immediately suspended, and they are hereby suspended.

And that there may be no pretence, for any of our Subjects to continue their illegal Meetings and Conventicles; we do declare; That we shall from time to time allow a sufficient number of Places, as they shall be deserved, in all parts of this our Kingdom, for the use of such as do not Conform to the Church of England; to meet and assemble in; in order to their Publick worship and Devotion; which Places shall be open and free to all persons.[33]

[31] *Great Britain, Public Record Office, Calendar State Papers Domestic, 1671-1672* (London, His Majesty's Stationary Office, 1912), 44-46.
[32] Charles II, *His Majesty's Declaration to All His Loving Subjects* (London, 1672), 5.
[33] *Ibid.*, 5-6.

Very wisely the Declaration finally contained provisions for Parliamentary control.

But to prevent such disorder and inconveniences as may happen by this our Indulgence, if not wisely regulated, and that they may be better protected by the Civil Magistrate, our express will and Pleasure is, That none of our Subjects, do presume to meet in any Place, until such Places be allowed, and the Teacher of that Congregation be approved by us.

And lest any should apprehend, that this restriction should make Our said allowance and Approbation difficult to obtain; we do further Declare, That this our Indulgence, as to the allowances of the Publick Places of Worship, and approbation of the Teachers, shall extend to all sorts of Nonconformists and Recusants, except the Recusants of the Roman Catholic Religion, to whom we shall in no wise allow publick Places of Worship, but only Indulge them their share in the common exemption from the Execution of the Penal Laws, and the Exercise of their Worship in their primate Houses only.[34]

The restriction imposed in the shape of license seemed necessary if the government expected to protect itself against the abuse of private conventicles for the hatching and maturing of plots. The licenses granted were of three kinds. First, the license allowing the use of a particular building as a meeting place for Nonconformists. To preachers licenses of two kinds were issued; one to "Teachers in general and at large"; otherwise, to itinerant preachers who went from town to town staying a night here and perhaps a week there. The holder of a license of either kind could preach in any licensed building.[35]

Though not a final solution to the standing problems of a hundred years, it was a distinct advance in the mutual relations of religious sects: dissenters won a security not hitherto experienced. But there was a more serious objection to the Declaration which Charles would have to face. Without the consent of Parliament he had suspended penal statutes in matters ecclesiastical. The supreme power of the sovereign had certainly never been strictly defined. As a result they had used the right in moderation; consequently, prior to the Stuarts, it had rarely been questioned. But at the beginning of the seventeenth century, politics in England were undergoing a decided change; the theory of government began to receive a vast amount of attention. It was with no little anxiety that Charles and his Cabal waited to see how the Declaration would be received.

The independents experienced doubts as to whether they should

[34]   *Ibid.,* 7.
[35]   *Calendar State Papers Domestic, 1671-1672,* 10, 17.

accept the provisions of the Declaration and return thanks to the King. They could see that the toleration therein granted rested on but a slender basis. Moreover, they queried, was it right and expedient to use a toleration which was extended to Roman Catholics, whom they hated and feared as greatly as did the bishops? The Catholics on the other hand, were overjoyed. For neither of these sects was there any possibility of comprehension within the national church. All that they could expect — toleration — was granted them there; they had no reason to refuse it. As usual, pamphleteers devoted page upon page to the discussion. Probably the best known were, Francis Fulwood's *Toleration Not to Be Abused*, 1672, and the anonymous pamphlet entitled, *Indulgence to Dissenters in Religion by Suspended Penal Laws in matters Ecclesiastical is Destructive both to Church and State*, 1673.

Nonconformists were not permitted to enjoy their new found liberty in complete security. They were surrounded by enemies who were prevented from continuing their persecuting efforts only because they feared the displeasure of Charles. Many of the bishops and clergy made no attempt to conceal their bitter hostility.[36] Informers, too, saw a lucrative profession slipping from their fingers if the penal laws were to remain in abeyance. All these were on the alert to catch Nonconformists transgressing but they complained that they were severely handicapped by the vagueness and generality of the Declaration.[37] Conforming clergy always had it in their power to harass Nonconformists by demanding from them church dues. Thus, for a brief period of twelve months the struggle went on. Nonconformists precariously enjoying their comparative freedom, their opponents for the most part jealously watching for opportunities to distress and annoy them. Few Nonconformists paused to wonder what the end would be, although many were aware of the slender foundation upon which their indulgence rested. Of those who did give it a moment's consideration, some thought a severe tax would be imposed by Parliament upon licensed persons and places.[38]

Unlike his father and his brother, Charles II could recognize revolution in the making. Unlike them, also, he had no deep convictions either religious or political. Upon one point he was determined: he would never set out again upon his travels. His character calls

[36] *Ibid.,* 457.
[37] *Ibid.,* 536.
[38] Henry W. Clark, *History of English Nonconformity, II* (London, Chapman and Hall, Ltd., 1913, 83.

forth no admiration, but at least it saved him from the disasters which overwhelmed Charles I and James II. In this case he knew that further remonstrance to the Commons would be worse than useless. Unwilling yet to acknowledge complete defeat, he sought the advice of his cabinet. The accounts of this council are somewhat conflicting. Burnet's version, colored perhaps by personal animosities, reveals three members of the Cabal deliberately plotting against the state.[39] Charles' minister, George Villiers, second Duke of Buckingham, advised that the army should be brought within striking distance of London, that refractory members should be expelled from both houses of Parliament, and that the conduct of affairs be entrusted to those favorable to the crown. Thomas Clifford, the Duke of Lauderdale, who had in 1663 raised in Scotland an army of 22,000 men, pledged to "march whither the king should desire it", mentioned the possibility of thus intimidating Parliament into submission. According to Burnet, Clifford also urged the king to presevere: the people could already see through his designs, so that he must make himself master at once or be henceforth subject to suspicion and contempt. Charles himself, with too much tact to act upon advice so reckless, inclined to the advice of Lord Shaftesbury and Henry Bennet, now Earl of Arlington, that Parliament should be appeased.

When King Charles issued his Declaration of Indulgence in 1672, the amount of liberty he provided for tender conscience was not excessive. The measure allowed freedom of worship to papists in their own houses, and to nonconformists in their own chapels, which had to be licensed for that purpose by the government. Charles proposed, in fact, to control Nonconformity with a system of supervision similar to that employed by modern governments to control smuggling. The House of Commons refused to sanction the Kings Declaration on the questionable grounds "that penal statutes in matters ecclesiastical could not be suspended, but by consent of Parliament".[40] The King was compelled to yield to the opposition, and on Friday March 7, 1673, he broke the Great Seal of his Declaration for Liberty of Conscience.[41]

His measure had failed, as it was bound to fail. He had underestimated the strength of the feeling against Roman Catholicism, and against the exercise by the King of his so-called prerogative. To the

---

[39]   Burnet, *Own Times*, II, 11.
[40]   *Journal of the House of Commons*, IX, 261.
[41]   *Great Britain, Public Record Office, Calendar State Papers Domestic, 1673* (London, His Majesty's Stationary Office, 1914), 24.

Commons the constitutional aspect of the Declaration appealed most strongly. Had the Declaration been issued by a sovereign whose protestantism was beyond doubt, it might have received a favorable reception. Yet, had Charles confined the benefits of the Indulgence to Protestant Nonconformists, the measure might still have been challenged. It is ironical that, perhaps, only for one purpose would the King have been allowed to exercise the rights he claimed: little or no objection would have been raised had he issued a proclamation increasing the severity of the laws against Roman Catholics.

The failure of the Indulgence is generally attributed to the efforts of the bishops and of the Court Party. The bishops certainly rejoiced that it failed. This brief session of Parliament had seen the failure of Charles' supreme effort to secure toleration for Roman Catholics and for Protestant dissenters. The Commons had asserted emphatically the constitutional maxim of legislation only by King in Parliament. The Commons had won for the nation another victory on behalf of Parliamentary legislation.

The Declaration had been cancelled, but the licenses were not yet recalled. It remained to be seen how the action taken by the Commons would affect Protestant Nonconformists. Some had continued their preaching arguing that since the Commons had proved themselves willing to grant toleration, no encouragement would be given to those who endeavored to prosecute or persecute them.[42] Unfortunately, the hope was vain. The clergy and the church wardens, country justices, constables and informers returned with fresh zeal to their cowardly and hateful work; [43] and those who, for a few months at least, had enjoyed the sweet taste of liberty, were to be persecuted more harshly than before.. Informers after a few years enforced idleness, were only too ready to ply their former trade. It was lucrative; it was easy. Many of the Anglican clergy had with difficulty endured the events of the past twelve months. To certain of their number it was very difficult to know that at the very hour when they were holding divine service, dissenting ministers were preaching and administering the Sacraments to congregations which were increasing daily. Other clergy there were, who, while in no way inclined to the kind of persecution which had prevailed since the Restoration, yet deplored the prevalence of sects, and longed for the union and uniformity of Christians. To such, Charles' withdrawal of the Declaration must have been welcome.

42   *Ibid.*, 101.
43   *Ibid.*, 613.

Many justices and ministers in persecuting and harassing Nonconformists, were running considerable risk of incurring the royal displeasure. In June 13, 1673, the justices of Oxfordshire were called
before the Council to give answer concerning an order made by them
at the quarter sessions, in which they declared that the penal laws
against Nonconformists were still in force because the King had no
power to suspend them.[44] The Lord Chancellor at the King's command, told them that Charles was convinced of their loyalty and
affection, but it were better for them hence forward to leave affairs
of state alone.

Largely as a result of the Treaty of Dover with France and some
other commercial aspects, England became involved in a war with
Holland. The Commons voted the money for the third Dutch war, but
they also imposed a restriction upon Charles which was very hard
indeed. They passed the Test Act.[45] By this Act every holder of any
civil or military office was to take the sacrament of the Lords Supper
according to the Church of England. They also had to take an oath
against transubstantiation, which would exclude all Roman Catholics,
and also to take the oaths of supremacy and allegiance to the State.
The most important consequence of this Act was the resignation of
the Duke of York, the future James II, from the Admiralty.

By the end of the Dutch war, Charles was gradually abandoning
the policy which had led to his numerous attempts at toleration.
Shaftesbury had been dismissed from office in November 1673, and
the King was drifting into an alliance with Sir Thomas Osborne,
created Earl of Danby in June 1674. The Anglican party, supporting
Danby, had formed an alliance which necessarily involved the strict
enforcement of uniformity in religion and no toleration either for
Roman Catholics or for Protestant dissenters. Hence it is not surprising
that in October 1674, for the first time during his reign, Charles summoned the bishops to give him advice.[46] Hitherto all such conferences
had been composed of dissenters as well as Conformists.

The Declaration of Indulgence and the licenses it had created were
things of the past; but not even the King could stay the movements
recently started. The Declaration was the culmination of a series of
efforts on the part of Charles to keep the promises made in the

[44] *Ibid.*, 369.
[45] Andrew Browning (ed.), *English Historical Documents, 1660-1714* (New York,
Oxford University Press, 1953, 389-391.
[46] *Great Britain, Public Record Office, Calendar State Papers Domestic, 1673-
1675* (London, His Majesty's Stationary Office, 1914), 390, 551.

Declaration of Breda; and though he failed to win Parliamentary approval for the policy, its results were permanent and certainly gave precedents to the actions of James II fifteen years later. The two or three years breathing space the Declaration had assured, gave the nonconformists an opportunity to organize and recover the ground they had lost during the period of persecution. Subsequently they were too strong for the repressive measures to be successful in putting them down. A vast number of dissenting congregations, existing even to this day, date their formation and continuous life from Charles II's Declaration of Indulgence.[47]

Had Charles been as religious as his brother, he was yet far too shrewd and too indolent to dream of entering upon a scheme which he well knew must involve him in a conflict from which he could not escape unharmed. He was thoroughly aware of the nation's deep rooted hostility to Roman Catholics and their creed: he was not ignorant of the history of his father's career. Unlike his father, he had sufficient imagination to enable him to estimate the effect that would be produced on the minds and temper of his people, were he to attempt anything so contrary to national sentiment. True, had he declared his own conversion, his position as supreme head of the English church would have been a questionable one. But Charles never seriously contemplated such a move.

The chances of toleration grew less and less as the year 1678 grew near. Never before, or since fortunately, did the country react to evidence largely based on supposititious findings. The credulity of the English populace was never so evident as during the years of the "Popish Plot." With the 1680's the hysteria died down and the people seemed to come to their senses. Titus Oates had been descredited, but much damage was already done. Toleration for Catholics or Dissenters was definitely out of the question.

The problem of toleration, therefore, at the accession of King James II, was an issue which appealed to the interest of a large minority of the population, probably one-fifth, or at least one-sixth, who could not conscientiously accept the State Religion.[48] This minority had suffered for twenty years the oppression of unjust laws, and was practically deprived of all its rights of citizenship; King James was determined with or without the consent of Parliament to put a stop to the scandal.

[47]   Bate, *Declaration of Indulgence (1672)*, 142.
[48]   Malcom V. Hay, *The Enigma of James II* (London, Sands and Co., 1936), 69.

CHAPTER II

THE MONMOUTH EPISODE

The death of Charles and the accession of James marked no deep transition in English political history. James, though his Catholicism would always be a hindrance and though he was known to be a sharp authoritarian man, had certain claims in the nation's esteem. He stood for authority and a firm hand. Though never popular, James in 1685 was in a strong position. With the help of the Tory Party and the Church he had triumphed over the Whig attempt to exclude him from the throne. More important, the English people felt that he was the lawful heir, in spite of his popery, and were for the time being content.

A few days after James accession, he had taken the initiative in calling the Archbishop of Canterbury and the Bishop of London to a private audience.[1] A frank discussion of the King's position as a Roman Catholic sovereign in a Protestant country would undoubtedly have been helpful, but the conversation, unfortunately, was disappointing to both parties. At the same time that James expressed his hope that churches might be full, he stated that there must be no preaching against Roman Catholicism; this was the first intimation of the coming storm. The following week James had instructions printed and addressed to William Sancroft, Archbishop of Canterbury, forbidding Anglican clergy to discuss controversial points of doctrine from the pulpits.

And whereas also sundry young Divines, and Preachers, either out of a spirit of Contention and contradiction, or in a vain ostentation of their Learning, take upon them in their Popular Sermons, to handle the deep Points of Gods Eternal Councils and Decrees, or to meddle with the Affairs of State and Government, or to wrangel about forms and gestures and other fruitless Disputes and Controversies . . . We out of Our princely care . . . by these Our Special Letters strictly Charge and Command you,

[1] Edward Carpenter, *The Protestant Bishop* (London, Longmans, Green and Co., 1956), 80.

to use your utmost Care and Diligence that these Directions which upon long and serious Consideration have approved and caused to be printed.[2]

James' most strenuous defenders admit that he was a poor judge of men; that he supplemented this constitutional disability by refusing to employ in the highest offices of state anyone who did not at least pretend wholeheartedly to support his policy. As a result he retained is his service two able but unscrupulous men: Robert Spencer, Lord Sunderland, and Lord Jeffreys, together with the three Catholic Lords who had been acquitted of complicity in the Popish Plot, Lord Arundell of Wardout, Lord Belasyse and the Marquis of Powis, men of good character, but all three well past the ordinary age of retirement. Lord Arundell was nearly eighty in 1685, and among them only Belasyse, who was an invalid, had more than moderate ability.

Immediately after Charles' death the chief ministers were Lord Guilford, Lord Keeper; Lord Rochester, Lord President of the Council; Lord Halifax, Lord Privy Seal; Lord Sunderland, Principal Secretary of State; and Lord Godolphin, First Commissioner of the Treasury. Both Godolphin and Sunderland had been Exclusionists but both seemed ready to switch to any side. Here, in fact, lay the future rift in the Cabinet, for it was eventually discovered that Sunderland received pensions from both King Louis XIV of France and James.[3]

The majority of the ministry was retained, but a few changes were made at James accession. Henry, Earl of Clarendon, Rochester's elder brother, displaced Halifax as Lord Privy Seal, and Halifax succeeded Rochester as Lord President of the Council — a position of dignity, but without great influence. The second Earl of Clarendon was a man about whom his contemporaries held conflicting opinions; he was a great friend of the bishops and a consistent royalist and Churchman; after the Revolution he was among the very few prominent men who refused to take the oaths of allegiance to William and Mary in 1689. Rochester moved up to become Lord Treasurer. The choice of Rochester was indeed not merely a compliment to the Tories, but has to be taken as part and parcel of James' early policy — to win liberty of conscience for his co-religionists through the agency of the

[2] James II, *Instructions to Ministers, To the Most Reverend Fathers in God, William Lord Archbishop of Canterbury, Primate of all England and Metropolis, and John Lord Archbishop of York* (London, 1685).
[3] Charles James Fox, *A History of the Early Part of the Reign of James the Second* (London, William Miller, 1808), Appendix, XXV, LXIV, CV.

Established Church.[4] His, he explained, to Barillon, must be a gradual process, but he looked on the dissenters as republicans, whereas many Anglicans seemed to him unconscious Catholics, who might be won without difficulty to the faith.[5]

In one very important matter James lost no time. He had for nine years been a Papist recusant and for thirteen years it had been known that he had absented himself from public celebration of the Sacrament. Suspicions that James was a Catholic had arisen not long after the Restoration and by the time of the Popish Plot had grown into a certainty in the public mind; it was only in deference to Charles' wishes that he had refrained from an open declaration of adherence to the old faith. Now that he was a free agent he determined, no doubt with the full approbation of his wife, Mary, to make an end of all concealment. Two days after his accession he attended mass publicly in the chapel of St. James palace, where the Queen worshipped.[6] This was the first public evidence of his change of religion. The following Sunday he had his own service at Whitehall. He did not go to the Royal Chapel where Dr. Tenison preached to the Household — but he opened an oratory attached to his own lodgings when Duke of York, and this oratory became for all practical purposes the Royal chapel.[7]

The regret which John Evelyn felt at the absence of the Sacrament at the coronation, was shared by many Englishmen.[8] Men also observed that while the queen expressed much devotion, the King showed little or none, and that at the responses he never moved his lips. The public worship, Barillon reported, did not produce any dangerous effects on the minds of moderate and reasonable men, but he felt bound to add that the London populace looked askance at their King thus comporting himself.[9]

To one of James' closest advisers and friends, Lord Ailesbury, this policy seemed, at best, a dangerous one. He had never hated Catholics, nor did he much fear those who chose to dissent from the official English mode of worship. He had no love for the Test Act or for any

---

[4]   Keith Feiling, *A History of the Tory Party, 1640-1714* (London, Oxford at The Clarendon Press, 1924), 204.

[5]   Fox, *History*, Appendix XXII.

[6]   T. S. Clarke (ed.), *Life of James II By Himself* (London, Longman, 1816), 79.

[7]   *Ibid.*, 80.

[8]   F. S. De Beer (ed.), *The Diary of John Evelyn*, IV (London, Oxford At The Clarendon Press, 1955), 418.

[9]   Fox, *History*, Appendix XLII.

other enactment which punished men for following their own beliefs. "It is never good", thought he, "to persecute anyone".[10] With these strong words, Ailesbury ranged himself, at least in principle upon the side of Toleration. He clearly saw, however, that there would be another issue at stake; that of legality and the authority of Parliament.

As Easter drew near a fresh problem arose. Hitherto James had had an informal escort of such members of his household as had no strong prejudices and were even in some cases willing to join in part of the worship in order to please the King. But he decided that the celebration on Easter Day must be accompanied by the pomp and ceremony of a full procession to and from the chapel not only of the officers of the Household, but also of the Chief Ministers of State. Rochester, who as Lord Treasurer, held the highest office, was in a quandary. Apart from his religious convictions he was anxious not to lose his position as head of the Church party; at the same time he could not afford to displease the King. He told James that he would not attend unless formally ordered to do so.[11] Barillon states that, "Rochester made so many difficulties that he was eventually given permission to retire to his country seat until after Easter." [12] James did say, however, that the ministers could remain in the antechapel if they so desired.[13] Rochester was apparently the only defection, for all other cabinet members took their places in the procession.[14]

Many Catholics had doubted James' assurances of his ultimate conversion to Rome, and such rumors multiplied during the early weeks of his reign. Such doubts were dispelled, however, on this Easter Sunday when James announced his intention of assisting at high mass in Whitehall Chapel.[15]

It was evident that at the commencement of the new reign there was no escaping the necessity of summoning a Parliament, but, as James knew full well, that was the very thing the French King most feared. Louis XIV had sought to make Charles financially independent of Parliament, so within a few hours of the death of Charles a courier had set out from Paris bearing about £37,000 to James in an attempt

[10]   W. E. Buckley (ed.), *Memoirs of Lord Ailesbury, II* (London, Roxburghe Club, 1890), 138.
[11]   Fox, *History,* Appendix LIII.
[12]   *Ibid.,* XLVI-LXVII.
[13]   Samuel W. Singer, *The Correspondence of Henry Hyde, Earl of Clarendon, and of His Brother, Laurence Hyde, Earl of Rochester,* II (London, Henry Colburn, 1826), 261.
[14]   *Ibid.,* 262.
[15]   Clarke (ed.), *James II,* II, 106.

to continue the policy.[16] Barillon's account, while often the only clue
to the contemporary scene, must be taken with some qualifications. He
was writing as the French Ambassador and therefore was writing to
please Louis. Barillon stated on this occasion that James led him into
his private room and there made the "most humble excuse for having
taken this step without the previous sanction of Louis".[17] This was
probably an exaggeration. He further added that James maintained
his zeal for Popery.

James realized that a Parliament, whether mistakenly or otherwise,
had passed the penal laws, and therefore a Parliament must repeal
them. In short, toleration must come, if at all, by constitutional means.
To push through such a policy assumed, as a first step, an agreeable
House of Commons, and the whole government influence was used at
the elections to secure the return of members loyal to the government's
interests. Thanks partly to the efforts of government agents, whose
great tricks and practices were exaggeratedly denounced by their
opponents, partly to the remodeled borough charters, but most of all
to genuine enthusiasm, the new Parliament that met in 1685 was even
more Royalist than that of 1661.[18]

The elections, which took place in April and early May, allowed no
time for long preparation. Lord Sunderland managed the campaign,
and letters to all parts of the kingdom urged local magnates to use
their influence. Apparently only one of these letters survived, but it is
no doubt typical of the rest.

His Majesty being well satisfied of your Lordships zeal for his Service,
and not doubting but you will use your utmost endeavours and employ
all your interest that good members may be chosen for the approaching
Parliament, commands me to tell you that he would have you take care
of the Leicestershire elections, so as to prevent all intrigues and disorders
which ill-affected persons may endeavour to set on foot.[19]

Although a convinced and declared Roman Catholic, James promised
a fair policy to the Church of England. In his speech to both Houses
on May 22, James said:

I will make it my endeavour to preserve this Government, both in Church

16   Fox, *History*, Appendix XXI.
17   John Dalrymple, *Memoirs of Great Britain and Ireland*, III (London, Strahan
and Cadell, 1773), Appendix, 103-106.
18   Narcissus Luttrell, *A Brief Historical Relation of State Affairs from 1678 to
1714*, I (London, Oxford At The University Press, 1852), 341.
19   *Historical Manuscripts Commission, Manuscripts of the Duke of Rutland*, II
(London, Printed for Her Majesty's Stationary Office (1888-1889), 86

and State, as it is now by law established. And, as I will never depart from the just Rights and Prerogatives of the Crown, so I will never invade any man's property. And you may be sure, that, having heretofore ventured my life in the defence of this nation, I shall still go as far as any man in preserving it in all its just Rights and Liberties.[20]

The harmony of the proceedings was disturbed by a violent speech from Sir Edward Seymour, Speaker of the House, bitterly attacking the Government for the way in which the elections had been conducted. He said that he did not oppose the grant of the revenues, but he urged that the question should be postponed until it was ascertained whether those present were in point of fact members of Parliament. He alleged that the elections, carried out by "intrigue and authority", violated the established principle of free election.[21]

The motion was not even seconded, for he had apparently not troubled himself to secure support beforehand, and though many members approved of his speech, no one was ready to follow it up for fear of revealing numerical weakness. The irregularity of the elections was again made the subject of a motion by Sir John Lowther, Whig leader in Parliament a few days later. This motion was supported by several members, but it led only to an inconclusive debate, largely because it was crowded out by the more burning question of rebellion.[22]

The inevitable storm was for the time being brushed aside by the invasions of Argyle and Monmouth. On May 22, James informed the House that Argyle had landed in the West. The wording and extremely hostile tone suggest that James had composed his speech without aid. In place of a request, if not humbly, at least politely, James accompanied his demand for supplies with a veiled threat.[23]

A unanimous report on May 27 from the Committee on Religion, whose chairman was the Whig politician Sir Thomas Meres, suggested a petition to the Crown for the enforcement of the laws against all Dissenters, whatsoever, and only extreme pressure on Bishops and members managed to quash it.[24] The House then proceeded to grant the King's revenue for life and everything else he had asked.[25]

[20] Anchitell Grey, *Debates of the House of Commons*, VIII (London, Henry and Care, 1763), 344.
[21] *Ibid.*, 345.
[22] John Reresby, *The Memoirs of the Honorable Sir John Reresby* (London, 1734), 160.
[23] Grey, *Debates*, VIII, 345-346.
[24] *Ibid.*, 346.
[25] *Ibid.*, 347.

The Duke of Monmouth, Earl of Argyle, and the numerous refugees, who, just before the death of Charles II, had thought themselves on the verge of triumphing over the Duke of York and the papists, saw all their hopes destroyed by the accession of James. Most of the refugees, having escaped from Scotland and England at a time when the Whig Party, notwithstanding its defeats, still retained courage and hope, thought that they had only to present themselves with arms to find soldiers. Subsequently, they resolved upon a double descent; the one on the West of Scotland, the other on the West of England. The Earl of Argyle departed in May for Scotland with three small vessels and five thousand men. Their secret had not been completely kept; so that when the Earl of Argyle arrived, the Earl of Perth and the Duke of Queensbury had assembled at Edinburgh and had taken other measures for isolating the Earl upon his debarkation. Some thousands of highlanders, his vassals, whom he collected, soon left him when they found that the royal troops, the militia, and the vassals of several great noblemen were marching against them. Deserted by most of his followers, he was already a fugitive by the time he crossed the Clyde at Renfrew, and on June 18 was captured. His execution followed twelve days later in accordance with a sentence of death passed on him nearly four years before.[26]

Parliament was still sitting when news came of the landing of the Duke of Monmouth at Lyme on June 11. The Duke had been detained nineteen days by contrary winds. The Commons at once took steps to ascertain the truth of this news, and when they had satisfied themselves, they brought in a Bill of Attainder against him for high treason; this bill passed both Houses within three days.[27] They also hastened to vote an extraordinary supply of £400,000 for the expenses of suppressing the rebellion, and put a price of £5000 on Monmouth's head.[28] The friction between King and Parliament was, for the time being, forgotten, and any member who wished to keep it alive was well advised to remain silent.

Monmouth had chosen his place of landing well, for the West of England was at best lukewarm toward James' interests, and the militia, which was the only military force available in those counties at short notice, was neither efficient nor anxious for the defeat of the invader. The Duke had not a hundred man with him when he landed,

[26]   Clarke (ed.), *James II*, I, 710.
[27]   Grey, VIII, 350.
[28]   *Ibid.*

but he had before him a full ten days to advance into the country and recruit. His landing was accompanied by the enumeration of a number of Whigs principles, such as annual Parliaments, security of tenure for judges, and no standing army.[29] About the same time a declaration, penned by Robert Ferguson, one of Monmouth's staunchest supporters, announced that Monmouth was the true heir to the throne, that James had started the Fire of London, and had poisoned his brother. He also concluded the declaration with a promise of all sorts of liberty both spiritual and temporal, to persons of all persuasions.[30]

Monmouth was personally far more formidable than Argyle. He assumed the title of King, a title which a large proportion of the population, in its hatred for popery, was quite capable of accepting, especially in the parts where Monmouth appeared.

The King, meanwhile, was occupied in summoning from Scotland the troops who had frustrated the enterprise of Argyle, and from Holland three English and Scottish regiments, which had been in the service of the States since the peace of 1678.

On July 6, 1685, Monmouth attacked the royal troops at Sedgmoor by night, hoping to surprise them. [31] Lord Feversham, however, had already managed to procure intelligence from some of the rebels, and was therefore on his guard. After a few hours fighting, the army of Monmouth composed mainly of peasants badly armed fled, leaving about fifteen hundred prisoners. Monmouth and all his followers were at James' mercy. After his capture Monmouth wrote to the King, and to everyone else who could be expected to influence the King, in a vain hope to save his life. But there could be no mercy for him; for not only had he waged war against the King, but he had taken upon himself the name of King and was doubly guilty of high treason. Monmouth was executed on July 15, 1685 on the basis of the June Bill of Attainder.

Such was the end of a rebellion, one might almost say an escapade, led by that favorite son of Charles II, whose popularity and Protestantism had made him, perhaps, the only Stuart who understood the common man. It was probably in these simple, straightforward things, that the explanation may be found why so many flocked to his standard. On the other hand, the reasons for Monmouth's failure are

---

[29]   *Ibid.*
[30]   *Ibid.*
[31]   Bryan Little, *The Monmouth Episode* (London, Wernie Laurie, 1956), 247-250.

easy to ascertain. First, there was a serious cleavage in his following: some supported his claim to the throne, while others, fired by ardent republicanism, regarded the Duke only as a means to an end. He also appears to have overrated the strength of the forces opposed to him, and by delay and much marching and counter-marching, he had sacrificed the one essential for success — surprise. Extravagant optimism in moments of success, and equally unwarrantable pessimism as soon as danger threatened were also qualities of character which led Monmouth to his doom.

The suppression of Monmouth's rebellion was followed by the judicial massacres known as the Bloody Assizes. Horrible as the executions were, they do not seem to have awakened public reprobation at the time. Throughout the seventeenth century the death penalty was inflicted for what we should call minor offenses; and no one can call rebellion a minor offense.

If James had kept his crown until his death, we would have heard far less about the Bloody Assizes. But in 1689 everyone was anxious to justify the Revolution, and the Bloody Assizes provide an obvious objective for an attack on James. The high handed behavior of Judge Jeffreys and his browbeating of witnesses and juries, had already earned him the hatred of the people of London. The many pamphlets which recounted the names and suffering of the victims were published in the winter of 1688-9 and were part of the revolutionary propaganda; it was not until many years later that English public opinion would have disapproved of any degree of severity against rebels taken with arms in their hands.

With respect to England one of the main points at issue during the Revolution was William of Orange's connection with the event. Unfortunately, this is a subject about which no positive statement can be made. The truth of the matter seems to be that while William may have encouraged Monmouth, he had neither helped or hindered him. He was certainly aware of Monmouth's presence in the country, and probably knew of his plans to invade England. An invasion and ultimate failure would benefit William.[32]

Upon the death of Charles II, William of Orange had endeavored to bring about a reconciliation with James and for this purpose sent over one of his trusted aides, M. Ouwerkerck from Holland.[33] James

---

[32] Lucile Pinkham, *William III and the Respectable Revolution* (Cambridge, Harvard University Press, 1954), 99-100.
[33] Singer (ed.), *Clarendon Correspondence*, I, 115.

received his advances in the same spirit in which he suspected they were made. Ouwerkerck's mission was to assure James that the Prince repented of his opposition to the late King, and also acknowledged his error in conduct toward James, when Duke of York: "to assure him that he would make all reparation in his power, and that his future conduct should be agreeable to what he could be pleased to prescribe." [34]

On March 5, 1685, the Prince of Orange wrote to the Earl of Rochester concerning the King's friendship and the Earl's:

I entreat you to continue your friendship to me, and to assist me in acquiring the Kings good opinion; assuring you that my conduct shall be such, that I doubt not the King will be satisfied with it, as also with the assurances that I have commanded Ouwerkerck to make him from me.[35]

On April 14, 1685, Rochester replied to the Prince of Orange advising him to remove the Duke of Monmouth from Holland.[36] James, as a matter of fact, wrote three letters to William protesting the fact that the Earl of Argyle was in Holland. According to a contemporary account, while Monmouth was in Holland, James had agents sent to kill him, but the Duke discovered his plans and William of Orange gave Monmouth money to go to Brussels.[37] This story has no positive substantiation. On the other hand, William did give positive assistance to James after the revolt started.[38] What else would William have done under the circumstances, especially for his father-in-law? He immediately sent the British regiments home which were in the service of the United Provinces, and he offered his personal assistance if needed.[39] James, very wisely, refused the latter offer. William wrote to Rochester on May 25:

I must confess to you that I never should have believed the Duke of Monmouth capable of such an action, after the assurances he made to me of the controversy when he took leave of me. I believe he is no longer in this country, at least, after all the pains that I have taken to discover that he is.[40]

In fairness to William, one must admit that much of the responsibility

---

[34] *Ibid.*, 116.
[35] *Ibid.*
[36] Dalrymple, III, Appendix, 120.
[37] David Jones, *The Secret History of Whitehall, from the Restoration of Charles II, Down to the Abdication of the Late King James* (London, 1689), 29.
[38] Dalrymple, III, Appendix, 130.
[39] *Ibid.*, 131.
[40] Singer (ed.), *Clarendon Correspondence*, I, 127.

and even the authority, for curbing Monmouth's activities lay not in the Prince but in the States General, in the provincial estates of Holland, and in the local government of the city of Amsterdam. James realized this also, and accordingly made his complaints through the English ambassador, Bevil Skelton, directly to the States General.[41]

James misinterpreted the rising. He took its failure to mean that henceforth he had a free hand to do what he liked, whereas in reality it should have served as a warning not to go too far or too fast. What the defeat of Monmouth meant was that the country was intensely loyal to the Crown, and in no mood for adventures; but the support which Argyle and Monmouth received demonstrated that an appeal to the Protestant sentiments of the English people could always meet with a ready response. The rebellion proved the necessity for proceeding slowly in religious matters, for many dissenters would oppose toleration if they had to share it with Roman Catholics. It was seriously to weaken the effect of the bid he was about to make for Nonconformists help in a policy of toleration; and it gave William of Orange a ready made body of supporters when he, in turn, landed in the West three years later.

After Monmouth's capture, the two Houses were prorogued until August 4 at which time they were further to be adjourned until November 9, 1685.[42] Without a Parliament James could still pursue his policy and his subjects had to watch helplessly the occupation of one power position after another by his adherents. What impressed London most was the new army. As early as April, 1685, James determined to have a large standing army. He told Barillon that he would raise it to twenty thousand men or more.[43] James regarded the possession of a well-equiped army, quite from its practical use, as an addition to his royal splendor; his frequent attendance at reviews, at first in Hyde Park, and later at Hounslow, show a liking for military display for its own sake. This attitude was probably due, in part at least, to James' admiration for the military might of France.

To the regiments raised to meet Monmouth's rebellion James had appointed Catholic officers.[44] He could not plead that they possessed qualifications which would give them preference over the many Protestant gentlemen who were ready to serve; for, except for the

41   Dalrymple, III, Book IV, 124-125.
42   Grey, VIII, 352.
43   Fox, *History*, Appendix LXI-LXII.
44   Clarke (ed.), *James* II, 110-115.

very few who had served abroad, they had been excluded both from the King's troops and from the militia, and had had no military experience. There was no provision in the Penal Acts about the enlistment of popish soldiers, however, and a chapel tent was provided for their use.[45]

He took interest in the publication of Catholic books and pamphlets, many of which were published at his own expense. He appointed Henry Hills, a convert, to be the King's printer.[46] A new controversial situation was thereby created. Hitherto the use of publicity had been confined to the Protestants, who had employed the privilege of press without restriction of competition. They had been able for generations to criticize their opponents without risk of retaliation. And consequently they had grown overconfident: they were neither able nor willing to retire in good order when the positions they had taken up became untenable. The King ordered the Catholics to confine their writings to a plain statement of doctrine, and the many books printed by Hills, which included such works as Bossuet's *Exposition of Catholic Doctrine*, show that the command was generally obeyed. The Protestants retorted with books denouncing popish plots, Jesuit intrigues, and the superstitions and idolatries of Rome.

The anonymous Catholic author of a tract entitled *Advice to a Confuter of Bellarmine*, made the new situation clear; he advised his adversary:

... when he treats of any Church, not to forget good manners, and he seems to have done when it is not content to charge the Church of Rome with errors only, but in plain English, with lies too. As if he thought an argument would not sound well in controversy unless it were put in the Billingsgate phrase.[47]

Most of the Protestant arguments popular in the seventeenth century have, of course, been long modified. Historical controversy at that time consisted of an appeal to secondary authorities. The doctrinal argument, which was given the most prominence, often degenerated into abuse. In a controversy of this kind, the Catholics had an easy victory, for, as Bossuet said in his Exposition, "... surely a Catholic bishop must be supposed to know the teachings of his own church".[48]

---

[45]   *Ibid.*
[46]   De Beer (ed.), *Evelyn Diary*, IV, 418.
[47]   *Advice to a Confuter of Bellarmine* (London, 1685), 5.
[48]   James Bossuet, *An Exposition of the Doctrine of the Catholic Church in Matters of Controversie* (London, 1685), 2.

This pamphlet was only forty-three pages, but it was a master of exposition and clarity and had already attained a large circulation on the Continent. It appeared at a time when people had begun to tire of long winded and almost unintelligible verbosity. Bossuet saw that religious disputes had now reached a point where further argument was a waste of time. He hoped that some understanding might be reached, some compromise might be possible, if all parties would state clearly what their essential religious beliefs really were. In writing this pamphlet he was not concerned with the doctrinal controversy. His purpose was to state briefly and plainly what the Church taught.

The Anglican theologians were not in a mood to enter into a discussion with Bossuet, except upon grounds of their own choosing. They were unwilling to admit that the greater part of their preaching against popery was based on misrepresentations; they could not be expected to acknowledge that they had been wrong. William Wake appeared as their champion. He answered Bossuet with a lengthy treatise entitled *An Exposition of the Doctrine of the Church of England*.[49] The contents did not fulfil the promise of the title. Wake used the argument that has so often been employed to discredit King James. He said that Bossuet could not be trusted; that he was insincere. He refused to admit that what the French Bishop had written really represented the doctrine of popery, in spite of the fact that the book had been published with a brief from the Pope himself.

If Englishmen were given time and opportunity to understand that their ideas about popery were founded on misrepresentation of the facts, then the cry of "no popery, no slavery, no arbitrary power," would lose much of its appeal.

John Gother, a Roman Catholic, came out with one of the most famous pamphlets of the year, in which he stated:

Those things which are brought about them, being as much detested by them as by the persons that lay the charge in their disfavor; and having no more relation to them, than the weeds and tares to the Corn amongst which it grows; or chaff to the Wheat, with which it lies mix'd in one heap. A Papist therefore is no more than he is above represented; and whom soever enters that Communion, had no obligation of believing otherwise, than as there specified.[50]

---

[49] William Wake, *An Exposition of the Doctrine of the Church of England* (London, 1685).

[50] John Gother, *A Papist Misrepresented and Represented: or, a twofold Character of Popery* (London, 1685), 123.

He went on to say that the Papists were as foully misrepresented as were the early Christians by the Gentiles.[51]

George Villiers, the Duke of Buckingham, also penned a short pamphlet; in it he set forth the Court's position.

I was forced to conclude with an opinion, which I have been long convinced of; that nothing can be more anti-Christian nor more contrary to sense and Reason, than to Trouble and Molest our Fellow Christians, because they cannot be exactly of our Minds, in all things relating to the Worship of God.[52]

He was immediately answered with a very fine pamphlet by Henry Maurice. Maurice stated that toleration, "therefore can serve to no other purpose than to be the Nurse of a Faction that is implacable; which as it grows up, will more and more despite this Infant Dispensation, and contend for mastery." [53] He also goes on to say that the dissenters and Catholics plead for an indefinite toleration, "For upon those terms the Indian Pagons may come and demand convenience for their Pagods, and the Mahometans may say that their Mosques may stand among our Churches." [54] Dr. Sherlock put the English point of view very clearly when he wrote that if people behave like idolaters "they will be judged not by enquiring into their private intentions but from the natural interpretation of such actions".[55]

The feeling of toleration seemed to be summed up with the publication of an anonymous pamphlet, probably written by the Duke of Buckingham.

It is not the will of the Great and Wise God, to appoint any Forcible Ways or causes to bring men and women to conform to his worship. If men conform to any worship or way thereof, with an unwilling mind, they cannot serve God, though the worship be Right, because the Heart of the Worshipper is not Right.[56]

The author's final point was that when the French King is blamed by English Protestants, and perhaps too by some English Catholics, for

[51] *Ibid.,* 126.
[52] George Villiers, *A Short Discourse Upon the Reasonableness of Men Having a Religion, or Worship of God* (London, 1685), preface.
[53] Henry Maurice, *The Antithelemite, or an answer to certain queries by the Duke of Buckingham and to The Considerations of an Unknown author concerning toleration* (London, 1685), 4.
[54] *Ibid.,* 5.
[55] William Sherlock, *A Papist not misrepresented by Protestants, being a reply to the Reflections upon the Answer to a Papist Misrepresented* (London, 1685).
[56] *Considerations Moving to a Toleration, and Liberty of the Conscience with Arguments inducing to a Cessation of the Penal Statutes against all Dissenters whatever, upon the account of Religion* (London, 1685), 10.

persecuting his peaceable subjects, "shall we do the same thing in our Kingdom which we condemn in another?" [57]

James had great hopes of the Parliament on its reassembly after adjournment, and in this opinion he was supported by Louis XIV, but these hopes merely provide further evidence that neither of them had even a rudimentary knowledge of the psychology of Parliament. The Crown's success in putting down the summer rebellion was partly responsible for the changed relations between James and this new Parliament. The incident had both frightened James and encouraged him. The former reaction led him in his speech from the throne to ask for an increase in the standing army; the latter caused him to admit that he had defied the Test Act by giving commissions to Catholic officers.

James indeed could hardly have made his request at a less favorable time. Only a few weeks before this, Louis had revoked the Edict of Nantes, and Huguenot refugees were beginning to stream out of France. The arrival of these refugees in England created a religious panic not less compelling, better justified, and wider in its appeal than that of the Popish Plot. The accounts of James' views on this revocation are conflicting. Barillon, reporting that while James was preaching sentiments of toleration to the people, he was congratulating the French King on the want of it, informed his court on October 4th, 1685, that

His Brittanic Majesty also heard with pleasure, what I told him of the wonderful progress with which God had blessed your Majesty's cares with regard to the conversion of your subjects; there being no example of a similar thing happening at any time or in any country with so much promptitude.[58]

Another source declared that James was appalled by the Revocation of the Edict and believed that Louis had injured the cause of Roman Catholicism by this rash act.[59] The English looked upon the Test and Penal Laws as safeguards against a similar situation in their own land. The days of peaceful relations between James and his Parliaments were over.

On November 9, James opened proceedings with a long speech. He congratulated Parliament and himself on the suppression of Mon-

---

[57]   *Ibid.*, 12.
[58]   Dalrymple, III, Appendix, Book IV, 177.
[59]   *Historical Manuscripts Commission, Manuscripts of the Earl of Lindsey* (London, Printed for Her Majesty's Stationary Office, 1895), 270-272.

mouth's rebellion, but he drew the moral that Monmouth's early successes had revealed the necessity for the strengthening of the defenses of the nation and he asked for a Parliamentary grant for the purpose of increasing the standing army; he was very explicit on the subject of the Catholic officers:

Let no man take exception that there are some officers in the army not qualified according to the late tests for their employments; the gentlemen, I must tell you, are most of them well known to me, and having formerly served with me on several occasions and always approved the loyalty of their principles by their practice. I think them now fit to be employed under me; and I will deal plainly with you that after having had the benefit of their services in such a time of need and danger I will neither expose them to disgrace nor myself to the want of them if there should be another rebellion to make them necessary to me.[60]

The debate on the Address opened on November 12, and it was clear from the outset that the opposition had grown in courage and in numbers. In the matter of employment of Catholic officers in the army both Houses were uncompromising. The King's ministers were unable to resist the evident desire of the House that an address to the King regarding the Catholic officers should be drawn up; they could only endeavor to make the Address as mild and innocuous as possible. A proposal that the House should acquiesce in the continued employment of these Catholics who already held commissions, on the understanding that no further unqualified officers would be appointed, was rejected.[61] A certain success, however, was achieved by the alteration of the words "that His Majesty would be pleased not to continue them in their employments" to "we therefore do humbly beseech Your Majesty that you would be pleased to give such directions therein that no apprehensions or jealousies may remain in the hearts of Your Majesty's good and faithful subjects." [62]

It then appeared to the promotors of the Address that its weight would be enormously increased if it went to the King as an address of both Houses, and not merely of the House of Commons; they accordingly moved that the Address should be sent up to the Lords. On November 16, the bill was rejected by a vote of 212 to 138.[63] James then made one of the most unfortunate speeches of his short reign.

[60] Grey, VIII, 353-354.
[61] *Journal of the House of Commons,* IX, 757.
[62] *Ibid.,* 758.
[63] *Ibid.*

I did not expect such an address from the House of Commons, having so lately recommended to your consideration the great advantages a good understanding between us had produced in a very short time and given you warning of fears and jealousies amongst yourselves.[64]

It was at this time in the House of Lords that Lord Halifax replied caustically that giving the King thanks for his Speech was a matter of common courtesy: "They had reason to thank His Majesty that he would speak to them at all, but they ought with greater reason to thank him when he spoke plainly to them." [65]

On Thursday, November 19, it was decided to enter on an examination of the King's Speech on the following Monday, but James had heard enough about the Popish officers. On Friday, November 20, Lord Jeffreys was sent to convey without speech or explanation the royal will that Parliament should be prorogued until February 10, 1686.[66] By this sudden action James lost the grant of £700,000; but he could not bear any more talk which implied that he himself was under the law and which insisted on the privileges of the Church of England. To expect Parliament to submit to a relation of the Test Act which would expose them to the free competition of their rivals was to expect from them a political maturity far beyond the grasp of seventeenth century England.

In the fall, James thought himself strong enough to dispense with Lord Halifax. He had hoped that love of office would incline him to support the royal policy in Parliament, or at any rate to restrain Halifax from active opposition.[67] James disliked Halifax on both personal and public grounds. His wit and subtility of mind, which had commended him to Charles, were to James a bewilderment; he disagreed with James in the three cardinal points of his policy, for he was against the French alliance, further extension of the royal prerogative, and against the repeal of the Test Acts.[68]

Halifax gave James occasion for dismissing him by moving in Council "that an order should be given to examine whether all the officers in Commission had taken the test or not";[69] he did not find a seconder, and the motion failed; but James could not pass over so

[64]   *Ibid.*, 759.
[65]   Helen C. Foxcroft, *A Character of the Trimmer* (London, Cambridge University Press, 1946), 223.
[66]   Grey, VIII, 371.
[67]   Foxcroft, *Character of the Trimmer*, 232.
[68]   Burnet, *Own Times*, III, 66.
[69]   Foxcroft, *Character of the Trimmer*, 340.

bold an expression of opposition on the part of one of the highest officers of state.

The King, after he had declared that he would be served by none but those who would vote for the repeal of the tests, called for the Marquis of Halifax and asked him how he would vote in the matter. He very frankly answered, he would never consent to it: "He thought the keeping up those laws was necessary, even for the King's service, since the nation trusted so much to them, that the public quiet was chiefly preserved by that means." [70] Upon this the King told him, that though he would never forgot his past services, he was resolved to let him go.[71]

Louis found Halifax's dismissal very helpful to the French cause. He wrote to Barillon on November 16, 1685, that:

.... you are well aware that it cannot but be very advantageous to my interest, that a Minister so devoted to Spain and so inimical to the Catholic religion, has been removed from the councils of the King of England.[72]

Halifax's post of Lord President was promised to Sunderland in addition to his Secretaryship of State, though the new appointment was not officially announced until December 4.[73] This advancement was the outward and visible sign of the progress which Sunderland had made since the beginning of the reign in the royal favor.

As already noticed, the King regarded anti-Roman preaching from the pulpit as a personal insult; as early in his reign as March 15 he had tried to deal with such affronts. Among the Bishops, Henry Compton, Bishop of London, stood pre-eminent as the determined enemy of Rome and the head of the Church of England opposition to the King's policy. The Archbishop of Canterbury, William Sancroft, though his devotion to the Anglican Church was deep and sincere, lacked the toughness and militant temperament which earned for his brother of London the title "The Protestant Bishop". Compton realized, of course, as did everybody else, that the King's desire to suppress the sermons arose solely from the anti-Roman Catholic sentiments which many of the lecturers did not hesitate to express.

James soon left no doubt as to what he thought of these indications of opposition. The King was furious at the Lords open criticism of his actions and particularly with Bishop Compton, who had said

[70] Luttrell, *Brief Relations*, I, 366-367.
[71] Burnet, *Own Times*, III, 67.
[72] Fox, *History*, Appendix, CXXXIII.
[73] Carpenter, *The Protestant Bishop*, 83.

during the debate on the Roman Catholic officers, that it was against the law.[74] By early December it was common talk that the Bishop of London had been removed from his place as Dean of the Royal Chapel, and his office was given to the more accommodating Bishop of Durham.[75] Nor was this all. As punishment for his share in the proceedings, the King announced two days before Christmas that the Bishop of London's name had been blotted out of the Council Book and he ceased to be a member of the Privy Council.[76] The fact was, of course, that Compton had become so personally obnoxious to James that the King determined to rid himself of his attendance at Court altogether.

As the year drew to a close, the future looked dim for the Anglican Church. James seemed to be in full command with a strong pro-Catholic cabinet, a subdued clergy, and a prorogued Parliament. The new year would bring startling developments.

[74] *Ibid.*
[75] *Historical Manuscripts Commission, Manuscripts of the Earl of Downshire,* I (London, Printed for His Majesty's Stationary Office, 1924), 83.
[76] *Ibid.,* 392.

CHAPTER III

THE HALES CASE AND THE ECCLESIASTICAL COMMISSION

The first few months following the prorogation of James' only Parliament was a period of very significant events but outward repose. This calm was only on the surface. Every action of James tended toward the same end: the improvement of the position of the Catholic Church and of its members. Opposition to James' policy, to his plan for establishing tolerance, developed not from any spontaneous clamor of popular opinion but from the organized hostility of a dominant political group composed of landowners and wealthy merchants, in Parliament or with Parliamentary influence, supported by many leaders of the Established Church. Men who controlled entry to all renumerative appointments in the government service had no desire to see the door opened to any rivals. Every step taken by James in favor of his religion either offended the personal interest of an individual and increased the number of his personal enemies or outraged Protestant prejudices. His inability to see that when loyalty is rewarded with disgrace, it ceased in most cases to exist, cost him support.

Three great fallacies provided the clue to the King's actions for the next two years: his belief that the Royalist reaction was favorable to a more authoritarian form of monarchy; his failure to perceive that the Nonconformists would not buy toleration themselves by supporting the abolition of penal laws against Catholics; his logical but mistaken conviction that the doctrine of non-resistance prevented Anglicans from actively opposing a Catholicizing policy. Such delusions were unforgivable in a man who had lived at the center of politics through the reign of Charles. The reception of Charles II's Declaration of Indulgence demonstrated that Dissenters preferred persecution to relaxation of the penal laws.

At the outset of 1686 the pamphlet warfare revived. Two papers, which set forth very concisely the arguments ordinarily used by Roman Catholics in controversy with Protestants, had apparently been found in Charles' strong box, and appeared to be in his handwriting. On the basis of these two papers James declared that Charles had lived and died a papist. The first paper, supposedly composed by Charles, described the authority of the Catholic Church:

The Discourse we had the other Day I hope satisfied you in the main, that Christ can have but one Church here upon Earth; and I believe that it is as visible as that the Scripture is in Print. That none can be that Church, but that which is called the Roman Catholic Church.[1]

The second, credited to the Duchess of York, prayed

That the poor Catholics of the Nation may not suffer for my being of their religion; That God would but give me Patience to bear them, and then send me any difficulties in this World, so I may enjoy a blessed Eternity hereafter.[2]

The religious controversy took several forms. Men debated whether the Roman Catholic Church or the Church of England was the true and universal church. The majority of the pamphlets early in 1686 attacked the Roman Catholic Church, not the monarchy. Even the more outspoken divines hesitated to attack James. Nicholas Stratford, High Churchman and Tory, early in March published an example of this type of publication:

The Church of Rome is not only fallible, but has actually erred; their errors were not slight, that no hope was left that the Church of Rome would either reform these errors in herself; that the right of the Church of England could reform herself without her leave.[3]

James on the other hand did not hesitate to exert direct pressure on the nobles. One such example was the futile attempt of Lord Melfort to persuade William Douglas, the Duke of Hamilton, to come around to the Crown's side. On March 4, 1686, Lord Melfort, writing from Scotland to the Duke concerning James' desire to repeal the Penal Laws, "... by which your Grace should see the fatherly care that His Majesty has of all the consciences of the people." [4] The writer adds that the King depended on the Duke to further his wishes.[5]

[1] James II, *Copies of Two Papers Written by the late King Charles of Blessed Memory; and also a copy of a Paper written by the late Duchess of York* (London, 1686), 3.
[2] *Ibid.*, 9-10.
[3] Nicholas Stratford, *The Necessity of Reformation with respect to the Errors and Corruptions of the Church of Rome*, Part II (London, 1686).
[4] *Historical Manuscripts Commission, Manuscripts of the Duke of Hamilton*, 11th Report, Appendix, Part VI (London, Printed for Her Majesty's Stationary Office, 1887), 172.
[5] *Ibid.*

The Duke of Hamilton would not hear of the repeal; on March 17 he received another letter from Melfort: "I was never more surprised than by your Grace's last to find the King's desires get such an answer." [6] Hamilton apparently had spoken out for toleration but was not prepared at this particular time to repeal the Tests.

Thomas Cartwright, Bishop of Chester, and Anglican, but the leading spokesman for the Roman Catholic Church in England, also supported James' side in a pamphlet printed early in February on the King's dispensing power. "So the King may, it seems, make use of his Prerogative, as God dares of his omnipotent, upon some extraordinary occasion." [7] He argued that those who broke the letter of the law for the government's sake could be pardoned: an interesting piece of logic. He goes on to say:

We must neither call him to account for his religion, nor question him for His policy in Civil Matters; for he is made our King by God and Law, of which the Law of the Land is only Declarative. It is God alone who can take vengence of him, if he does amiss; and proportion Punishments to his Person.[8]

In January of 1686, Edward Stillingfleet, Bishop of Worcester, one of the most outspoken critics against toleration for Catholics, analyzed the authority of the Catholic Church. Stillingfleet, "generally acknowledged to have occupied the very first place among those illustrious men, who, in that important crisis of history, brought great talents and learning to bear upon the exposure of Popery",[9] stated that "The Saviour would not permit the Church to give the Communion in one kind, if it were not lawful so to do." [10] In his opinion the argument was stronger the other way; the Church of Rome forbids the doing of that which Christ enjoined: "Therefore it cannot be infallible, since the Command of Christ is so much plainer than the Promise of Infallibility by the Church of Rome."[11]

John Rawlet wrote a supposed dialogue between two Protestants in answer to a Popish pamphlet. The members of the Church of England, to Rawlett, were true Catholics and the Church of England was

[6]   *Ibid.*, 173.
[7]   Thomas Cartwright, *A Sermon Preached Upon the Anniversary of the Happy Inauguration of our Dread Sovereign Lord King James II* (London, 1686), 20.
[8]   *Ibid.*, 15.
[9]   James Welwood, *Memoirs of the Last Hundred Years Preceding the Revolution of 1688* (London, 1736), 180.
[10]   Edward Stillingfleet, *An Answer to Some Papers Lately Printed, Concerning the Authority of the Catholic Church* (London, 1686), 72.
[11]   *Ibid.*

a sound part of Christ's Holy Catholic Church, "In whose Communion therefore the people of England should be most strictly bound in conscience to obey." [12]

The attacks on the Catholic Church also assumed another aspect with disagreement over the praise due to the Virgin Mary and the Church of England's views on the subject. George Hickes, English scholar, whose brother had been executed after the Monmouth rebellion, penned a pamphlet on this subject early in March, 1686, stating that the Roman Catholics paid too much attention to the Virgin Mary and not enough to Jesus Christ.[13] Hickes criticized the Roman Catholics for praying to the Virgin as though she were God. "in a word, let us admit her singular Purity and Holiness though we cannot admit her innocence." [14] William Claggett echoed this sentiment in his pamphlet published on March 10, 1686.

Now this is a very popular way to save themselves from blame, but by no means sufficient. For there is a concurrence of other reasons to make it profitable, to desire the prayers of our Brethren upon earth besides these two, and that they are our Brethren and that we love one another.[15]

It was his contention that if the Catholic prayed to the Virgin Mary he was going against the scripture "worship the Lord thy God, and Him only shalt thou serve".[16]

Many pamphlets tried to inject a note of peaceful non-resistance into the picture. Such men as Thomas See,[17] Louis Maimbourg,[18] and Thomas Thurlin, implored the English Protestant and English Catholic to obey the King and unite. "Unity is the band of the Religion, the Spirit of Christianity, and the distinctive sign of that one Church which God has established as a Society." [19]

While James was desperately trying to persuade the English popu-

[12]   John Rawlett, A Dialogue Betwixt Two Protestants, In Answer to a Popish Catechism Called a Short Catechism Against all Factions (London, 1686).
[13]   George Hickes, A Discourse of the Due Praise and Honors of the Virgin Mary (London, 1686), 39.
[14]   Ibid.
[15]   William Clagett, A Discourse Concerning the Worship of the Blessed Virgin and the Saints (London, 1686), 5.
[16]   Ibid.
[17]   Thomas See, Seek and you will find; or a search into the Grounds of Religion (London, 1686).
[18]   Louis Maimbourg, A Peaceable Method for the Reuniting Protestants and Catholics in Matters of Faith (London, 1686).
[19]   Thomas Thurlin, The Necessity of Obedience to Spiritual Governors, Asserted in a Sermon, May 10, 1686 (London, 1686), 34.

lace that Roman Catholicism was basically good, his relations with the Papal See were not completely harmonious. The Pope, Innocent XI, took a more moderate view of bringing England to a pro-Catholic point. The Pope was farsighted enough to realize that any great amount of pressure would end in some sort of revolt. A complete re-Catholizing policy would take many years. The unofficial representative at Rome of the English Catholics, Cardinal Philip Howard, popularly known as the Cardinal of Norfolk, was entirely of the Pope's opinion on James' religious policy, and for that reason was not completely in James' favor. For the first few months of his reign James carried on an unofficial correspondence with the Roman Curia through Cardinal Howard, but as early as the fall of 1685 he had told Barillon that he had decided to inaugurate regular diplomatic correspondence with Rome and asked for his opinion on the advisability of such action.[20] A few weeks later Barillon heard that the first ambassador would be Roger Palmer, Earl of Castlemaine.[21]

The choice of such a man is an example of the extra-ordinary short-sightedness of James; for though Castlemaine was a staunch Catholic and had endured imprisonment during the Titus Oates Plot, his violent character alone was pointed out by the French Ambassador as enough to disqualify him. On the other hand, the sense of ridicule handicapped the mission of a man whose wife had been Charles II's mistress with the consent of her husband. To a man of such strict moral principles as Innocent XI, such personage could hardly be acceptable.[22]

Castlemaine's first business in Rome was the securing of a red hat for Queen Mary's uncle, Prince Rinaldo d'Este,[23] an object contrary to papal policy, which was averse to making princes cardinals. He also hoped to persuade the Pope to confer a titular bishopric on Edward Petre, an English Jesuit of noble family, who, though not formally the King's confessor,[24] had more influence on his mind than any other ecclesiastic. The honor for Petre was desired in order to qualify this gentleman for performing with more dignity the duty of Dean of the Royal Chapel.[25] These requests, ironically, as the King knew from

[20]   Thomas See, *Seek and you will find*, 5.
[21]   Dalrymple, II, 20.
[22]   Campana di Cavelli, *Les Derniers Stuarts à Saint Germain en Laye*, II (Hamburg, 1871), 82.
[23]   Ernest Graf (ed.), *History of the Popes*, XXXII (St. Louis, B. Herder Book Co., 1940), 503.
[24]   This office was held by a learned Jesuit named Warner.
[25]   Campana di Cavelli, II, 120.

an earlier letter from the Pope, were unacceptable to the pontiff.[26] Innocent declined, on the ground that the Jesuits were prohibited by their institution from accepting bishoprics, and that he would sooner make a Jesuit a cardinal than a bishop. But as the Popes had often dispensed with this prohibition, Petre himself rightly conjectured that the political pressure by the Austrian party at Rome was the true cause of the refusal.[27]

Castlemaine had his first audience jointly with Cardinal Norfolk on April 19, and it was obvious from the very beginning that his mission would be a failure.[28] After a few audiences the Pope began to treat Castlemaine with contempt, and when the ambassador became importunate the Pope would terminate the audience by pretending to have a coughing fit.[29] To the Pope, a direct affront from a foreign ambassador must have been a new experience. When the Pope refused his request, Castlemaine became more and more insistent; on July 26, he announced that if Renaldo d'Este were not given the red hat he would have to depart.[30] The Pope was in no way disturbed by this announcement, though in September he thought it expedient to comply with the request of the King of England as far as d'Este was concerned.[31] He would not hear of the elevation of Petre to the episcopal dignity, however. To do so he repeatedly explained, would be to go against the rules of the Society of Jesus; these rules permitted its members to accept ecclesiastical dignity only by exception and at the express approval of the Pope. He would never lend a hand to such breach of discipline.

The Pope instructed his minister to complain of the conduct of Castlemaine, as "very ill-becoming the representative of so pious and so prudent a King";[32] and d'Adda made the complaint to James at a private audience at which the Queen and Lord Sunderland were present. That zealous princess, with more fervor than dignity, often interrupted his narrative by exclamations of horror at the liberty with

[26]   Joachim J. Berthier (ed.), *Innocentii PP XI Epistolae Ad Principes*, II (Rome, 1895), 260.
[27]   Fox, *History*, Appendix, CLVI.
[28]   Campana di Cavelli, II, 120.
[29]   James Welwood, *Memoirs of the Last Hundred Years Preceding the Revolution of 1688*, 185.
[30]   James Macpherson, *Original Papers; Containing the Secret History of Great Britain from the Restoration to the Accession of the House of Hanover*, I (London, W. Strahan and T. Cadell, 1774), 120.
[31]   *Ibid.*
[32]   Campana di Cavelli, II, 132, 147.

which a Catholic minister had spoken to the successor of St. Peter. James professed the most undoubted devotion to the Holy See, and assured d'Adda that he would write a letter to his Holiness to express his regret for the unbecoming conduct of his ambassador.[33] This he did the next year.

After Castlemaine left for Italy, James received the Papal nuncio, Ferdinand, Count d'Adda. He made no secret of his presence or of his position, but he was not publicly recognized, and the rumor circulated that he was a foreign visitor of private station.[34] James agreed with the Pope that at first d'Adda should only appear as a distinguished foreigner who had come to study English life. On January 5, 1686, Father Petre impressed on d'Adda that on no account must he pose as a papal nuncio; whether he should wear clerical or lay attire for the time being was left to his discretion.[35] D'Adda, who promptly won the King's confidence, was not content with this modest role; he desired to become an ambassador.[36] In March 1686 the Pope felt compelled to yield on this point. D'Adda was obliged by his station and by his intercourse with Lord Sunderland, to keep up friendly appearance with Petre; but Barillon easily discovered that the Papal minister disliked that Jesuit and his order, whom he considered as devoted to France.[37]

By the beginning of the year Lord Sunderland had established himself in power to the exclusion of all rivals. As noted, James had signified his increasing reliance on his services by appointing him in December of 1685 Lord President of the Council while retaining the post of principal Secretary of State. With such advisers as Sunderland and Petre, James in the spring of 1686 began a policy of infiltration. As his father had done from 1629-1640, James now turned to the courts of law for judicial endowment of those powers which his Parliament had denied him. Thus commenced a political device invented by James and used systematically by him and no other English King, the device later known as "Closeting"; an attempt by the King to secure the conversion of individuals to his own opinion in a personal interview and by means of argument and the awe of majesty. By the summer of 1686 James had twelve judges pledged to return a verdict agreeable to himself. It does not appear that James received in

---

[33] *Ibid.*, 127-128.
[34] *Ibid.*
[35] Graf, *History of the Popes*, XXXII, 502.
[36] Fox, *History*, Appendix, CXLV.
[37] *Ibid.*

audience all the twelve judges, but he certainly received Sir Thomas Jones, the Chief Justice of the Common Pleas, who, when James told him that he was determined to have twelve judges who took his own view of the prerogative, made the famous rejoinder that "His Majesty might find twelve judges of his mind, but hardly lawyers." [38] He was dismissed with three other judges in April, 1686.[39] The judges were first consulted on the question whether the King could dispense with laws relating to religious disabilities. The only ground on which such action could be justified was in cases where the royal prerogative superseded the law, and James' endeavor was to find judges who would take this view of constitutional law; he could then dismiss the judges who were not of his mind and replace them by those who were.

The first basis on which James justified his overriding of the penal laws was his dispensing power: an ancient and undoubted right of the Crown to dispense individuals from the operation of statutes when hardships or inconvenience made exceptional treatment desirable. The judges had always found it difficult to define and limit this right, but, through the centuries careful judgments had hedged it about with rules and restrictions which prevented any serious misuse. Though no separate administrative jurisdiction any longer existed, the courts of the restoration period, it must be remembered, were staffed by judges still holding permanent offices.

In one of the most famous of cases, that of *Godden vs. Hales*, Lord Chief Justice Herbert swept all the carefully built up safeguards away.[40] The action in this case was collusive, brought simply to test the validity of a dispensation which exempted a man from the legal penalties on Catholics. Sir Edward Hales was made governor of Dover, the nearest port to France, and in June, 1686, his servant Godden brought action against him for not taking the sacrament and the oaths according to the Test Act. This action was brought with a view of establishing the prerogative power claimed by the Crown to dispense with the operation of the statute. When Hales was indicted and convicted at the Rochester Assizes, action was brought to recover the £500 awarded the state to the informer.[41] It was argued before twelve judges in the King's Bench, where Hales pleaded royal pardon and dispensation in bar of the action. Eleven judges, Justice

[38] Reresby, *Memoirs of the Honorable Sir John Reresby*, 422.
[39] *Ibid.*
[40] 2 James II, *Robertson*, 245-248.
[41] *Ibid.*

Street alone dissenting, agreed that the Crown had the power to dispense.[42] The case is important when seen in the arguments explicitly laid down by Lord Chief Justice Herbert. On Monday, June 21, after having consulted with all the judges, his lordship delivered their opinions in open court:

Truly, upon the argument before us, it appears as clear a case as ever came before this court: but because men fancy I know not what difficulty, when really there is none, we were willing to give so much countenance to the question in his case, as to take the advice of all the judges of England ... To these judges there is one dissenter, brother Street, who yet continues his opinion. That the King cannot dispense in this case: but that's the opinion of one single judge, against the opinion of all.[43]

Herbert went on to lay down five points upon which the court based its decision: that the King of England was a sovereign prince; that the laws of England were the king's laws; that therefore this is an inseparable prerogative in particular cases, and upon particular necessary reasons; that of those reasons and those necessities the King himself is sole judge, which is consequent upon all; and finally. "That this is not a trust invested in, or granted to the King by the people, but the ancient remains of the sovereign power and prerogative of the Kings of England; which never yet was taken from them, nor can be."[44] Hales kept his commission and the next year was made governor of the Tower of London and master of the Ordinance.

A contemporary poem typifies some of the feeling of the public:

> Dignify'd things, may in your leave implore,
> To kiss your hands, and your high Heads adore;
> Judges you are, but you are something more
> May I draw near, and with a rough hew'd Pen
> Give a small Draught of you, the worst of men;
> Tell of your merits, and your mighty skill,
> And how you chain all courts of Justice still.
> Your Louis, far stronger than the Commons Votes,
> So freely flow from your Dispensing Throats.
> What Rome will ask, you must not here deny:
> If Hell command you too, you must comply.
>
> Worse than fanatick Priests, for they being prest
> by a wise Prince, Preach'd to Repeal the Test
> Then how's difference 'twixt you Popish Tools,
> You're downright Rogues, they only Knaves and Fools.[45]

[42] *Ibid.*
[43] Howell, *State Trials*, XI, 973-975.
[44] *Ibid.*
[45] Miscellany Poems, *The Muses Farewell To Popery* (London, 1690), 41.

The case of *Godden vs. Hales* presents a number of interesting features. The fact that several judges left their posts rather than concur in the verdict does not necessarily mean the verdict was bad; it was, however, unpopular, and fear of Parliament quite probably explained the refusal of these judges to undertake in advance to uphold it. But whether or not the verdict was bad in law, the case is a typical example of Stuart failure; an inability to win public opinion. The Stuarts found constitutional law in a fluid state and based on mutually contradictory precedents; James procured a judicial decision favorable to the Crown and congratulated himself on his success. The unsatisfactory opposition had been reached by legal but unprecedented means, of an *ad hoc* tribunal, set up not only to try a particular case, but to find a particular verdict. In all probability one of the first activities of a Parliament, if James had called one, would have been to attack the pregogative as it has been defined by the judges. In the absence of a Parliament, this decision was, through the use the King made of it, one of the main causes of the Revolution.

After the revocation of the Edict of Nantes and the persecution of French Protestants, special collections were taken up for the relief of refugee French Huguenots in most of the Anglican churches. When the brief for the collection for the Huguenots was read in churches throughout the land, William Sancroft, the Archbishop of Canterbury, was very apprehensive that the exhortations to subscribe would be reinforced by violent diatribes against the Catholics, and he did what he could to restrict the clergy to a bare reading of the brief. But he had no effective control over them in this matter, except that in a few cases he was able to show his displeasure by dismissing some of them from posts, and by stopping their pensions.[46]

In April 1686, a history of the persecution of the French Protestants published in France in both English and French circulated.[47] The French Ambassador, very disturbed about the distribution of this pamphlet, subsequently complained of it to the King and Council. An order for burning a copy was obtained and the burning carried out on Friday, May 8, at the Exchange in London, by the hangman.[48] On May 2 and May 9, Dr. John Sharp had preached two sermons against Roman Catholics at his church, St. Giles-in-the-Fields. Sharp

---

[46] Burnet, *Own Times*, III, 76.
[47] John Claude, *Account of the Complaints and Civil Persecution of the Protestants of France* (London, 1686).
[48] Burnet, *Own Times*, III, 77.

was a man of high character and attainments who, in addition to his metropolitan living, held the Deanery of Norwich.[49] He had received an anonymous letter purporting to have been written by a man whose Protestant faith had been shaken by Catholic arguments, and the sermon in question was intended to solve the doubts of his correspondent. Sharp argued that Papists were idolaters and had reflected on certain aspects of Charles II's handwriting which had been found among the late King's papers and which summarized the reasons for which he had embraced the Roman faith.[50] In the report which was made to the King, it was alleged that Sharp had been less discreet than a man of his wisdom could be expected to be. There was nothing in the sermons in any way reflecting on the King, but Henry Compton, Bishop of London, in whose diocese the sermon had been delivered, was ordered by Lord Sunderland to suspend Sharp; Compton replied that it was not in his power to suspend anyone from his ecclesiastical functions unless he had been found guilty of offence by the appropriate ecclesiastical tribunal; and, at the same time he privately requested Sharp to desist from preaching pending a settlement of his case.[51] Sharp, unable to obtain permission to speak with the King, went to Norwich to await further orders.[52]

James was furious and he determined to make this a test case. This was the first challenge to James' policy, and the challenge was accepted. James was determined to strengthen his hands against the clergy by instituting a Commission with summary powers. In July 1686, he declared in Council his intention to set up this tribunal, and gave as his object "the prevention of indiscreet preaching".

His Majesty was this day pleased to declare that for the prevention of Indiscreet preaching (His many exhortations having proved ineffectual) he had granted a Commission for the inspecting Ecclesiastical Affairs.[53]

But James had much more in mind than the pulpit attacks on Catholicism, and the powers of the Commission were actually so wide that it superseded all other ecclesiastical courts. By it James was enabled to make effective his powers as Head of the English Church, a position which as a Catholic he ought to have repudiated as an encroachment

---

[49] After the Revolution he became Archbishop of York.
[50] Thomas W. Bramston (ed.), *The Autobiography of Sir John Bramston* (London, Camden Society, Nichols and Sons, 1845), 324.
[51] *Ibid.*
[52] *Ibid.*
[53] De Beer (ed.), *Evelyn Diary*, IV, 524.

on the rights of the Pope. Through these powers, at least from Baril-lon's point of view, James planned to subvert the English Church and to further the Church of Rome.

That God had permitted that all the laws which have been passed for the establishment of the Protestant, and to destroy the Catholic religion, should now serve as a basis for what he wished to do for the re-estab-lishment of the true religion and should give him the right to exercise a power still greater than Catholic Kings, in other countries exercise over ecclesiastical affairs.[54]

To d'Adda he wrote that the unlimited authority granted by Parlia-ment over ecclesiastical affairs should be employed with an aim contrary to what was intended, that is to say, to the advantage of the Catholics.[55]

The Commission consisted of the Lord Archbishop of Canterbury, William Sancroft, who, out of respect to the Church, would not act; this gave an opportunity of putting the Bishop of Chester, a prelate less scrupulous, in his place.[56] Other members were the Bishop of Durham, Nathaniel Crewe; the Bishop of Rochester, Thomas Sprat; the Lord Chancellor, Jeffreys; the Lord Treasurer, Lord Rochester; the Lord President, Lord Sunderland; and Lord Chief Justice Herbert.[57] This group had power and authority to visit and correct all offenses, to enquire of any misdemeanors against the Ecclesiastical laws, and to punish the offenders by suspension, deprivation, and excommuni-cation, and other Church censures, as they saw fit. They also had the power to examine all irregularities and immoralities punishable by Church laws, and even into disorders in marriages; and to call before them and punish any offenders, or anyone suspected. They could cite and swear witnesses; punish the obstinate and disobedient; and tax and condemn in costs the party prosecuting or prosecuted. They had a registrar, Mr. Bridgman, and a common seal.[58] The universities and colleges, with eleven collegiate churches and schools, were expressly included within the scope of the Commission, and it was declared that the statutes of these bodies might be amended.[59]

If Parliament had been sitting, the Ecclesiastical Commission would

---

[54] Fox History, Appendix, XLVIII.
[55] Campana di Cavelli, II, 280.
[56] Dalrymple, II, 77.
[57] The History of King James Ecclesiastical Commission (London, 1711), 2-3.
[58] Henry Ellis, Ellis Original Letters Illustrative of English History, 2nd Series, IV (London, Harding and Lepard, 1827), 96-98.
[59] Ibid.

probably never have come into being, for the Restoration Parliament when it re-established the other ecclesiastical courts, had expressly and in unequivocal terms refused to reconstitute the Court of High Commission. It was recognized for what it was; an instrument in the King's hand for the exercise of arbitrary power over the clergy. Archbishop Sancroft, who ought undoubtedly to have been consulted before it was decided to set up the Commission, did not, as he certainly should have done, state that he considered the Commission illegal, but excused himself on the grounds of ill-health and pressure of other business. Lord Rochester lost much of his prestige as the chief lay supporter of the Church by accepting a seat on the Commission — he could hardly have done otherwise if he expected to continue to be Lord Treasurer; he excused himself on the ground that he could in that position best serve the interests of the Church, an excuse rather specious than sound.[60] The two other Bishops were Crewe of Durham, always servile to James, and Sprat of Rochester, a man of no violent religious principles, but one who deserves to be known in the annals of literature as one of the chief precursors of the Augustan age of English prose.[61] Sunderland represented the Catholic interest; Lord Chief Justice Herbert and Jeffreys were the last two members. In many respects Jeffreys dominated the Commission and expected silent acquiescence from his colleagues; such clearly was James' intention, for it was laid down in the rules that no quorum should be complete without him.[62]

Jeffreys proceeded at once to the prosecution of Compton, opening the trial on August 4. At an adjourned session on August 23, the Bishop claimed that he should be tried by his suffragans. This being rejected, council pleaded on his behalf that he had disobeyed the King because on receiving the royal mandate he had advised Sharp to desist from preaching. To suspend him would have been unlawful, and no man can be required to do an unlawful act.

The Bishop would have been better advised to have treated the Commission as an illegal tribunal and to have ignored the summons. He gained nothing by his attendance except a short delay for the preparation of his case, for the Commission would not allow itself to fail in the very case for which it had been appointed. If, however, Compton had deliberately absented himself and taken as his ground

60   *History of Ecclesiastical Commission*, 6.
61   F. C. Turner, *James II* (New York, The Macmillan Company, 1948), 318.
62   Howell, *State Trials*, XI, 1123-1165.

that the King had no right to set up courts condemned by Act of Parliament, the Commission would have been in dilemma; it could either have compelled attendance by sending a messenger to apprehend the bishop, or have condemned him in absentia; in either case Compton could have sought his remedy in the civil courts. On September 6, sentence of suspension on the Bishop of London was pronounced by the Commissioners,[63] but the Commissioners did not dare to expose themselves to action in the King's Bench by depriving him of the emoluments of his See.[64]

The later Stuarts, who seldom violated the law outright, were working in a vast, marginal domain, where it was by no means certain what was law and what was not. It can even be argued that James was quite within his rights. This claim rests on three things: the distinction between a commission and a court; the limitation of a commission's power to a certain class of person, usually a highly placed person; and the difference in the kind of penalty imposed.

As regards the first, it has already been seen that James' Commission was never a "Court"; as regards the second, whereas the Court of High Commission had dealt mainly with laymen, now persons of ecclesiastical or semi-ecclesiastical status were considered. As to the third point, the old Court had locked people in, whereas James' Commission, by suspension and deprivation, merely locked them out. Accordingly, there is reason to think that a tribunal such as James' was not in the minds of either of the two legislatures which had abolished the old Court of High Commission. Indeed, the old visatorial power was still exercised over universities and colleges, in some cases by the sovereign, in others by bishops or laymen or committees. Compton's trial was the first time James had challenged the Church of England which had been the strongest supporter of his dynasty. In past conflicts between church and state, the churchmen had usually shown themselves more than a match for the laymen.

Why then did James' exercise of this power cause such disquiet and opposition? Because what may be acquiesced in so long as it is haphazard and intermittent, may be resisted when it becomes constant and purposeful. James, in contrast to his predecessors, was obviously working on a definite policy. His nominees were even more disreputable than their predecessors, but that did not matter, since the Stuarts were almost expected to have a preference for such

63 Bramston (ed.), *Bramston Autobiography*, 265.
64 *Ibid.*

persons; what did matter was that they were all Roman Catholics.

During the summer John Dryden turned Catholic.[65] It was no light thing to have secured the cooperation of the greatest living master of the English language. The first service which he was requested to perform in return for his pension was to defend the Church in prose against Edward Stillingfleet. But the art of saying things well is useless to a man who has nothing to say; and this was Dryden's case. He soon found himself unequally paired with an antagonist whose entire life had been one long training for controversy. The veteran easily defeated the novice. A very caustic poem appeared at this time concerning Dryden's conversion:

> On all religions present, and on past,
> Long hast thou rayl'd — and chose the worst at least.
> 'Tis like thyselfe; 'tis what thou didst before;
> Rayl'd against all women, — and then married a whore.[66]

Through the use of the prerogative and dispensing power, every person and institution could be subject to the King's wishes. The dispensing power was employed for the purpose of enabling Roman Catholics to hold ecclesiastical preferment. One of the most flagrant examples of these warrants was in favor of a wretch named Edward Sclater, who had two benefices which he was determined to keep at all costs and through all changes. He administered the sacrament to his parishioners according to the rites of the Church of England on Palm Sunday, 1686; on Easter Sunday, only seven days later he was at mass.[67] The royal dispensation had authorized him to retain the emoluments of his benefices.[68]

Another form of penetration was seen in the large number of new religious establishments set up in London, to the horror of the populace. The Franciscans established their headquarters in a mansion in Lincoln's Inn Fields;[69] the Carmelites had their convent in the city;[70] the Benedictines were established in St. James' Palace; while in the

---

[65] Llewelyn Powys (ed.), *The Life and Times of Anthony a' Wood* (London, Wishart and Company, 1932), 250.
[66] *Ibid.*
[67] *The Reasons of Edward Sclater, Minister of Putney, for his Conversion to the Catholic Faith and Communion* (London, 1686).
[68] On Rogation Sunday, May 5, 1689, he made public recantation of the Catholic Religion, and was received into the communion of the Church of England in the Savoy Church.
[69] Clarke (ed.), *James II*, II, 80.
[70] *Ibid.*

Savoy the Jesuits had a church and a school.[71] From the King's London printing press, under the direction of Henry Hills, there poured forth a mass of Roman Catholic literature, which provided good game for such controversalists as Tillotson, Tension, Stillingfleet, Sherlock and Wake.[72] In Oxford Obadiah Walker busied himself with the printing and publishing of books advocating the claims of his faith.[73] Roman Catholic chapels rose all over the country; cowls, girdles of ropes, and strings of beads constantly appeared in the streets. A convent rose at Clerkenwell on the site of the ancient cloister of St. John.[74] To make matters worse for the London populace, the army camped on Hounslow Heath became larger and more active. There were constant rumors of quarrels between the Protestant and popish soldiers.[75] A short tract had been actively circulated throughout the ranks.[76] The writer Samuel Johnson exhorted the troops to use their arms in defense, not of the mass book, but of the bible. Johnson, a priest of the Church of England, had been chaplain to Lord Russell. He was one of those persons who are mortally hated by their opponents, and less loved than respected by their allies.[77] On November 21 he was tried at the Court of Kings Bench upon charges of libel, and on December 16th was sentenced to stand in the pillory, to pay a fine of 500 marks, and to be whipped from Newgate to Tyburn. The means of communication were being tightened up throughout England.[78]

On the foreign front things were no better. The relations between James and William of Orange during the greater part of the year 1686 appear, from the few reports between them, to have been amicable. During the middle of January, for instance, James wrote to the Prince to ask him to give more protection to regular priests in Holland. He asked that they no longer be banished out of Rotterdam and other towns.[79] On January 26 James was pleased to note that the Prince had saved the Priests.[80] In May the situation began to get worse. James

[71]   David Ogg, England in the Reigns of James II and William III (London, Oxford At The Clarendon Press, 1955), 168.
[72]   Historical Manuscripts Commission, Manuscripts of the Earl of Downshire, I, 173.
[73]   Ibid.
[74]   Ogg, England in the Reigns of James II and William III, 169.
[75]   Luttrell, Brief Relations, I, 380.
[76]   Samuel Johnson, A Humble and Hearty Address to all English Protestants in the Army (London, 1686).
[77]   Thomas B. Macaulay, The History of England From the Accession, II, 96.
[78]   Luttrell, Brief Relations, I, 381, 388.
[79]   Dalrymple, III, Book IV, Appendix, 176.
[80]   Ibid., 177.

wrote three letters to the Prince on the subject of English refugees in Holland.[81] In these letters he assumed that William would agree that it was undesirable that James' enemies should be allowed to congregate so near to the English coast; and he requested him to use his influence with the States General to prevent the abuse of the right of asylum.

Towards the end of the summer, however, trouble commenced in a disagreement between the King and the Prince regarding the appointment of a new commander for the six British regiments which were in the pay of the States General. On July 23, James wrote to William saying that he had been unable to find a man of the necessary qualifications but now he was decided on Francis Taafe, Earl of Carlingsford.[82] The wording of this letter is significant in view of what subsequently occurred, for James at this state made no claim to do more than recommend, and by implication he admitted William's right to object to the appointment. To William the recommendation was embarrassing: the chief object of his policy was to avoid giving any sort of offense to James, but commands in the Dutch army were given by the Captain-General, and the appointment of a Catholic would seriously injure him with his own people. William wrote that it would hurt him extremely if he gave the commands of these six regiments to a person of that religion.[83]

James replied through Sunderland in uncomprising terms, saying that, "He cannot but desire that my Lord Carlingford may command these regiments and thinks the alterations of times and persons ought to be considered." [84] To this letter William replied on September 2 with a polite but stubborn refusal.

It would not be decent and I have too much respect for His Majesty to enter further into reasonings on that matter, and therefore I have only to beg you will humbly intreat His Majesty on my part to have the goodness not to insist upon this affair.[85]

The situation in England at the end of the year 1686 can best be described in the words of Barillon:

The discontent is great and general, but the fear incurring still worse evils

[81]   Dalrymple, I, Book II, Appendix, 54-56.
[82]   Turner, *James II*, 349.
[83]   A. J. Mazure, *Histoire de la Revolution de 1688 en Angleterre* (Paris, 1825), 409.
[84]   Dalrymple, II, 30-31.
[85]   *Ibid.*, 31-32.

restrains all who have any thing to lose. The king openly expresses his joy at finding himself in a situation to strike bold strokes.[86]

The Ecclesiastical Commission was still sitting; the opposition pamplets were being suppressed; and James' dispensing power cast a gloom over England as the year closed.

---

[86]   Fox, *History*, Appendix, LVII.

CHAPTER IV

DECLARATION OF INDULGENCE, 1687

The dilemma facing the Tories at the beginning of the year also plagued the Prince of Orange. Two courses of action presented themselves to the Prince. He could maintain the policy he had adopted in the closing years of Charles II, that is, wait for the natural run of events to bring him his wife's inheritance. With most people he did not expect the interval to be long, as James was not particularly robust and there was no reason for thinking he would long survive his brother. The possibility that a rival heir might be born was slight; even more unlikely was it that James might try to divert the succession to Anne, or to one of his illegitimate sons. The other choice would be to plan the overthrowal of James and take the throne by conquest; during the early months of 1687 William chose the former.

During January William was able to state his views to still greater advantage. In December of 1686, James had sent his Quaker friend, William Penn, to The Hague on a special mission to sound out the Prince on the subject of religious toleration, and to persuade William and Mary to declare publicly in favor of the repeal of the penal laws and the Test Act.[1] Penn had no official status, but his position in the English Court was well-known and the probability that he might be acting without the King's knowledge was negligible, even if he were not under express orders. As a member of a dissenting group that believed in complete separation of Church and State, Penn opposed Anglican toleration. Although to his way of thinking the state should have nothing whatever to do with religious affairs, concessions to political necessity could be made through a division of the public offices so that one third of them should be reserved to the Anglicans and the remainder be divided equally between the Roman Catholics and the Protestant Dissenters. Penn, anxious for William's approval of this plan, gave him to understand that he had been commissioned

[1]   Burnet, *Own Times,* I, 693-694.

by the King to make this request.[2] Gilbert Burnet, who was then at
The Hague and had conversations with Penn, alleged that, as the price
of William's acquiescence, James offered to join the coalition against
France.[3]

Even if Penn's proposals had been workable, William could not have
accepted them without abandoning the support of the Anglican party
against which they were directed. Such a declaration would forfeit all
claim to his leadership of the English Protestants. Neither could he
afford to oppose the suggestions outright; the situation was delicate.
William, a Calvinist himself, was well aware that Dissenters comprised
a substantial part of his strength in England.

The Prince met the problem astutely. He told Penn — and Burnet
saw to it that the right people in England knew the nature of his
answer — that he favored religious toleration even for Roman Catholics, but that he regarded the Test Acts as political safeguards of
Protestantism and that nothing could induce him to take a different
stand. He would not join those who intended to repeal those laws.[4]
Penn's visit therefore hurt James instead of helping him, in that it
gave William the chance to pronounce views that would attract Dissenters, and even those Catholics who wanted only the right to
worship freely. At the same time, it gave assurance to the Anglicans.

In this contest for the support of the Dissenters, James, however,
had many advantages. He could offer release from the humiliation
and abuses of the Clarendon Code; he could perhaps even give that
release the sanction of enacted law, provided, of course, that he could
assemble Parliament willing to take such a step. But offsetting that
lay his supreme disadvantage: he was a Papist. Whatever dispensation
he granted to the non-Anglican Protestants would go also to the
Catholics whom most of them hated bitterly. No matter what he might
say or do about liberty of conscience for all, he would always be open
to the charge of insincerity and of acting primarily in the interests of
his co-religionists.

James' weakness was William's strength. The latter could speak
safely of religious toleration, for no one could suspect him of being
pro-Romanist. He drew additional support from his home country's
record in maintaining religious toleration for all Protestants and even,

---

[2] Ibid.
[3] Ibid.
[4] Thomas Clarkson, Memoirs of the Public and Private Life of William Penn
(London, Bradshaw and Blacklock, 1849), 173.

to a degree, for Roman Catholics at the same time that political authority rested safely in the hands of the Calvinists. His own devotion to Calvinism was another great drawing card, especially among the leaders of the English Presbyterians, who, like their Anglican rivals and would-be friends, disliked Anabaptists and Quakers only slightly less than they disliked Papists. Finally, the Tory leaders had good reason to believe that William's views on the English constitution corresponded with their own, and that, as heir to the Crown whether by virtue of his own claims or those of his wife, he was the natural defender of that constitutional aspect against Parliament or against Republicans. In what other man could there be found such a happy combination of attributes?

James' second attempt to win over William followed almost immediately after Penn's failure. It was carried out through the Marquis of D'Albeville who was sent to The Hague in January to replace the objectional Bevil Skelton, as ambassador.[5] He was not an improvement on his predecessor. In fact, James could scarcely have done worse. An Irish Catholic, D'Albeville had a reputation in his own time for incompetence and unreliability, and his nationality and religion made it easy for contemporaries to cast doubts upon his integrity. The primary reason for Skelton's dismissal had been the suspicion that he had been spying on William; consequently it was difficult to find a successor who would at once be acceptable to the Prince and would not attach himself to William's interests.[6] D'Albeville had orders to protest to William his open favors to Burnet and to try to get him to announce his approval of the repeal of the Penal Laws.[7] D'Albeville succeeded somewhat in his first task but failed, of course, in the second. The Prince was growing tired of the self-important divine, and probably too of Burnet's violent antagonism towards James. At any rate, he complied to the extent of sending him from the Court; he did not, of course, break off correspondence with this valuable contact.

Meanwhile a change in the domestic scene further weakened James' hold over the Anglican Church. At the suggestion, it is said, of Lord Sunderland, anxious for the downfall of his rival, the King dismissed his brother-in-law, the Earl of Rochester, for no better reason than his refusal to turn Catholic, and entrusted the Treasurership to a Board of

[5] Burnet, *Own Times*, I, 707-708.
[6] *Ibid.*
[7] Dalrymple, Part I, Book II, Appendix, 54-55.

Commissioners.[8] Rochester had been steadily losing influence since the summer of 1685, and for a year his activities had been confined largely to his own department. But he was still Lord Treasurer, and nominally, at least, the chief adviser of the King; he was also one of the chief lay supporters of the Church of England, and it was felt that he was in a position to prevent the most serious breaches in the defenses of that Church. Publicly, James gave as his reason for the dismissal his belief that the Treasury was too great a charge for one man.[9] Although a sound reason, it was one which might have occurred to him prior to June 1685, when James first mentioned his intention. James further said in Council that he was not acting from any dissatisfaction against the late Lord Treasurer, for he had served him very well both before his coming to the Crown and since.[10] But James weakened the value of his tribute by not appointing Rochester to the new Commission of Treasury. He did show a certain gratitude by securing to him a considerable income, £4000 a year from the Post Office for ninety-nine years or three lives, in addition to the £16,000 granted him six months earlier, but he cut him off entirely from the royal counsels.[11]

Rochester had been put to a different test from that which was employed in the other cases. He was not asked whether or not he would support legislation in favor of the Catholics, but actually to join the Roman Catholic Church himself, and it was no doubt understood that his retention of the Lord Treasurership depended on his decision. Rochester's enemies had persuaded James that the Lord Treasurer had been behind the nation's obstinate resistance to his designs for toleration.[12] In James' opinion the claims of the Church of Rome were so unassailable that it was only by a persistent refusal to listen to the arguments of the priests that Protestants were able to keep their faith; he was unaware that appeals to reason are of small effect in conversions, and he pressed Rochester to allow two priests to attempt to convert him. Rochester could not frustrate the King in a harmless design on which he had set his heart, but he asked that two priests of his own Church should be present to uphold their own views.

[8]   Bramston (ed.), *Bramston Autobiography*, 234.
[9]   *Historical Manuscripts Commission, Manuscripts of the Duke of Rutland*, II, 109.
[10]   *Ibid.*
[11]   De Beer (ed.), *Evelyn Diary*, IV, 533.
[12]   Sybil Rosenfeld (ed.), *The Letterbook of Sir George Etherage* (London, Oxford University Press, 1928), 172.

James agreed and there were two conferences, at the first of which James was present and took part. As is usual in religious controversy there was no agreement on basic beliefs, merely assertion and counter-assertion.[13]

The expected result followed, and the new Commission for the Treasury was headed by a Catholic, Lord Belasyse, who was seventy-two years of age and a cripple, and another Catholic, Henry Jermyn, a man of notorious incompetence.[14] The three other Lords of the Treasury were Lord Godolphin, Sir Stephen Fox, and Sir John Ernle; these three were good appointments as they had all been on the Commission in the reign of Charles II, and the presense of Godolphin particularly was a guarantee of efficiency.

Very shortly afterwards, Rochester's brother, the Earl of Clarendon, was recalled from Ireland, and was succeeded by the Earl of Tyrconnel as Lord Deputy.[15] Clarendon had hoped to be allowed to retain his post as Lord Privy Seal, the duties of which had been performed during his absence in Ireland by three members, but the King relieved him of that also, and made no provision to provide for his maintenance.[16]

Through these dismissals James hoped to appease both the "low" and the "high" Catholics. The former argued that he ought to give up the idea of establishing the Catholic religion in the Kingdom in his lifetime, "that it was enough for his glory to have begun the work, and that he compromised it by seeking to urge it forward by violent means." [17] The high Catholics, on the other hand, besought James to remember that the Catholic religion had already been established once, and that to lose, by scruples such as those which had restrained Queen Mary, the opportunity of extirpating the Protestant heresy from the Kingdom would be a weakness unworthy of a King. They added that history gave ample evidence how little the wishes of Kings were respected, that the revolutionists under the late King, by doing their utmost to exclude his present majority from the succession, had shown how they viewed the question between the two religions.

This state of affairs continued for some months, but James resolved

---

13   *Ibid.*
14   *Ibid.,* 139-140.
15   Lister (ed.), *Clarendon Correspondence,* III, 136.
16   But nothing could shake his loyalty. He alone of those who had held high office under James in the early part of his reign refused to take the oaths to William and Mary.
17   Lister (ed.), *Clarendon Correspondence,* III, 140.

to go on in his design of toleration for all. On February 12th, 1687, he sent a proclamation of Indulgence to Scotland.[18] It proposed that the King had an absolute power vested in him, so that all his subjects were bound to obey him without reserve; by virtue of this power the King repealed all the severe laws that were vested in his grandfather's name during his infancy.[19] He took off all disabilities on his Roman Catholic subjects and made them capable of all employments and benefices. He also slackened the laws against moderate Presbyterians and Quakers:

In the first place, We allow and tolerate the moderate Presbyterians, to Meet in their Private Houses, and there to hear all such Ministers, as either have, or willing to accept of Our Indulgence; . . . In the meantime, it is Our Royal Will and Pleasure, that Field Conventicles, and such as Preach or Exercise at them, shall be prosecuted according to the utmost Severity of our Laws made against them . . . . In like manner, We do hereby tolerate Quakers to meet and exercise in their Form, in any Place or Places appointed for their worship.[20]

The Declaration was strangely drawn, and liable to much just censure. By this Declaration, the King raised his power to a new high, not only of suspending, but of repealing laws, and of enacting new ones by his own authority. Gilbert Burnet, still in exile, penned a pamphlet on the Scottish Declaration.[21] Here he argued that the English people ought not only to consider what consequences were now drawn from them, but what might be drawn from them in the future: "for if they are on force to justify that which is now inferred from them, it will be full as just to draw from the same Premises an Abolition of the Protestant Religion." [22] In other words, Burnet maintained that through this declaration James was asserting that he had rights over his subjects to command what he wanted and the obligation on the part of the subjects to obey.[23] He further attacked James's premise that since the laws were enacted in King James the sixth's minority they should be abolished.[24]

[18]   James II, *A Proclamation for a Toleration in Scotland, February 12, 1687* (London, 1687).
[19]   *Ibid.,* 1.
[20]   *Ibid.,* 2.
[21]   Gilbert Burnet, *Some Reflections Upon His Majesties Proclamation of the 12th of February 1687 for a Toleration in Scotland, together with the said Proclamation* (London, 1687).
[22]   *Ibid.,* 1.
[23]   *Ibid.,* 2.
[24]   *Ibid.,* 3.

Burnet also referred to the judges' decision the previous year. "For if twelve Men, that get into Scarlet and Furs, have an Authority to dissolve all our laws, the English Government is to be hereafter looked at with as much scorn, as it had hitherto drawn admiration." [25]

This Declaration thus gave toleration to Catholics. The Quakers had little reason to complain; but the Indulgence given to the Presbyterians, who constituted the majority of the Scottish people, was burdened with conditions. In place of the old test, which excluded Catholics and Presbyterians alike from office, a new test admitted Catholics but excluded most Presbyterians. The latter were prevented from worshipping God anywhere but in private dwellings; they were not to build meeting houses; they were not even to use a barn or an out-house for religious exercises; and it was distinctly stated that if they disobeyed any of the provisions they would be prosecuted to the full letter of the law.[26]

There is reason to believe that when James published this proclamation he had by no means fully made up his mind to a coalition with the Puritans, and that his object may have been to grant just so much favor to them as might suffice to frighten the Anglican Churchmen into submission. He therefore waited a month, in order to see what effect the edict put forth at Edinburgh would produce in England. It was expected that the Parliament would shortly meet for the dispatch of business and many members were in London. The King proceeded to canvass them individually. He believed the Whigs would find it difficult to resist his earnest request, addressed to them not from the throne, but in the familiarity of conversation. Through these "closetings", however, James ascertained the impossibility of obtaining the consent of a majority of the Commons to a repeal of the Test and Penal laws. If Parliament met, it would, even during the King's life, abolish his dispensing power which he had established. On March 18 the King informed the Privy Council that he had determined to prorogue the Parliament until the end of November, and to grant by his own dispensing authority entire liberty of conscience to all his subjects.[27]

On April 4, 1687 the King set out his declaration of toleration and liberty of conscience for England. It was drawn up in much more modest terms than the Scottish proclamation had been. In the pre-

[25] *Ibid.*
[26] James II, *A Proclamation for a Toleration in Scotland* (1687), 2.
[27] *London Gazette*, March 21, 1687, 1.

amble the King expressed his aversion to persecution on account of religion, and the necessity that he found of allowing his subjects liberty of conscience, in which he did not doubt the concurrence of his Parliaments.[28]

The Declaration began with a short statement concerning religious conformity during the last four reigns. "It is visible the Success has not answered the Design, and that the Difficulty is invincible." [29] He swore allegiance and protection to the Church of England and her clergy:

In the first place We do Declare, That We will Protect and Maintain Our Archbishops, Bishops, and Clergy, and all other Our Subjects of the Church of England, in the free Exercise of their Religion, as by Law Established, and in the quiet and full Enjoyment of all their Possessions, without any Molestation or Disturbance whatsoever.[30]

The next major provision concerned the suspension of the Penal Acts.

We do likewise Declare, That it is Our Royal Will and Pleasure, That from henceforth the Execution of all manner of Penal Laws in Matters Ecclesiastical, for not coming to Church, or not receiving the Sacrament, or for any other Non-conformity to the Religion Established, or for any Reason of the Exercise of Religion in any manner whatsover, be immediately Suspended; And the further Exclusion of the said Penal Laws is hereby Suspended.[31]

James went on to assure the Dissenters and Roman Catholics that the Crown would do everything in its power to see that this protection was carried out. "That no Disturbance of any kind be made or given unto them, under Pain of Our Displeasure, and to be further proceeded against with the uttermost severity." [32]

The Declaration closed with further assurances of the oaths of Supremacy and Allegiance and also assurances to Non-Anglican property holders.

That it is our Royal Will and Pleasure, That the Oaths commonly called, The Oaths of Supremacy and Allegiance, and also the several Tests and Declarations mentioned in the Acts of Parliament made in the 25th and 30th years of the Reign of Our Late Royal Brother King Charles the Second, shall not at any time hereafter be required to be Taken, Declared,

---

[28] James II, *His Majesties Gracious Declaration To All His Loving Subjects for Liberty of Conscience, 1687* (London, 1687).
[29] *Ibid.*, 1.
[30] *Ibid.*
[31] *Ibid.*, 2.
[32] *Ibid.*, 3.

or Subscribed by any Person or Persons whatsoever, who is or shall be employed in any Office or Place of Trust either Civil or Military, under Us or in Our Government. And We do further Declare it to be Our Pleasure and Intention from time to time hereafter, to Grant Our Royal Dispensations under Our Great Seal to all Our Loving Subjects so to be employed.

And although the Freedom and Assurance We have hereby given in relations to Religion and Property, might be sufficient to remove from the Minds of our Loving Subjects all Fears and Jealousies in relation to either; yet We have thought fit further to Declare, That We will Maintain them in all their Properties and Possessions, as well of Church and Abby-Lands, as in any other their Lands and Properties whatsoever.[33]

The Declaration of Indulgence of April evoked from Gilbert Burnet some further reflections, the more important in that Burnet subsequently represented this Declaration as the real justification for the English Revolution. To the principle of toleration, Burnet showed himself openly favorable. He regarded a Parliamentary revision of the severe penal laws against Papists as eminently to be desired.

But I will take the boldness to add one thing that the Kings wholesale suspending of laws strikes at the root of the whole government and subverts it quite; for though the executive power of the law is entirely in the King; and the Law . . . . has . . . . made it unlawful upon any pretence whatsoever to resist it . . . . yet the Legislative power is not so entirely in the King . . . . or which is all one, suspended, but by consent of Parliament.[34]

The noble doctrine of universal toleration could not be held in theory, or applied in practice, without restrictions. No governor had the right to tolerate people whose religion commanded them to overturn his government. Toleration of any kind was impossible unless people behaved tolerably. The problem of toleration was always one of degree. James had faced this problem since his accession to the throne. In England the Nonconformists were regarded by every single member of the King's government as men who were irreconcilable enemies of the monarchy. Many of them had openly sympathized with Monmouth; and many had taken an active part in the rebellion.

The King had made a public gesture of friendship to the Dissenters in November of the previous year; he remitted a sentence of imprisonment, which had been inflicted for a seditious libel, upon the

[33] *Ibid.*, 2-4.
[34] Gilbert Burnet, A *Letter Containing Some Reflections on His Majesty's Declaration for Liberty of Conscience Dated the Fourth of April, 1687* (London, 1687), 6.

Nonconformists minister, Richard Baxter.[35] Although the English Nonconformists as a whole were grateful to the King for his efforts on their behalf, the Scottish Presbyterians were naturally inclined to be suspicious of clemency shown by a Popish Prince. The credulity of these people was beyond measure. Richard Baxter, for instance, was honestly convinced that Catholics recognized no authority, whether of God or man, except the Pope of Rome; that the Jesuits were men who would commit any crime with a special skill and enthusiasm, for the sake of the Church. Baxter believed that these Jesuits had set fire to the city of London in 1666 and he believed the whole of the fantastic inventions of Titus Oates.[36]

The Declaration of Indulgence, although not unexpected, was greeted with consternation by James' opponents. Macaulay described the situation a little naively: "The Anglican party", he wrote, "was in amazement and terror. This new turn of events was indeed alarming. The House of Stuart leagued with the republican and regicide sect against the old Cavaliers of England." [37]

From the distance in time it is almost impossible to establish the Dissenters feelings. Whatever their inner-convictions, however, their immediate response, except for a few stubborn souls like John Bunyan, was either passive acceptance or outright joy. Several declarations of gratitude were sent to the Court, especially from the more radical sects such as the Quakers and the Anabaptists, so that James had very good reason to believe that his action was meeting with approval. This approval was expressed by the people in the only possible way, since Parliament, when it sat represented mainly the landed interests. Hundreds of addresses of thanks were sent to Whitehall from all over the country. Behind this impressive revelation of public opinion there was no political organization at work collecting signatures; no pressure was exerted upon public bodies.[38]

Some of the addresses and James's subsequent answer to them are important in judging whether this enlightened move was a plan to establish popery. The thanks of the Presbyterians to James were presented by a Mr. Hurst. James received him graciously and answered:

[35] Frederick J. Powicke, *A Life of the Reverend Richard Baxter, 1615-1691* (Boston, Houghton Mifflin Company, 1924), 260-261.
[36] *Ibid.*
[37] Macaulay, *History of England*, II, 198.
[38] Between April 13, 1687 and July 18, 1688, a contemporary estimated the number of representations of witnesses at over 200. Luttrell, *Brief Relations*, I, 298-451.

I have already found two good effects of my declaration; the easing and pleasing of my subjects you speak of, and my restoring to God the Empire over conscience: .... And, gentlemen, I hope to live to see the day when you shall as well have Magna Carta for the liberty of conscience, as you have had for your properties.[39]

The King's anxiety to obtain approval for his favorite measure of a general indulgence led him to accept addresses from almost every class of men. Even the Master of the Incorporated Body of Cooks about London was graciously received upon this occasion. The language was professional; for he compared the Declaration to the "Almighty's Manna", which suited everyone's "Palate", and professed the penal laws might be as well employed "to regulate men's taste in eating as their ideas of religion." [40]

Political and religious skeptics naturally made fun of the Declaration. Probably the best known was the thanks from the Atheists, or the Sect of the Epicureans.

We are sure there is no party of men more improved and advanced by your indulgence, both as to principles and proselytes of England, and our cabals are as full as your Royal Chapel; for your unlimited toleration has freed the nation from the troublesome bigoties of religion and has taught men to conclude, that there is nothing sacred or divine but trade and empire, and nothing of such eternal moment as secular interest.[41]

In an address of thanks to James the Quakers emphasized their general expectations that this Declaration of Indulgence would result in peace, increased trade, and prosperity of the Kingdom. Penn declared that the King was now upon a principle that has good nature, Christianity, and the good of society on its side.[42] "By this grace he has relieved the distressed subjects from their civil sufferances, and raised to himself a new and lasting empire, by adding their affections to their duty." [43] James answered this presentation, "... and that all men ought to have liberty of their conscience: and what I have promised in my declaration I will continue to perform as long as I live." [44] He also went on to say that he hoped that he would be able to settle

---

[39] *Thanks of Presbyterians to James II*, IX, reprinted in *Somers Tracts* (London, Cadell and Davies, 1813), 35.

[40] *Ibid.*, 46.

[41] *To the King's Most Excellent Majesty The Humble Address of the Atheists, or the Sect of the Epicureans* (London, 1687).

[42] *Somers Tracts*, IX, 34.

[43] *Ibid.*

[44] *Ibid.*

the religious question so that after ages should have no reason to alter it.[45]

On account of his intimacy with the King, and his support of the Declaration, Penn was accused not only of being a papist but a Jesuit; reports spread that he had been educated at the Jesuit College of St. Omer, that he had taken orders in Rome, and had obtained a dispensation to marry.[46] In replying to these accusations, Penn gave a fine testimonial to the sincerity of James:

In the presence of almighty God I do delare that the King never did once, directly or indirectly, attack me or tempt me upon that subject, the many years that I have had the advantage of free access to him . . . . In his honor as well as in my own defence, I am obliged in conscience to say that he has ever declared to me it was his opinion (That conscience should be free); and on all occasions, when Duke, he never refused me the repeated proofs of it.[47]

In place of the expressions of gratitude early summer saw a pamphlet war with Dissenter fighting Dissenter, and the Anglican Church joining the fray. Hot words and exaggerated accusations flew wildly from both sides, but the most cogent arguments came from the opponents of the Crown. James' sincerity was questioned. This misgiving was clearly expressed in what is considered the most famous pamphlet of the seventeenth century, and certainly one of the most influential during this period. It was Lord Halifax's *A Letter to a Dissenter upon occasion of his Majesties late Gracious Declaration of Indulgence.* Halifax's object was to prevent that discussion between Protestant Nonconformists and the Church of England which the Declaration was so likely to produce, and to unite them firmly against the papists. All the arguments which could convince a Nonconformist that it was his duty and his interest to prefer an alliance with the Church to an alliance with the Court were illustrated with lively eloquence unmatched by any other appeal of its time. "Men who are sore, run to the nearest Remedy with too much haste to consider all the consequences. It is like telling Lovers, in the beginning of their joys, that they will in a little time have an end." [48] Halifax hoped that the Dissenters had not gone so far in the new found liberty but that they

[45]   *Ibid.*
[46]   Thomas Clarkson, *Memoirs of the Public and Private Life of William Penn,* 160.
[47]   *Ibid.*
[48]   George Savile, *Marquis of Halifax, A Letter to a Dissenter upon Occasion of his Majesties late Gracious Declaration of Indulgence* (London, 1687), 2.

would still listen to reason.[49] He offered two suggestions: first was to suspect their new friends, "Consider that notwithstanding the smooth language which is now put on to engage you, these new Friends did not make you their choice, but their Refuge." The second, "the Duty incumbent upon you, in Christianity and Prudence, not to hazard the Public Safety, neither by desire of Ease, nor of Revenge." [50]

Halifax said that the alliance between liberty and infallibility brings together the two most contrary things in the world: Roman Catholics and the tolerating of liberty of conscience. The Roman Catholics would not give liberty to heretics.

Suppose then, for Arguments sake, that the Mediators of this new alliance, should be such as have been formerly imployed in Treatises of the same kind, and there detected to have Acted by Order, and to have been Impower'd to give Encouragements and Rewards. Would not this be an Argument to suspect them?[51]

He went on to say that because of the desire of enjoying Liberty which had long been denied them, they tended to overlook some of the strings attached. He warned them to think twice before they went any further in a losing bargain.

It is time for you to look into the Danger of the Means: The same Reason that made you desirous to get Liberty, must make you solicitous to preserve it; so that the next Thought will naturally be, not to engage yourself beyond Retreat, and to agree so far with the Principles of all Religion, as not to rely upon a Death-Bed Repentence.[52]

The effect of this pamphlet was immense, for more than 20,000 copies were circulated during the first year and it went through three printings.

An anonymous pamphlet immediately came out in answer to Halifax's *Letter to a Dissenter*. It was probably written by Sir Roger L'Estrange endeavoring to save his consistency, by declaring that though he had for twenty years resisted religious liberty as a right of the people, he acquiesced in it because it was now a gift from the King. Why should it be a crime to be thankful for a favor granted? "Every citizen is bound in conscience to attend the call and the service of their Prince, for the precept is positive, without any qualifications, Limitations, or condition whatsoever." The question was raised as to

---

[49] *Ibid.*, 2.
[50] *Ibid.*
[51] *Ibid.*, 5.
[52] *Ibid.*, 9.

whether or not the Penal Laws were just and equitable laws, and consistent with the law of God.[53]

For if the Church of England for once would lay wide that Idol Interest, and consider what is agreeable to God, and what not, and remember that Golden Rule, of doing unto others as they would be done by, I am confident she could never be so eager an advocate for the continuing of these un Christian laws.[54]

The author injects an element of shame into the pamphlet also. He says that as long as the King complied with the Church of England's interests and desires, the prerogative was strained to the highest, but as soon as the King acted contrary to their interests, "though in the most just and necessary occasion that ever was", great was the cry.[55] Just because the Dissenters addressed the King for legal dispensation, they should not be charged with giving a blow to all law.

An anonymous author immediately answered this work. In it he said, "I will believe that a chaste Dissenter may live in the same Kingdom with the Romanist without the hazard of a Rape." The author asserted that he wished the Church of England, instead of criticizing James, would put out her own declaration of repentance and indulgence.[56]

A Letter in answer to Two Main Questions of the First Letter to a Dissenter, also published anonymously, posed the question, "Whether Protestant Dissenters ought to refuse the proposed legal toleration, including Catholic Dissenters?" The proposed answer stated that they should take what they could get and that they should not be excluded in prudence or in conscience; second, "whether Protestant Dissenters ought to expect the said Toleration, until the next Succession upon the suggested hopes of Excluding Catholics?" The author claimed that there was good reason why they should defer it until the next Succession.[57]

The King hath granted you a present Toleration, and intends with your concurrence to make it his Legacy to you, and Your perpetual inheritance,

---

[53]   Roger L'Estrange, An Answer to a Letter to a Dissenter upon His Majesties Late Gracious Declaration of Indulgence (London, 1687), 2.
[54]   Ibid., 1.
[55]   Ibid., 4.
[56]   Remarks upon a Pamphlet stiled, a Letter to a Dissenter, In another Letter to the Same Dissenter (London, 1687), 4.
[57]   A Letter in Answer to two Main Questions of the first Letter to the Same Dissenter (London, 1687), 13.

by a fundamental law. The sum of all is this; an equal toleration if any, is most just. The present time, the most eligible.[58]

This pamphlet was answered by another, probably written by L'Estrange also. "The Letter itself is like a Pleasure-Boat, richer in the Trimming than in the Sailing." [59] The author goes on to assure the readers that James' motives were pure. "We can never trust our lives and Fortunes in safer Hands than his, to whom by our Addresses we have so unanimously tendered them." [60]

The Bishop of Oxford, Samuel Parker, one of James' strongest supporters, declared his "Utter abhorrence of the Test Act; he regarded its abettors as the sworn enemies to the peace of Christendom".[61] He reminded his readers that the Test had been originally devised by Shaftesbury, and recast with a more stringent wording at the time of the Oates Plot, chiefly as a political instrument to be used against the Duke of York.[62] The Bishop's main, and most lengthy, argument was theological; he asserted that to take the test involved a denial of dogmas regarded as an essential part of the Christian faith:

And I date appeals to the Honourable members of both Houses, if (when they consider seriously with themselves they have any distinct ideas or Notion in their minds of the thing they were so solemnly renounced) I fancy if every man were obliged to give his own account of it, whatever Transubstantiation may be, it would certainly be Babel.[63]

This was the first occasion since the Reformation that a controversy on a religious and political question had been held with freedom to print allowed on both sides. Members of the Protestant party, followers of Tillotson and Stillingfleet who had always taught the idolatry of Rome as if it were an article of faith, were furious with the Bishop. They professed to regard him as a traitor. Many felt that James could establish liberty of conscience not by law but by a questionable use of the prerogative which, if allowed to remain unchallenged, could well be used later to deprive the Dissenters of their newly acquired privileges once the established religion was beaten and the Papist was in control. Even should the King give his deeds the sanction of enacted law,

---

[58]   *Ibid.*, 17-18.
[59]   A Modest Censure of the Immodest Letter to a Dissenter (London, 1687), 3.
[60]   *Ibid.*, 9.
[61]   Samuel Parker, *Reasons for abrogating the test imposed upon all members of parliament* (London, 1687), 5.
[62]   *Ibid.*, 6-7.
[63]   *Ibid.*, 9.

the fact remained that he had issued the Declaration before, not after taking such a step.

In the spring of 1687, just after the Declaration was issued, rumors that some sort of printed statement from the Prince might appear had gone about England.[64] The diplomatic situation in Europe, where Catholic princes and the Papacy itself, none of whom William could afford to antagonize, might well view a negative attitude on William's part unfavorably also had to be considered.

The sincerity of James in offering freedom of conscience to all his subjects is apparent from the honesty of his letters to his son-in-law, who, at the very time, was waiting for the propitious moment to move against him.

For my dear son the Prince of Orange. . . . . I am very glad all things continue to be quiet on your side of the water, they are so here, and I find my declaration contributes much to it, the generality of the nation being satisfied with it, and at ease by it.[65]

Toward the latter part of May he added two letters which confirm this opinion. "My Declaration has put people's minds much at ease, and I have great reason to be well pleased with having put it out." [66] On May 27, James added, "I am satisfied I have not made one step but what is good for the Kingdom in general as well as for the monarchy, and have more reason every day than other to be pleased with having put out my Declaration." [67]

The King's confidence was not altogether unjustified. Had he been able to dissemble his purpose or postpone his plan to obtain complete emancipation for the Catholics, he might have won the permanent support of the Dissenters. It seemed to him that the foundations of peace had been firmly laid.

King James expected that his son-in-law would approve of proposals which provided for Dissenters and for Catholics in England some measure of the freedom they had long enjoyed in Holland; he was very soon disappointed. The Prince of Orange could not support the Declaration because James' supposed attack on English liberties had to be one of the pretexts for his invasion of England.

James was not deceived by the peculiar logic of his son-in-law's letters. He had to contend in England with people who used the same

---

[64]   Ogg, *England in the Reigns of James II and William III*, 197.
[65]   Hay, *Enigma of James II*, 84.
[66]   *Ibid.*
[67]   *Ibid.*

sort of argument. When William, who was not a member of the Church of England, wrote, "I am averse to all persecution, but I cannot agree to do anything contrary to the benefit or interest of the religion I profess," [68] he was obviously avoiding a straight answer to the question he had been asked.

In England the King's enemies at first opposed his liberal measures on political grounds. They said that the Tests were essential to the peace of the Kingdom, and that it was the duty of every citizen to see that those laws were maintained for the security of the realm. The pamphleteers made the mistake of supposing that peace and happiness can be obtained by compacts and regulations, by the mere fact that legislation is imposed with such an object, whereas law is effective in producing the desired result only when, not merely in appearance but in fact, it is founded on justice.

These pamphleteers merely succeeded in emphasizing the moral weakness of opposition to the Kings plan. But the Whigs did not waste much time in argument. The success to the people was partly due to the fact that the papists, who had for generations been driven out of public life and public notice, made an indiscreet, and spectacular use of the new freedom. They regarded, and the King encouraged them to regard, this new liberty to preach and to practice their religion in public, this recognition of an unrestricted citizenship, not as concessions graciously accorded to an offending and perhaps repentant minority, but as rights restored to a much injured and long suffering community: the fulfilment of the promise which King Charles II had made at Breda in 1660.

It must be recognized, however, the mistrust of King James's Declaration was something more than a political pretext. According to the prevailing theory of government, the interests of tender conscience were always subordinated to the interests of national security. And national security then demanded, and seemed to many people at the time to require, conformity, or at least an outward submission of all citizens to the State Religion.

From the furious verbal warfare of the summer of 1687 the two major issues upon which the Revolution was to be fought and won emerged. The first of these was the repeal of the Test Act, and the second was the terms on which religious toleration should be effected. They were narrow issues, to be sure, but on them hung a host of others; political and constitutional, and even social and economic.

[68] Burnet, *Own Times*, I, 709.

CHAPTER V

JAMES AND THE UNIVERSITIES

After the issuance of the Declaration of Indulgence, James went ahead with his plan of toleration for Roman Catholics and Dissenters. The mission of the papal nuncio d'Adda was important in this respect in that it furnished an opportunity for affirmation of his adhesion to the Church of Rome, and for presenting the outward appearance of the return of England to her ancient allegiance. On May 1, 1687, in St. James Chapel, d'Adda was consecrated Archbishop of Amasis, and two months later there was a splendid ceremony at Windsor on the occasion of his public reception as papal nuncio.[1] It had been James' intention from the first to give him a public character, but d'Adda had on various pretexts successfully avoided this move, for fear of attracting too much attention to a Catholic visitor.[2]

James decided not to hold the ceremony in London, where the mob could only be checked by a considerable military force, but he nevertheless had to endure one of his most unfortunate personal encounters. Anxious that a peer of the highest rank should perform the office of introduction, James had no reason to think that the Duke of Somerset, who as gentleman of the bedchamber had attended him to his own public worship, would be scrupulous in the present instance. When, however, he ordered the Duke to introduce the nuncio in the public audience he received an uncompromising refusal. Somerset had received legal advice, and he refused on the ground that to recognize the jurisdiction of the Pope in England was high treason, and that a royal pardon given in advance was invalid:

He humbly desired of the King to be excused; the King asked him his reason; the Duke told him he conceived it to be against law; to which the King said he could pardon him. The Duke replied he was no very

[1] Joseph Hunter (ed.), *The Diary of Dr. Thomas Cartwright Bishop of Chester* (London, Camden Society, Nichols and Son, 1843), 52.
[2] Campana di Cavelli, II, 81-82.

good lawyer, but he thought he had heard it said that a pardon granted to a person offending under assurance of obtaining it was void.[3]

It was easy to punish Somerset by depriving him of his office and to substitute James' nephew, the Duke of Grafton, but Somerset's action was widely applauded and the implication of the terms of his refusal was clearly seen, namely, that the Declaration of Indulgence was legally null and void. Barillon wrote to Louis, "The refusal of the Duke of Somerset to conduct the nucio to the audience shows that the anti-Catholic laws are still in force." [4]

These events did not pass unnoticed across the Channel. William of Orange did not depend for information solely on the emigre colony which had collected around him, nor on the letters that came to him from London. From time to time he sent trusted envoys to England to feel the pulse of the nation and to report on events. Such a visitor was Everard Dykvelt who made a special mission to England from February to June, 1687.[5] This mission was of paramount importance in the history of England, for though he was nominally the envoy of the States General, he was, as James was aware, closely in William's confidence. He carried instructions from the Prince, and he was the means of establishing William's position as head of the opposition to James' religious policy and of concentrating the hopes of that opposition upon the ultimate succession of William to the throne. William's instructions to Dykvelt were:

To expostulate decently but firmly with the King upon the methods he was using both at home and abroad, to assure all the Church party that the Prince would ever be firm to the Church of England and to all our national interest . . . to assure them of a full toleration and likewise of a comprehension, if possible.[6]

Dykvelt, so James complained bitterly to William, "Had not taken the right measures of affairs here, by giving so much credit to some that do not wish me and the monarchy well.[7] The King could not conceal his distrust of the Prince's intentions even from the Prince's servant.

Among the people whom the Dutch envoy especially approached was the Bishop of London, Henry Compton, still suffering under the frustrations of his suspension. Compton gave him a brief note to take

[3]   Bramston (ed.), *Autobiography*, 280-281.
[4]   Dalrymple, III, Book V, Appendix, 283.
[5]   Andrew Browning (ed.), *Thomas Osborne Earl of Danby*, II (Glasgow, Jackson, Son, and Company, 1944, 116.
[6]   Burnet, *Own Times*, I, 708.
[7]   Dalrymple, III, Book V, Appendix, 285.

back to his master, which, however general, had great significance in the light of subsequent events.

I was very glad to receive so good assurances of your welfare as Monseiur Dykvelt brought over. It is not only for your near relation to the Crown that you are so much prayed for here, but for your usefulness to it. For if the King should have any trouble come upon him, which God forbid, we do not know any sure friend he has to rely upon abroad, besides yourself, whom God therefore long preserve.[8]

Dykvelt brought assurance to the few with whom he established contact, but a curious and much discussed letter reveals the current uneasiness in the minds of others. This letter, dated March 7, 1687, was sent with elaborate precautions for secrecy to William from Anne, the wife of Lord Sunderland and the mistress of William's close friend, Henry Sydney. The writer informed William that her circle had discussed the possibility that he might yield to the pressure which she knew was being put on him, and that any indication of his doing so would be of great damage to him in England.

Your highness is not ignorant, I am sure, what endeavors have been used here to gain votes in Parliament for repealing the test and penal laws upon which I suppose you know several have and do quit their places rather than submit to; which makes the Roman Catholics see they are not likely to carry it that way, which brings me to that which I think it is of importance you should know, that the last essay they will put in practice as to the Parliament is to flatter M. Dykvelt with a great many fine things, that there shall be an entire union between England and Holland.[9]

This last piece of information was particularly valuable to the recipient, for, taken in connection with the Bishop of London's letter, it strengthened William's conviction that he could not remain neutral in England's politics, and that support of the Test Act must be the one sure and indispensable plank in his platform.

Almost simultaneously with the Declaration of Indulgence another development enabled James to make full use of his dispensing power. The Universities, which on the one hand were the sole recruiting ground of the English clergy and on the other were entirely staffed by clerics, were regarded as the Church's dearest possessions. The first inkling of trouble came in February 23, when Dr. Pechell, Vice-Chancellor of Cambridge, wrote to his friend Samuel Pepys:

8   Edward Carpenter, *The Protestant Bishop*, 115.
9   R. W. Blencowe (ed.), *The Diary of the Times of Charles II* (London, Henry Colburn, 1843), II, 258.

I must not conceal from such a friend as you what before this comes will be known in Court and City. His Majesty was pleased to send a a letter directed to me, as Vice-Chancellor, to admit one Alban Francis, a Benedictine Monk, M. of A. without administering any oaths or oath to him.[10]

The University subsequently rejected this mandate as contrary to the statutes, and the Ecclesiastical Commission summoned Dr. Pechell to appear before it. Dr. Pechell defended himself by setting forth the statute which required all graduates to take the oath of supremacy and allegiance, and to recite the oath of supremacy at large.[11] Jeffreys told Pechell that he was guilty of great disobedience to the King's command and other crimes, and that because of his contempt of Court he would be deprived of his office.[12] It does not appear, however, that Francis succeeded in obtaining his degree.

It was at Oxford, rather than at Cambridge, that the most vicious assault was made on the Colleges. The master of University College, Obadiah Walker, having declared his conversion to the Roman faith, was allowed by royal dispensation to retain his post; he set up an oratory in his college, and with the aid of three Fellows, and in spite of systematic persecution by the undergraduates, managed to maintain a Catholic nucleus in the University.[13] Further, the Deanery of Christchurch, which was in the royal gift, was bestowed on John Massey, a junior Fellow who had nothing to recommend him except his change of religion, and by a royal dispensation he was installed without taking the oaths.[14]

The matter of the presidentship of Magdalen was even more important and extended over a longer time. On March 24, 1687, Dr. Henry Clarke, President of Magdalen, who had been on sick leave from the College since February 7, died, and the College was officially informed of this occurrence on March 29. On March 31, the Vice-President, Dr. Aldworth, convened the Fellows; a meeting for the election of a new President was called for April 13, and the text of a letter was agreed upon to Peter Mews, Bishop of Winchester, the visitor of the College. In this letter the Bishop was asked to agree with

10 Richard Braybrooke, *Diary and Correspondence of Samuel Pepys* (London, George Bell and Sons, 1890), IV, 236-237.
11 Bramston (ed.), *Autobiography*, 274.
12 *Ibid.*, 275.
13 Burnet, *Own Times*, I, 731.
14 John Gutch, *Collectanea Curiosa: or Miscellaneous Tracts*, I (London, Oxford, At The Clarendon Press, 1781), 294-295.

the Fellows in the choice of a President according to directions of the Founder's Statutes, a form which asked his Majesty's "Grace and Favour," and prevented any stranger being set over them.[15] On April 2, the Bishop's reply was received and he advised the College to proceed to an election at once.[16] On April 5, Lord Sunderland signed a royal mandate to the College, ordering it to elect Anthony Farmer to the office of President, "any statute, custom or condition to the contrary in any wise notwithstanding, wherewith we are graciously pleased to dispense on his behalf".[17] The King also stated that he was "well satisfied with Farmer's piety, loyalty and learning", but there was no mention of the oaths in the mandate or that Farmer would have to declare himself a good Protestant.[18] On April 8 the Bishop of Winchester wrote to Sunderland:

I am informed that great endeavours are used with His Majesty to recommend one Mr. Farmer, who is not at present, nor ever was Fellow of that College, to be President of it, which is directly contrary to the Statutes of the Founder, as I am confident some who promote Mr. Farmer's interest cannot be ignorant of.[19]

The same day the Bishop wrote to the College advising it to petition the King against the mandate and, either on that advice or independently of it, the College on April 9 agreed on a petition representing that "the said Mr. Farmer is a person in several respects incapable of that character according to our Founder's Statutes".[20] This petition was sent by the College to London by a member, Captain Frances Bagshaw, and on the following day he and Dr. Thomas Smith, another Fellow living in London, waited on Lord Sunderland and delivered it to him. On April 12, Smith and Bagshaw again waited on Sunderland for news of the success of the petition; they were given an appointment on the next day, and Sunderland said to them, "I have addressed the Bishop of Winchester's letter and your address to the King: the King has sent down his letter to the College, and expects it to be obeyed." [21]

Meanwhile, this second mandate had reached the College by the

15   J. R. Bloxam, *Magdalen College and King James II, 1686-1688* (Oxford, Printed for the Oxford Historical Society, 1886), 13.
16   *Ibid.*
17   *Ibid.*, 14-15.
18   *Ibid.*
19   *Ibid.*, 15.
20   *Ibid.*, 16.
21   *Ibid.*, 22.

hand of Robert Charnock, the only Fellow who was a Catholic. The mandate was considered at a meeting on April 11 and the Fellows decided to hold to their intention of proceeding to election on April 13.[22] The election was adjourned, however, until April 15 when Dr. Thomas Smith, who had hurried down from London, moved for a delay to provide time for the dispatch of a second petition to the King, but was overruled. In the election which followed Dr. Smith's motion, Dr. John Hough was declared President; and the following day he went with the Vice-President to Farnham, where the Bishop as Visitor confirmed the election.[23]

The various points on which more information up to this date are required are three. Had James any plan to interfere in the election before the death of Dr. Clarke, when he was known to be very ill? On the basis of his own reflections we must conclude that he did not.[24] Secondly, did James see the petition which Smith and Bagshaw handed to Sunderland? Smith had his doubts at the time, and, from reports of conversations in which James took part when he was at Oxford later in the year, we must very strongly suspect that Sunderland kept the petition in his own hands and that his answer to it was without authority.[25] Finally, had James any previous knowledge of the candidate who was put forward in his name for the presidentship? If he had not, as appears likely, he must be convicted of acting very irresponsible in failing to inquire into Farmer's suitability for so important a post. Anthony Wood appears to have known something about him before his character had been fully investigated, for on April 9 he wrote in his diary:

Was there ever such a ridiculous thing that a mandamus for such a person should come from the King! Sure if the King had a right understanding of things and men he would not have recommended such a person.[26]

It seems likely that Farmer was well and not favorably known at Oxford; indeed, the words of the petition, "A person in several aspects incapable of that character" reveal that the Fellows of Magdalen knew more than that he had not qualified for candidature by becoming a fellow of Magdalen or New College. His most obvious disqualification, which could be ignored only if balanced by exceptional scholarship

22 *Ibid.*
23 *Ibid.*,24.
24 T. S. Clarke, *James II*, II, 265-267.
25 Bloxam, 84-88.
26 Wood, *Diary*, III, 217.

or strength of character, was that he was under thirty years of age.[27]

The King took notice of Dr. Hough's election merely by a short letter of expostulation addressed to the Vice-President and Fellows and demanding an explanation of their conduct.[28] To this letter reply was sent in very loyal terms and a statement was made to the effect that they had been bound by their statute neither to postpone the election nor to elect Mr. Farmer, who had never been a Fellow of their College or of New College.[29] No answer was made to this letter, and the College was left in uneasy security for over two months.

On May 28 the Vice-President and Fellows were cited to appear before the Ecclesiastical Commission.[30] They appeared on June 6, and were allowed to wait a week to prepare their case; on the 13th they put in two statements, one of their legal position, the other containing their allegations against Farmer's character; on June 22 the Commission declared the election of Dr. Hough null and void and suspended the Vice-President for contempt in disobeying the royal mandate.[31] On May 27 the Commission considered the allegations against Farmer, and it was noticed that at the meeting which followed its attitude had changed; it no longer harassed the Fellows, but treated them with deference, for the members had probably become aware of the weak position in which the King had put himself by offering such a man as President.[32]

The College had justified itself as far as Farmer was concerned and persisted in refusing to acknowledge the validity of the declaration by the Commission that the election of Dr. Hough was null and void. But it was far from the nature of James to admit defeat. On August 14, the King, abandoning Farmer, issued a new mandate, no mention being made of the previous one to elect Farmer, calling upon the Fellows to elect Samuel Parker, Bishop of Oxford, to the vacancy which the Commission had declared to exist.[33] After a fortnight's delay the Fellows replied submissively in form but stubbornly in essence, that "They humbly conceived the place of the President to be full." [34]

[27]   Stephen Leslie and Sidney Lee, *The Dictionary of National Biography*, VI (London, Oxford University Press, 1922), 1073. Farmer matriculated at Trinity College Cambridge in 1672.

[28]   Bloxam, 52-53.

[29]   *Ibid.*, 53.

[30]   *Ibid.*, 49.

[31]   *The History of King James's Ecclesiastical Commission*, 37.

[32]   *Ibid.*

[33]   Bloxam, 37.

[34]   *Ibid.*

In the autumn of 1687, James toured the West and Midlands, where he had ample opportunity to assess the damage he had already done. He also determined to try to overawe the Fellows by his personal presence. On his arrival at Oxford he was met on the Woodstock Road by the University and the City and conducted to his lodgings.[35] The following afternoon James sent for the Fellows of Magdalen, and in the Dean's lodgings was enacted a scene in which he exhibited to the full that lack of royal dignity which the Earl of Ailesbury admitted to be his gravest fault.[36] After obtaining the decision of Alexander Pudsey, the Senior Fellow, that the Fellows had received the mandate to elect Dr. Parker, he addressed them as follows:

Then I must tell you and the rest of your Fellows that you have behaved yourselves undutifully to me and not like gentlemen; you have not paid me common respect; you have always been a stubborn and turbulent college, I have known you to be so these six and twenty years myself; you have affronted me, know I am your King and I will be obeyed. Is this your Church of England loyalty? One would wonder to see so many Church of England men got together in such a thing. Go back and show yourselves good members of the Church of England. I am hearing nothing from you, get you gone. I command you be gone, go and admit the Bishop of Oxford, Head, Principal, or what do you call him as President of the College. Let them that refuse it look to it. Go and obey me or you shall feel the weight of your sovereign's displeasure.[37]

And as they were going out James called them back to reprimand them again for having confirmed a probationary Fellow in contravention of a royal mandate to elect no new Fellows. When they attempted to justify their actions he cut them short by a fresh outburst.[38]

There followed a short period of bargaining. The Fellows held that they could not elect Parker, even if Hough made way for him by resigning, without violating their oaths and committing perjury.[39] The King hesitated to create a new precedent by making the direct appointment. Whatever reservations James had had he overcame by the middle of October, when he appointed as Lord Commissioners for visiting Magdalen College, William Cartwright, Bishop of Chester, Robert Wright, Chief Justice, and Sir Thomas Jenner, Baron of the Exchequer.[40] These Commissioners sat at Magdalen from October 21

[35] Wood, *Diary*, III, 226.
[36] Buckley (ed.), *Ailesbury Memoirs*, II, 131.
[37] Bloxam, 85-86.
[38] *Ibid.*
[39] *Ibid.*, 92.
[40] *Ibid.*, 107.

to 28; they repeated the old arguments, but finding the Fellows still obdurate, they forcibly entered the President's lodgings on October 24 and left in possession a chaplain of the Bishop of Oxford as proxy for the Bishop.

> By virtue of the King's Commission to us directed, we do order and decree the Right Reverend Father in God, Samuel, Lord Bishop of Oxon, to be installed by his Proxy, Mr. Wickens in the president's stall in the chapel of this college forthwith, and the chapel doors to be opened for that purpose. . . . Then we propound you will submit to the Bishop of Oxon, now installed your President by the King's mandate, in *licitis et honestis*. And they desired till the afternoon consult together, and to give in their answer in scriptis, which was granted them.[41]

On the afternoon of the same day the Commissioners received a declaration by all the Fellows except one that they would only obey Dr. Parker as President "so far as is lawful and agreeable to the Statutes of the said College";[42] otherwise they would not sanction the decision at all. On November 15 the three Commissioners returned to Oxford, and on the following day dismissed the twenty-five recalcitrant Fellows. Of the Fellows, only two, Charnock and Dr. Thomas Smith, submitted to receive the Bishop to be their President; the remaining twenty-five were deprived of Fellowships, and declared incapable of being admitted to any ecclesiastical dignity or benefice.[43] On December 31 James wrote to Dr. Parker ordering him to admit twelve new Fellows; six of these are known to have been Catholics, and quite probably the others were of the same faith.[44]

As in other cases, James's victory was less complete than it appeared. The College was indeed in Catholic hands and the Fellows had been driven to dependence on charity, but they had defied the royal will for nearly seven months. Even at the end of that time the King had been unable to persuade them or to scare them into electing his nominee, and had to use force to attain his ends. The worst feature of the proceedings, however, was the destruction of the unanimity of the Ecclesiastical Commission, which up to that time had been willing to go to any lengths to further James' plans. In all probability had the headship of another College at Oxford or Cambridge fallen vacant, James would not have entered on a second conflict of the same

41　*Ibid.*, 147.
42　*Ibid.*, 153.
43　*Ibid.*, 185.
44　*Ibid.*, 225-230.

nature, not least for the reason that Jeffreys would not have advised such a step.

During the summer James intended to summon a new Parliament as soon as he could anticipate the election of members to his liking. He still felt that he could influence a new Parliament sufficiently to get the Test Act repealed. His closeting now had a different aim: instead of trying to influence the votes of existing members, he exercised pressure on everyone who possessed local influence in elections. In August, 1687, he began to inquire into attitude of the Lords Lieutenant to his proposed reforms and, where necessary, to replace them by persons more amenable.[45] As a man of very great local consequence the Lord Lieutenant was the natural leader of country society and generally the largest landowner in the county. As commander of the county militia he held military rank and though he was, as matter of form, appointed by the King, it could almost be said that he appointed himself by his natural predominance in the county.

The occasion of the changes in the Lords Lieutenant was an attempt by James to ascertain in advance from prospective members of Parliament and from voters what support he was likely to get from a Parliament to his efforts to favor the Catholics. In the autumn of 1687 every Lord Lieutenant was ordered to go down to his county and to put three questions to Deputy Lieutenants, sheriffs, justices of the peace, mayors and members of corporations, Government officials such as customs and excise officers, forty-shilling freeholders, and any other who could influence or take part in an action, and to demand a separate answer from each individual.[46]

Among some uncalendared State Papers in the Record Office are the secret instructions to the King's agents. In them James said that they should weigh well the difficulty of their work, and consider that they would meet with all manner of deceit and combination.

Inform yourselves what Members each Corporation intends to choose, and if they are contrary to his Majesties interest, and you find the Corporation resolved upon them out of prejudice, consider then how to give a diversion to their intentions, by seeming to promote such persons Election, which they discerning may create an aversion to them, and dispose them to elect others, which they are inclined to, as suspecting those they before designed, to have privately warpt to the Kings interest.[47]

[45] Luttrell, *Brief Relations*, I, 412-413.
[46] Burnet, *Own Times*, III, 182-183.
[47] Reprinted in George Duckett, *Penal Laws and Test Act, Questions Touching their Repeal Propounded in 1687-8 by James II*, I (London, 1882), 197.

The first two questions were, from a political point of view, far too simple and straightforward; they would never have been put to the electors by anyone who knew the art of politics and the ways of men when asked questions. Charles II for instance would have avoided all mention of the Act and would probably have obtained a majority in favor of any proposal to repeal the penal laws. The questions put to the Lords Lieutenant were:

1. If in case he shall be chose Knight of the Shire or Burgess of a town, when the King shall see fit to call a Parliament, whether he will be for taking off the Penal Laws and the Tests.
2. Whether he will assist and contribute to the election of such members as shall be for taking off the Penal Laws and the Tests.
3. Whether he will support the King's Declaration for Liberty of Conscience by living friendly with those of all persuasions, as subjects of the same Prince and good Christians ought to do.[48]

To the first question, a few said plainly that, if elected, they would not vote to repeal the Test Act, while others more cautiously said that they would come to no decision until they had heard the matter fully debated in Parliament.[49] To the second question, the gentlemen mostly replied that they would not wish to limit the freedom of their members to make their own decisions on such a matter.[50] A few, such as Charles Leigh of Leighton, expressed their sentiments more clearly, saying that "they would vote for such as have approved themselves to be of the most constant unshaken loyalty . . . those that are ye truest sons of ye Church of England".[51] Some went further and declared themselves against the questions. The Earl of Northampton, who was then Lord Lieutenant of Warwickshire, told the gentlemen he had received the King's commands to lay some proposals before them; which he thought it was his duty to obey; but at the same time thought himself obliged to acquaint them that he did not plan to comply with them himself, but would make a faithful report to his majesty of those that would.[52] Many county spokesmen answered very boldly in the negative; and others refused to give any answer, which was understood to be equivalent to a negative. The mayor and most of the new aldermen of London refused to answer and some were turned out of their commissions.[53]

[48]   *Ibid.*, 29.
[49]   Luttrell, *Brief Relations*, I, 420-421.
[50]   Burnet, *Own Times*, III, 183.
[51]   Reresby, *Reresby Memoirs*, 478.
[52]   Burnet, *Own Times,* III, 182-183.
[53]   Luttrell, *Brief Relations*, I, 410-411.

Only to the third question was the answer almost unanimously in the affirmative. There were only a few, and those persons of very little character, who professed themselves unwilling to live on friendly terms with their Catholic neighbors. There was one such, a Mr. Pocklington from Huntingdonshire, and his intolerant attitude was so much resented that Lord Salisbury very soon turned him out.[54]

There was, indeed, a fairly numerous minority which was willing to satisfy the King. In this minority were many in whom the light of loyalty burned bright, but there were many also who would sign anything rather than let their wives and children starve, and others who thought they could better their fortunes by a display of loyalty. The majority in some localities refused to give any pledge that they would assist in returning a Parliament of James' mind on the religious question. They took their stand on the sound theory of members in accordance with the facts of democratic government, that they should assemble with open minds and should give their votes to the side which produced the more convincing arguments. Here is a typical answer:

1. If I be chosen a member of Parliament, I conceive myself obliged to give my vote according to the reason of the debate of the House and not otherwise.
2. If I shall concern myself in the election of any to serve as Members of Parliament I shall give my vote for such as to the best of my judgment will serve the King and Kingdom faithfully and honestly.
3. I think it is my duty to live friendly and peaceably with all men as becomes a good Christina and a loyal subject.[55]

This reply a courtier at Whitehall characterized as a "civil and politic denial".[56]

A notable feature of the answers was that while they were of a sort calculated to displease James, they none the less were couched in the language of loyal and reasonable men. From an examination of the reports it is clear that many favored repealing the penal laws, and perhaps, if left to themselves, without the constant pressure from the pulpits, would have voted for a repeal, and even of the Test Act, provided that legislation secured Protestant religion and property, which many believed to be in danger. Even among the stoutest

---

[54] Earl of Cardigan, *The Life and Loyalties of Thomas Bruce* (London, Routledge and Kegan Ltd., 1951), 118.
[55] *Historical Manuscripts Commission, Manuscripts of Le Fleming,* XII (London, Her Majesty's Stationary Office, 1890), Appendix 7, 208.
[56] *Ibid.,* 209.

Protestants who gave a direct refusal to the first two questions, some signified their disapproval of oppressing conscience. A few did not understand anything of what was asked and voted blindly against popery. John Dryden added this postscript: "I do sincerely promise to venture my life and fortune for the preservation of his Majesty's person, His Crown and Dignity, whom God grant long to reign over us." [57]

The next move was up to Sunderland, who sent a written order to Lord Ailesbury in the King's name, commanding him to dismiss all Deputy Lieutenants and to supply a new list for his Majesty's consideration. [58] Ailesbury obeyed orders as to the dismissals, but as to the new list, he sent in one containing exactly the same names. Sunderland was furious. Ailesbury replied that he could only recommend men of the first quality, for whose patriotism and integrity he could personally vouch. He refused to put forward others of inferior calibre. [59] Sunderland, in the King's name, submitted a list and named names. One exception of the quality was Samuel Pepys, whom Ailesbury had not proposed. He liked Pepys but considered him a Londoner. [60]

The questions themselves were without precedent, and an attempt to pledge Parliament in advance to a course of action was, constructively at least, a breach of the privileges of Parliament; besides, there was an implied intention that a Lord Lieutenant who put the questions was to use his influence to secure favorable answers to them. A few consented to obey the royal command, relying on their local reputations to avoid suspicion of Catholic bias, but put the question in such a colorless manner as to discourage rather than to encourage affirmative replies. One of the few exceptions was the Earl of Rochester, who lost whatever reputation he had earlier gained from his refusal to continue in office at the cost of changing his religion, by attempting to obtain the adherence of his county of Hertfordshire to James' views. According to Barillon he had concealed his true feelings from fear of the royal displeasure, [61] and there is no doubt that he was in danger of losing his pension of £4000 a year.

James himself was entirely unaware that he had sustained a major disaster. He did not realize that he had consolidated the opposition and increased his difficulties by the ill-conceived attempt made to

[57]   Cardigan, *Life and Loyalties of Thomas Bruce,* 118.
[58]   *Ibid.,* 119.
[59]   *Ibid.*
[60]   *Ibid.*
[61]   Luttrell, *Brief Relations,* I, 422.

solve them. The effect of imposing on everyone of local importance the obligation to declare his opinion for or against the repeal of the laws against the Catholics was to reveal the overwhelming determination of the country to give the King no assistance in the matter. What had hitherto been a matter of conjecture now became a matter of fact; even the moderate men, who were averse to persecuting for religion, disapproved of the means used to secure repeal, suspected James' ultimate aims and kept their principles in abeyance.

Simultaneously with the issuance of the three questions James attacked the Corporations. The last three years of Charles II's reign had seen a revision of the charters of towns and cities throughout England, and the process continued in the early part of James' reign. By the legal means of *quo warranto* the charters were forfeited and new charters granted, ostensibly because of irregularities committed by the Corporations, but actually for the purpose of replacing Whigs and Dissenters with Tories and Churchmen. Hitherto the aim had been to man the Corporations with adherents of the old Court party: now James was concerned with the contemplated general election, and wanted Corporations which would influence the borough elections in favor of the principles of the Declaration of Indulgence. In November, 1687, a Commission again headed by Lord Jeffreys and including Lord Sunderland, and four Catholics, Lord Powis, Lord Castlemaine, Father Petre, and Sir Nicholas Butler, was appointed to deal with them.[62] This Commission's purpose was to purge the corporations and the other local organizations of all people who would not give a definite and affirmative reply to the three questions.[63] A timely cartoon came out in Holland at this time. It pictured the Church of England in the shape of a goose, the Papist plucking one wing and the Dissenter another, with the label from her mouth, "Passive obedience".[64]

One thing badly needed in England was education. Yet when James allowed the Jesuits to start a school in London his action was represented at the time, and for a long time after, as an attack not on ignorance but on Protestantism. The first of these free schools was opened at the Savoy in June of 1687, and in October of that year was inspected by the King, who was met on the steps by the Provincial who conducted him to the Chapel and schools. James was so pleased

[62]   *Ibid.*, 420-421.
[63]   *Ibid.*
[64]   *Letters of Eminent Men Addressed to Ralph Thoresby,* I (London, Henry Colburn and Richard Bentley, 1832), 91.

with the Greek, Latin, and English speeches that he gave the students gowns and said they should be called his "scholars".[65] At the end of the year a school for girls was opened by the Queen under four nuns. No religious distinction was to be made; poor and rich were to enjoy the benefit provided they came in clean and decent habits.[66]

James, refusing to take as final the Prince of Orange's repeated answer that he would not approve the repeal of the Tests, made one more attempt to win him over to the family standard. The go-between this time was one James Stewart, a Scottish covenanter, a refugee for some years in the United Provinces. One of the many who had gone to England after the Declaration of Indulgence, he had, like the others, talked to William before his departure and had given assurances that he would act in the latter's interests. Unlike the others, however, shortly after his arrival in London he seems to have become sincerely convinced that the best interest not only of William but also of all the Dissenters themselves lay in accepting James' offer of toleration. He volunteered his services to the King and after they had been accepted, opened a correspondence with Mijn Heer Fagel, pensioner of Holland and adviser of William, who had been Stewart's close friend while he was in the Netherlands, to use his great influence to get William to change his mind. His two principal arguments were that the Roman Catholics were too few in number to be dangerous, and that the Dissenters were faced with a return of the persecution which they had suffered under the Penal Laws if the Tests were not repealed.[67] James was determined not to give up the one without the other.

It is not clear whether Stewart was acting in this matter on his own responsibility or as the agent of the English Court; but his letters were shown to William, who saw that they provided him with an excellent opportunity both of publicly defining his attitude to the religious question in England and of refuting a charge, which Whitehall had been sedulously spreading, that the intention on the succession of Princess Mary was to extirpate the English Catholics. William therefore decided that Fagel should write a reply to be translated into

[65]   *Historical Manuscripts Commission, Manuscripts of the Earl of Downshire,* I (London, His Majesty's Stationary Office, 1924), 272.
[66]   *Ibid.,* 282.
[67]   Gilbert Burnet, *Bishop Burnet's History of the Reign of King James the Second* (Oxford, At The University Press, 1852), 242-243.

English by Gilbert Burnet.[68] The reply dated November 4 emphasized the devotion of the Prince and Princess to the cause of religious toleration.[69] They were willing that it should be extended not only to Dissenters, but even to Catholics, although the latter ought not to be given the privilege of public worship.[70] On the question of the Tests, however, they were unyielding, for they looked upon them as the great safeguard of the Protestant religion, and since they laid no punishment upon anyone, but simply disqualified certain persons from office, they could not be looked upon as unduly severe.[71]

Within a few weeks after it had been sent the letter had been translated into four languages, printed and scattered in broadsheet form throughout England and Western Europe. On the mainland it assuaged the fears of the Catholic enemies of France by its tolerant attitude toward their religion. People, it was said, were "in rapture to find the sentiments of Your Highness and the Princess in matters of religion not only so equitable, but so agreeable to the unrest and to the taste of all this nation." [72]

It was against the background of these worsening relations between Whitehall and The Hague that the first rumors of the Queen's pregnancy began to circulate throughout Whitehall. The first whispered rumor that the Queen might be pregnant reached Barillon on October 24, 1687, and by November 3 it was the talk of the Court.[73] On November 14 the news was finally confirmed. [74] To every statesman, minister, and politician, the tidings brought new hopes or new fears. After landing in England at the end of November, Sydney at once went to London to organize pro-Dutch intelligence in England and the distribution of propaganda.[75]

As for the Anglicans and the anti-Catholic Dissenters, their first instinct was to temporize. Mary Beatrice had miscarried more than once, the children she had borne had all died in infancy, and she might well bear a dynastically useless daughter: it was better to await the child's birth before making any move. The moderate Catholics

[68] Mijn Heer Fagel, *A Letter writ by Mijn Heer Fagel, Pensioner of Holland, to James Stewart, Advocater* (Amsterdam, 1687).
[69] *Ibid.*, 2.
[70] *Ibid.*, 3.
[71] *Ibid.*, 4.
[72] Dalrymple, III, Book V, Appendix, 295.
[73] *Ibid.*, 297.
[74] *Ibid.*
[75] Burnet, *Own Times*, III, 277.

were in a much worse quandary. If they threw themselves unreservedly onto the King's side they would probably forfeit any chance of reaching an advantageous accommodation with William in the event of the Queen's giving birth to a girl. On the other hand, if the child were a boy, and they had not given James their unqualified cooperation, they were in danger of being pushed aside by the Catholic extremists. A policy of watchful waiting was adopted by all parties concerned.

By the close of the year, James might have boasted that he had accomplished almost everything that had been in his mind at his accession. He had enjoyed almost unrestricted power for almost two and one-half years and he had used this power in the interests of the Roman Catholic religion; there were Catholics in every sort of public position; the Lord Privy Seal, five members of the Privy Council, and two Commissioners of the Treasury were Roman Catholics. In only one matter had he been thwarted: conversions to the Catholic faith had been few. James had not only failed to carry the people with him but had antagonized them at nearly every step. Consequently his political dynasty was without foundation.

CHAPTER VI

1688 DECLARATION OF INDULGENCE

During the first few weeks of the new year Whitehall was plagued with inner dissension. The party which now had the undisputed ascendant was the "High Catholics", as a term of reproach, called "Jesuits" by the enemies of that famous society, as well as by the Protestants. This group was largely led and dominated by Father Petre. To exalt the Papal power this group had revived the scholastic doctrine of the popular origin of governments; rulers might be subject to the people, but the people themselves, on all questions as difficult as those relating to the limits of obedience, were to listen with reverential submission to the judgment of the Sovereign Pontiff, the common pastor of sovereigns and subjects. The moderate Catholics, particularly Lord Powis and Lady Middleton, Catholic wife of James' leader in the House of Commons, were bitterly critical of the Jesuits in public.[1] The feeling of tension was further aggravated by the appearance of a court-sponsored pamphlet entitled *Parliamentum Pacificum* written by John Northleigh. Northleigh, an ardent supporter of James II, was a medical doctor who devoted more attention to polemical theology than to his profession. This pamphlet suggested that the Heer Fagel pamphlet, which had appeared in the fall of 1687, did not have the approval of the Prince and Princess of Orange, and certainly did not represent their views on the repeal of the Test and Penal Laws.[2] Northleigh, licensed by Lord Sunderland in the middle of February, maintained that until the Protestants could prove that repealing the laws would make more Papists in England than Protestants, they "only made many words, but no arguments".[3]

This tract was written primarily to prepare the way for what was

[1] John P. Kenyon, *Robert Spencer, Earl of Sunderland, 1641-1702* (London, Longman, Green and Co., 1959), 193.
[2] John Northleigh, *Parliamentum Pacificum: or the Happy Union of King and People in an Healing Parliament* (London, 1688), 45.
[3] *Ibid.,* 52.

called "A Healing Parliament", but chiefly attracted notice by its tone of insult and menace. It reminded the United Provinces that their commonwealth was the result of an absolute rebellion, revolt, and defection from their prince. Northleigh also threatened Burnet, stating that he might be taken from Holland and cut up alive, in imitation of a supposed example in the reign of Queen Elizabeth.[4] This threat was the more alarming because it was well known that the first part of such a project had been long rumored, and that attempts had already been made for its execution.[5]

Concerning the possibility of the calling of a new Parliament in 1688, Northleigh wrote:

I will close with two exhortations to those that are to choose our Representatives, and offer one consideration to those that are chosen. Whenever the King sends you his Summons, let your Electors be carried with moderation and your Choice of such men, as one either concern'd to repeal these laws for their own sakes, or inclin'd to do it for the Reasons that require it.

Let your Retinues be made as fairly as Possible; for that which is a Sound Parliament, will the sooner be an healing one. And may that Peaceful Assembly, when it Sits, consider how to pacify the Nation, and grant too, His Majesties propositions for Peace. Let them consider, that their present Prince does only desire a repeal by law, does allow them all that Liberty of Debate, which even an Henry the eighth did indeed make but a merit of obedience.[6]

This pamphlet, like the Fagel letter to Stewart, was printed and circulated in England.

Naturally, Fagel was very angry that his letter was not accepted as genuine, and that he was accused of lying. He told the ambassador d'Albeville that not only did the letter represent the views of "Their Mightiness", but that it had been published by their command. He assured Stewart that William and Mary had often declared that no Christian ought to be persecuted for his conscience or be ill-used because he differed from the public and established religion.

And as for the Dissenters, Their Highnesses do not only consent, but do heartily approve of their having an entire Liberty, for the full exercise of their Religion, without any trouble or hindrance; so that none may be able to give them the least disturbance upon that account.[7]

[4] *Ibid.*, 57.
[5] David Jones, *The Secret History of Whitehall*, 29.
[6] Northleigh, *Parliamentum Pacificum*, 76.
[7] Mijn Heer Fagel, *Their Highnesses the Prince and Princess of Orange's Opinion about a General Liberty of Conscience* (Amsterdam, 1688), 1-2.

He went on to say, however, that William and Mary would not be able to consent to any repeal of the Tests because these Tests pertained to the security of the Protestant religion. Fagel maintained that the Tests were only provisions qualifying men to be members of Parliament, or to be capable of bearing office, and that they were not for the Protestant religion and could not be said to carry in them any security against the Roman Catholics. The Penal Laws were only a protection for the Protestants against the Catholics.[8]

One of Stewart's basic premises had been that the toleration could be granted because there were only a small number of Roman Catholics; consequently they were not strong enough to harm the Government. Fagel answered him by saying:

> I know it is commonly said, that the number of the Roman Catholics in England and Scotland is very inconsiderable; and that they are possessed only of a very small number of the places of Trust: though even as to this, the case is quite different in Ireland: yet this you must of necessity grant me, that if their numbers are small, then it is not reasonable that the public Peace should be disturbed on the account of so few persons.[9]

This statement was also widely circulated and the Government felt it was so detrimental that by late spring its selling was prohibited and booksellers caught were prosecuted.[10]

Gilbert Burnet, who had been taken under the protection of the burghers of Amsterdam, joined Fagel in an answer to Northleigh's work. Burnet stated that peace was a very desirable thing, but every state that is peaceable is not blindly to be counted. Burnet urged the English people to consider the differences between the English case and the Dutch case. In Holland the government was wholly in the hands of Protestants, but in England the situation was dangerous because she was under a Popish King.[11]

During the spring of 1688 James and his cabinet encouraged pamphlets urging the repeal of the Test and Penal Acts. One of the active Catholic authors during the last few months of 1687 had been Samuel Parker, Bishop of Oxford, who had died in late fall of that year. After Parker's death many of his works were published by the Government and widely read. Parker, a man of many talents and activity, became involved with Gilbert Burnet over the dispute of the Colleges and

8   *Ibid.*, 2.
9   *Ibid.*, 5.
10 Luttrell, *Brief Relations*, I, 440.
11 Gilbert Burnet, *Reflections on a Late Pamphlet Entitled Parliamentum Pacificum* (Amsterdam, 1688), 4-5.

doctrine of the Church. Burnet had the poor taste to carry on this feud after the Bishop's death. Burnet's account of the controversy is as follows:

He wrote a book against the tests full of petulant scurillity, of which I shall only give one instance. He had reflected much on the popish plot, and on Oates evidence; and upon that he called the test the sacrament of Oatesian villany. He treated the Parliament that enacted the tests with a scorn that no popish writer had yet ventured on; and he said much to excuse transubstantiation and to free the Church of some of the charge of idolatry.[12]

Another of the pamphleteers was Thomas Goodwin, a dissenting London minister, who wrote in the *Preface to his Examination of the New articles of the Roman Creed by Catholic tradition* that the year before Parker had managed, very unsuccessfully, the design of proving transubstantiation to be the peculiar doctrine of the Church of Rome.[13] This pamphlet was answered by William Wake who was long and actively engaged in controversy with the papists. Of all the great divines who stood forward in defense of the Church of England in this protracted contest, Wake, after Edward Stillingfleet, was the most astute, stolid and judicious in the argument of his cause. His gentle spirit usually led him to be moderate, but on this occasion he wrote:

That the Church of Rome thus worshipping images is truly and properly guilty of idolatry. . . . Of the Adoration of the Host he says, the Church of England, consequently to her principles of the Bread and Wine remaining in their natural substances, profess that she thinks it to be Idolatry, and to be abhorred of all faithful Christians, Of the Sacrifice of the Mass, justly esteemed one of the greatest and most dangerous errors that offend us.[14]

Wake set out to refute the Roman interpretation and instruction of this sacrament.

Our Savior Christ spoke to his apostles not as the representatives of the holy body of the Church, but as those whom he was about to consecrate to the peculiar office of the ministry in it; and therein gave them power in celebrating the rite, to offer a true and proper offering made for the satisfaction both of the dead and the living.[15]

[12]   Gilbert Burnet, *Own Times*, III, 137-138.
[13]   Thomas Goodwin, *Examination of the New Articles of the Roman Creed by Catholic Tradition* (London, 1688), 1.
[14]   William Wake, *A Discourse Concerning the Nature of Idolatry* (London, 1688), 1.
[15]   *Ibid.*, 2.

A very interesting anonymous pamphlet came out at this time concerning a fictitious conversation between *Harry and Roger Concerning the Times.* Roger was Sir Roger L'Estrange, and Harry, Henry Care, the Dissenting printer who changed sides during the reign of James. A contemporary poem entitled *The Epitaph of Henry Care* provides us with the regard in which he was held.

> A true Dissenter here does lie indeed.
> He ne'er with any, or himself agreed:
> But rather than want subjects to his spite
> Would snake-like turn and his own tail would bite.
> Sometimes, 'tis true, he took the faster side,
> But when he came by suffering to be tried
> The craven soon betrayed his fear and pride,
> Thence, Settle-like, he to recanting fell,
> Of all he wrote, or fancied, to be well:
> Thus purged from good, and thus prepared by evil,
> He faced to Rome, and marched off to the devil.[16]

In this pamphlet, Roger asks Harry, "How camst thou to be either beloved by the Papists, or believed by the Dissenter's?" Harry answers:

I perceive you don't understand the virtue of Holy Water; this powerful sprinkling will immediately restore a Man to the State of Innocence: Had Adam but known this easy recipe, he would never have been at the Expence of Figleaves. You must know I have all my old sins forgiven me, and I am now as clean as if I had been over head and ears in Jordan.[17]

He goes on to say "I fill the Peoples Heads so full with Penal Laws, that there is no room left for the Inquisition; and if any one blabs about Queen Mary's Days, I immediately stop his Mouth with the thirty-fifth of Elizabeth." [18] Roger asserted that he was not for trusting the Dissenter too far, for they were "slippery creatures".[19]

In the course of the story Roger departed and "An honest Dissenter" came up to Harry. The discussion centered around the penal laws, of course, and Harry after calling them "mud-walls", went on to say:

Is it not unreasonable that the Papists should be debarred of those privileges and advantages which they are born to? And since they are

[16] *The Muses Farewell to Popery*, 162.
[17] *Heraclitus Ridens Redivivus: or, a Dialogue Between Harry and Roger Concerning the Times* (London, 1688), 4.
[18] *Ibid.*
[19] *Ibid.*, 5.

under an equal obligation of duty with other Subjects, why should not they have the same right?

The Dissenter answered him:

Prithee shew me but one Country where there are but four Papists to one Protestant, and the Protestants allowed to enjoy equal Privileges with the Papists: If this cannot be done, why then should the Papists of our Nation look upon it as unequal dealing in this Government to keep them from Offices, when their number is not as yet perhaps as above one in two hundred? Unless they assume some extraordinary Privileges to their Persons as well as their Religions, and pretend that their very Civil Rights are Catholic?[20]

Harry: I do assure you, it has been the constant judgment of Papists, that men all ought to have Liberty of Conscience: and they are very ill men, and you ought not to join with them who would persuade you to the contrary.

Dissenter: Divide and conquer, I know is the Papists rule, as well as the Politicians. Prithee Harry, he is but eight and twenty years old, has lived long enough to see their methods of destroying the Protestant Religion: and it is mostly by playing fast and loose with the Dissenters.[21]

In an attempt to combat the anti-Court works, William Penn came out with a pamphlet favoring abolition of the Laws and Tests. He stated the basic principle that no man ought to be persecuted for matters of religion. "Nothing that does not tend to the ruin of the government, or to the prejudice of the people, which is but one and the same thing, should be made the occasion of laying any restraint upon any Man." [22] Penn agreed with the criticism that the Dissenters must have liberty with security of its continuance. But he then asked whether or not it could be demonstrated that the penal laws, and test too, might be taken away without exposing the nation to any hazard of persecution by the Roman Catholics. He answered his own question by saying no, "if a better security may be provided".

The Security we demand must be considered either as it lies naturally in the thing itself; I mean in the Repeal of all Old Penal Laws and Tests, and in the Sanction of a New Great Charter for Liberty of Conscience; or else as it may be fortify'd by such Expedients as the Wisdom of a Parliament may think fit to propound and His Majesty's Goodness may vouchsafe to grant.[23]

[20]   *Ibid.*, 8.
[21]   *Ibid.*, 10.
[22]   William Penn, *The Reasonableness of Toleration and the Unreasonableness of Penal Laws* (London, 1688), 9.
[23]   *Ibid.*, 10.

Penn went on to ask what were the advantages that Protestants, or the nation in general, pretended to receive by this exclusion.

The best defence that I know against those imaginary fears, and the most becoming dutiful Subjects, is to comply cheerfully with his Majesty in all things reasonable; that so an unreasonable Refusal may not force him upon new Methods, and make us feel in the end what we are perhaps too slow to conceive, that *Omnia dat qui justa negat.*[24]

His final and most important proposal was to have a law enacted which would abolish all the Penal Laws and Tests and establish a universal and equal liberty of conscience. "Let that Liberty be declared to be the Natural Right of all Men, and any violation thereof be therefore accounted Criminal." [25] Penn stated that if such a law were enacted, it would protect the Protestants against persecution a great deal better than the present Tests. It would, in the first place, secure all the Dissenting Protestants from the Penal Laws, which the Tests did not do; it would also secure all parties against all persecution, in every respect far better than they did. The new law would do it in a direct manner and also upon the solid grounds of religion, truth, and equity.[26]

Penn desired a Parliament, as the only mode of establishing toleration without subverting the laws, and tried to persuade the King to spare the Tests, or to offer an equivalent for such parts of them as he wished to take away. Lord Halifax said to a friend, who argued for the equivalent, "Look at my nose, it is a very ugly one, but I would not take one five hundred times better as an equivalent, because my own is fast to my face." [27] He made a more serious attack on these "dangerous and seductive experiments", in his masterly tract entitled *The Anatomy of an Equivalent.* Halifax stated that an equivalent must have several qualifications.

The first must be that the appraisers be indifferent, else it is only a sound, there can be nothing real in it. For where the same party that proposeth a Bargain, claimeth a Right to set the value; or which is worse, hath power too to make it good, the other may be forced to submit to the Conditions, but he can by no means ever be persuaded to treat upon them.[28]

[24]   *Ibid.*, 13-14.
[25]   *Ibid.*, 16-17.
[26]   *Ibid.*, 17.
[27]   Foxcroft, *Character of a Trimmer*, 250.
[28]   George Savile, *Marquis of Halifax, The Anatomy of an Equivalent* (London, 1688), 1.

Another thing necessary to making a fair bargain was that there must be an exact equality, as far as it related to the full liberty of taking or dissatisfaction: "for it is impossible to treat it as an affront to differ. The way of bargaining must be equal, else the Bargain itself cannot be so." [29] He went on to say bluntly that in the language of the Catholic Church, "The *writ de Haeretic Comburendo* is a Love Letter, and burning men for differing with them in Opinion howsoever miscalled Cruelty, is as they understand it, the persecution of flaming Charity." [30] He next attacked the institution of Kingship on the grounds of infallibility:

But there is one Circumstance annexed to their Glorious Calling, which in this respect is sufficient to outweigh all those Advantages; it is that Mankind, divided in most things else, agree in this, to conspire in their endeavors to deceive and mislead them; which maketh it above the power of human understanding, to be so exactly guarded as never to admit a surprise, and the highest applause that could ever yet be given to the greatest Men that ever wore a Crown, is that they were no oftender deceived. . . . Where Distrusting may be the cause of provoking Anger, and Trusting may be the cause of bringing ruin, the Choice is too easy to need the being Explained.[31]

Another pamphlet along these same lines exposed the inconsistency of the Church's recent independence with her long professions and solemn decrees of non-resistance, and hinted that "His Majesty would withdraw his royal protection, which was promised upon the account of her constant fidelity." [32] Such menaces were very serious at a moment when d'Albeville, at The Hague, told the Prince of Orange that upon some occasions princes must forget their promises; being reminded by William that the King ought to have more regard for the Church of England, which was the main body of the nation, he answered that "the body called the Church of England would not have a being in two years." [33]

The moderate Catholics, and William Penn, desired a Parliament, hoping that if its convocation were not too long delayed it might produce a compromise, in which the King might for the time be contented with a universal toleration of worship. On the other hand, the Anglican Church was convinced by James' conduct that his aim

[29]   *Ibid.*, 2.
[30]   *Ibid.*
[31]   *Ibid.*, 3.
[32]   *A New Test of the Church of England s Loyalty* (London, 1688), 7-8.
[33]   Burnet, *Own Times*, III, 207.

went far beyond toleration and that ultimately he wished to bring England to Rome and to reduce the Church of England to the position of a mere sect. For their part the Jesuitical party also desired a Parliament, because they hoped that it would produce a final rupture, and a recourse to more vigorous means.

With the advice of the "High Catholics", and particularly Father Petre, James early in April sent out Government agents with £10 each for a horse, and twenty shillings a day for expenses, to seek out the leaders of the Court party in each locality whose names they had been given.[34] From them, and by private inquiry, these agents were to obtain all possible information on the chances of the royal candidates in the coming elections and the reliability of the sheriffs, magistrates and other local officials. They were to counter opposition propaganda as much as they could, and check on the correspondents whose duty it was to distribute government pamphlets and information sent from London; where none existed they were to select one. They were also to correspond regularly with Robert Brent, James' court lawyer, at Whitehall.[35] The appointment of these agents is significant, for it shows that the Court, and Lord Sunderland in particular, distrusted the loyalty or ability of the new Lord's Lieutenants, sheriffs, and magistrates appointed the previous winter. Meanwhile, the preliminary reports from the Parliamentary agents, presented to the King in precise form on April 19, forecast a two-thirds majority for the Government in elections held in the autumn, and there seemed no reason to modify the plan to hold a Parliament at that time.[36]

As early as March 13, 1688, *The Gazette* printed the rumor that another declaration for liberty of conscience would soon be forthcoming to second the first and to extend farther that of 1687. It would include a provision that all Protestant churches should remain the true Church established by law and never be altered to any other form of worship nor be exempt from taking the oaths. The essential defect in this Declaration was confessed rather than obviated by the impractical remedy recommended in a tract which, for the security of the great charter of religious liberty, proposed:

That every man in the Kingdom should, on obtaining the age of twenty-one swear to observe it; and that no Peer or Commoner should take his seat in either House of Parliament until he had taken the oath; and that

34   *Ibid.*
35   Duckett, *Penal Tests*, I, 194-197.
36   Duckett, *Penal Tests*, II, 218-219.

all sheriffs, or others, making false returns, or Peers or Commoners, pre-suming they should moreover mention anything in or out of Parliament, that might tend to the violating or altering the liberty of conscience should be hanged on a gallows made out of the timber of his own house.[37]

It seems not to have occurred to this writer that the Parliament which he thus proposed to restrain might have begun their operations by repealing his penal laws.

On April 27 the King renewed the Declaration that he had set out the former year for liberty of conscience; in addition, he declared that he would adhere firmly to it, and that he would put none in any public employment but such as would concur with him in maintaining it. It was approved in Council on April 28 and published May 3. James began this second Declaration by stating that he was still firm and constant in his resolutions and he felt that his Declaration for liberty of conscience issued in 1687 was a just and right declaration. He there-fore reissued the 1687 Declaration in its entirety.[38] He went on to say, however.

Ever since we granted this indulgence we have made it our principle care to see it preserved without distinction, as we are encouraged to do daily by multitudes of addresses, and many other assurances we receive from our subjects of all persuasions, as testimonies of their satisfaction and duty; the effects of which we doubt not but the next Parliament will plainly show, and that it will not be in vain that we have resolved to use our utmost endeavours to establish liberty of conscience on such just and equal foundation as will render it unalterable, and secure to all people the free exercice of their religion forever, by which future ages may reap the benefit of what is so undoubtedly for the general good of the whole Kingdom. It is such a security we desire, without the burden and con-straint of oaths and tests, which have been unhappily made by some governments but could never support any; nor should men be advanced by such means to offices and employments, which ought to be the regard of services, fidelity and merit.[39]

In conclusion James maintained that he was still the "father of his people", and then added the sentence on the calling of a Parliament in November.

We recommend these considerations to all our subjects, and that they will reflect on their present happiness, how far above three years that

---

[37] *The New Test of the Church of England's Loyalty, Examined by the Old Test of Truth and Honesty* (London, 1688), 7-8.

[38] James II, *His Majesties Gracious Declaration for Liberty of Conscience* (London, 1688), 1.

[39] *Ibid.*, 2.

it hath pleased God to permit us to reign over the Kingdoms we have not appeared to be that prince our enemies would have made the world a-fraid of; our chief aim having been not to be the oppressor but the father of our people, of which we can give no better evidence than by conjuring them to lay aside all private animosities as well as groundless jealousies, and to choose such members of Parliament as may do their parts to finish what we have begun for the advantage of the monarchy over which Almighty God has placed us, being resolved to call a Parliament that shall meet in November next at furthest.[40]

In general substance the 1687 and 1688 Declarations were alike. Both safeguarded the Anglican establishment and secularized Church lands; both suspended penal laws on ecclesiastical matters, the obligation to take the Tests and the oath of supremacy, and restraints upon liberty of worship. Where the second differed from the first was that in order to give the Declaration wider publicity than could be afforded by *The Gazette*, James added an Order-in-Council on May 4, publicly commanding the bishops to distribute the Declaration and have it publicly read by their clergy.

It is this day ordered by his Majesty in Council, that his Majesty's late gracious declaration, bearing date 27th of April last, be read at the usual time of divine service, upon the 20th and 27th of this month, in all churches and chapels within the cities of London and Westminster and ten miles thereabout, and upon the 3rd and 10th of June next in all other churches and chapels throughout this kingdom. And it is hereby further ordered, that the right reverend the bishops cause the said declaration to be sent and distributed throughout their several and respective dioceses to be read accordingly.[41]

Whether the insertion of this unusual clause was casual, or intended to humble the bishops, it is now difficult to conjecture. It was naturally received and represented in the offensive sense. On the other hand the King already had every reason for expecting the clergy to submit for there was nothing new in an order to the clergy to read important public pronouncements from their pulpits. In 1641 the House of Commons had caused their declaration to be read in churches.[42] Charles had employed the same means to make known his reasons for dissolving Parliament in 1681,[43] and the Exclusion Bill provided that

[40] *Ibid.*
[41] Reprinted in Grant Robertson (ed.), *Select Statutes Cases and Documents*, 249.
[42] *The Journal of the House of Commons*, II, 362-363.
[43] Charles II, *His Majesties Declaration to all His Loving Subjects, touching the Causes and Reasons that moved him to dissolve the last two Parliaments* (London, 1681), 2.

James' ineligibility should be annually announced in the same manner.[44] In both instances the King claimed this power as supreme
ordinary, and in accordance with the rubric. James further maintained
that it was the good Christian's duty to join in the Declaration. James
not unnaturally expected the same obedience, but apparently forgot
that whereas his brother's declaration had been issued as a general
command to the clergy as a whole, he was now attempting to saddle
the bishops with the odious task of distributing and then enforcing the
reading of the Indulgence in their own dioceses, and so would compel
them to bear the dishonor of submission. The clergy had no objection
whatever to reading from the pulpit proclamations concerned with
secular matters, but they held to the point of fanaticism the doctrine
that any concession to the Dissenters, particularly to the Catholic Dissenters, injured the Church. By this injunction the King was endeavoring to make every clergyman *particeps criminis* and this was more
than they could stand.

One of the chief objections was that the Order had not been
transmitted in the usual and less ostentatious manner, through the
Primate.[45] It has been alleged that this divergence from the precedents
was deliberate and can be attributed to Father Petre. So strongly did
the belief prevail that insult was intended that Petre, to whom it was
chiefly ascribed, was said to have declared in the gross language used
of old by Rabshakeh to the deputies of a besieged city, that they
should eat their own dung.[46]

The first obvious effect of this order was to place the prelates who
were then in the capital or its neighborhood in a situation of no small
perplexity. They must have been taken by surprise much more than
the more moderate ministers; and, in that age of slow conveyance and
rare publication, they were allowed only sixteen days from the Order,
and thirteen from its official publication (April 7) to learn the sentiments of their brethren and of their clergy. This incident fixed the
eyes of the whole nation on the prelates, rendering the conduct of
their clergy visibly dependent on their determination, and so concentrating on a small number the dishonor of submission which would
have been lost by dispersion among the whole body. The time factor
may have been a carefully designed move, since, for obvious reasons,

[44] Reprinted in Grant Robertson (ed.), *Select Statutes Cases and Documents*,
424.
[45] Arthur Tindal Hart, *William Lloyd, 1627-1717* (London, Printed for the
Church Historical Society, 1952), 94.
[46] 2 Kings, XVIII, 27.

resistance would only be formidable if it were general. Consequently, a great responsibility rested upon the men on the spot. Distinguished Anglican laymen like Rochester, Clarendon, Nottingham, and Halifax refused to commit themselves.

The clergy was placed in a deeply embarrassing position. To refuse to carry out the order was to deny the principle of nonresistance to obey it was to recognize the legality of acts by which the King could destroy the safeguards of the established religion. There can be little doubt that the clergy of the Church of England had created a difficulty for themselves by their extravagant utterances on the royal prerogative since the Restoration. They felt they had been deceived by James' promises to uphold their church, and had not realized that it was not altogether possible for a Catholic monarch to keep these promises. The edict for the reading of the second Declaration they considered to be a direct attack on the Church as a whole. The English public had not been too deeply stirred by the fine points of legality, but the affront to the dignity of the Church fanned already kindled excitement into flame.

The second Declaration of Indulgence and the ensuring Order-in-Council caused the pamphlet warfare to be once again renewed. Arthur Anglesey, the Earl of Annesley, one of James' staunchest supporters, strongly defended the King's right of indulgence in spiritual matters.

By indulgence I do not mean that a toleration should be granted by the King of any known blasphemy or sins, I mean a permission of liberty of mens conscience, in matters not sinful of themselves, and whereby there is no disturbance of the Public Peace. That they may not be punished in their Estates or Liberties, much less in their Lives, for Nonconformity. This is that Indulgence which is meant in matters spiritual.[47]

This view was held by most moderate Catholics and many Protestant Dissenters. The Earl maintained that it was the persecuting of different opinions, and not the dissenting in opinion, that caused schism and divisions in the Church. "No good Christian but will heartily pray for this uniformity; yet as the Chancellor Bacon notes, unity and uniformity are two things." [48]

In contrast, Lord Halifax wrote a pamphlet urging the ministers

[47] Arthur Anglesey, *Earl of Annesley, The King's Right of Indulgence in Spiritual Matters with the Equity thereof, asserted* (London, 1688), 3.
[48] *Ibid.*, 50.

not to read the declaration. "But yet we judge, and we have the concerning Opinion of all the Nobility and Gentry with us, who have
already suffered in this their cause, that to take away the Test and
Penal Laws at this time, is but one step from the introducing of
Popery." [49] He went on to point out that by reading the Declaration
the clergy would, in the eyes of the nation, be giving their consent
to it in all its ramifications. Halifax stated that the Declaration was
against the constitution of the Church of England, which was established by law, and to which he had subscribed. Therefore he was
bound in conscience to teach nothing against it, while this obligation
lasted.

It is to teach my People, that they need never come to Church more, but
have my free leave, as they have the Kings, to go to a Conventicle or
to Mass. The most material objection is that the Dissenters, whom we
ought to not provoke, were spared our not reading it, to be the effect
of a Persecuting Spirit. [50]

Andrew Poulton, a Jesuit of the Catholic College in the Savoy, answered Halifax. He attacked Halifax for writing that because a person
followed the direction of the King, he followed ill-counsel and planned
the ruin of the Church of England. Poulton maintained this was not
true and failure to read the Declaration was an unequivocable act of
disobedience to the command of the sovereign authority.

If he means that the order, or rather the Declaration is contrary to the
Law of the Land, that is to say, to the Penal Laws, and the Law enforcing the Test, that is absolutely to deny the King's Royal Powers of
Dispensation, which has already rendered them invalid. For if the King
of England may be deprived of his undoubted Right of altering, Repealing,
or Suspending such laws as are inconsistent with these Maxims of Rule
which he finds destructive to the greatest part of his Subjects, he loses
one of the greatest advantages which he enjoys, to preserve those Methods
of Government which he deems most proper for the renouncing his Reign
in future History. [51]

Poulton maintained that proposing the reading was one thing, and
commanding the reading another, the difference being a "Sovereign
Command".

[49]   George Savile, Marquis of Halifax, *A Letter from a Clergy-man in the City, to
His Friend in the Country, containing his reasons for not reading the Declaration*
(London, 1688), 1.
[50]   *Ibid.*
[51]   Andrew Poulton, *An Answer to a Letter From a Clergyman in the City, to His
Friend in the Country, Containing his Reasons for Not Reading the Declaration*
(London, 1688), 8.

This pamphlet was seconded by an anonymous one entitled *An Answer to the City Conformists Letter from the Country Clergyman, about Reading His Majesties Declaration*. The author declared that reading the Declaration was not the same as reading the Mass, or professing the Catholic faith. Therefore there was no harm in reading it.

To suffer for such a refusal is not to fall like confessors, but to suffer as criminals, for disobeying the lawful commands of our Prince. And to prevent any change of this law, we shall have the help of all the Dissenting Protestants to join with us, who were afraid any alteration should be made on it lest thereby they also lose their Security.[52]

Obviously a diversity of opinion prevailed among the clergy. On one side men urged that a refusal was inconsistent with the professions and practice of the Church; that it would provoke the King to desperate extremes, expose the country to civil confusions, and be represented to the Dissenters as a proof of the incorrigible intolerance of the Establishment. Further, the reading of a Proclamation implied no assent to its contents and that it would be presumption on the Dissenters part to pronounce a judgment against the legality of the dispensing power, which the competent tribunal had already adjudged to be lawful. Those of better spirit answered that the danger of Romish examples was now so apparent that they should be considered warnings rather than precedents; that compliance would bring command after command until at last another religion would be established; that the reading, unnecessary for the purpose of publication, would be understood as an approval of the Declaration by the contrivers of the Order and by the body of the people; and, finally, that the Parliamentary condemnations of the dispensing power were reason enough to excuse them from a doubtful and hazardous act.[53] Many felt it was better to fall under the King's displeasure when supported by the consolation of having performed their duty than to fall a little later, despised. As one of the middle courses suggested, it was proposed to gain time and smooth the way to a compromise by entreating the King to revert to the ancient methods of communicating his commands to the Church.[54]

The majority appeared at first to lean toward submission. In these dire straits a message from leading London Dissenters was published

[52] *An Answer to the City Conformists Letter from the Country Clergyman, about Reading His Majesties Declaration* (London, 1688), 8.
[53] William Sherlock, *A letter from a Gentleman in the City to a Friend in the Country* (London, 1688), 1-6.
[54] *Ibid.*

imploring the clergy not to read the Declaration and promising to stand by them for the sake of religion and liberty.[55] Some of the chief ministers and laymen among the Nonconformists earnestly besought the clergy not to judge them by a handful of their number who had been influenced by the Court, but to be assured that, instead of being alienated from the Church, they would be drawn closer to her, by her making a stand on the authority of lawyers. Edward Stillingfleet, for instance, declared that reading the Declaration would be as offensive as the publication of an unlawful document, but he excused himself from being the first subscriber to an agreement not to comply, on the ground that he was already proscribed for the prominent part which he had taken in the controversy against the Romanists.[56] Dr. Edward Flower, Vicar of St. Giles, Cripplegate, summed up much of the feeling by these courageous words, "Let every man say Yea or Nay. I shall be sorry to give an occasion to schism, but I cannot in conscience read the Declaration." [57]

Symon Patrick in his autobiography described the decision by the London clergy:

We had many meetings about it: twice at Ely house with the Bishop, and on the 11th of May, where at the Master's house we came to this resolution, that the Bishops should be desired to address to the King, but not upon any address of ours to them. For we judged it best that they should lead the way, and we follow them. And on the 13th we went there again, everyone resolving for some reason or other, not to read the Declaration. There were twenty of us, as I remember, who were desired to feel the pulse of all the ministers in London, how they stood affected, and if they were generally so resolved as we were. His Grace of Canterbury promised to petition the King not to exact it of us. Accordingly Dr. Tenison and myself were appointed to go to all the ministers at one end of the town, and know their minds. . . . I wrote a list of them who promised not to read it fairly with my own hand, and carried it to the Bishop of Peterborough . . . and he carried it to Lambeth that night.[58]

Meanwhile, Sancroft had also convened a meeting at Lambeth on Saturday, May 12, which was attended by Henry Compton, Bishop of London, Francis Turner, Bishop of Ely, Henry Mordaunt, Earl of Peterborough, Thomas Cartwright, Bishop of Chester, and William Watson, Bishop of St. David's. The last two named were known to be

[55] John Mackintosh, *History of the Revolution in England in 1688* (London, Longman, Brown, Green and Longmans, 1846), 246.
[56] Hart, *William Lloyd*, 94.
[57] Mackintosh, *History of the Revolution*, 247.
[58] A. Taylor (ed.), *The Works of Symon Patrick*, IX (London, 1858), 509-511.

in sympathy with the royal policy. Clarendon recorded in his diary:

Saturday I dined at Lambeth; where likewise dined the Bishops of London, Ely, Peterborough, Chester and St. Davids. The last two discomposed the company, nobody caring to speak before them. Quickly after dinner they went away. Then the archbishop and the rest took into consideration the reading of the declaration in the churches, according to the order of council: and, after a full deliberation, it was resolved not to do it. Dr. Tenison was present at all the debate. The resolution was, to petition the King in the matter; but first to get as many bishops to town as were within reach; and, in order thereunto, that the Bishops of Winchester, Norwich, Gloucester, St. Asaph, Bath and Wells, Bristol and Chichester should be written to, to come to town.[59]

Special messengers were dispatched immediately with copies of the following letter:

My Lord: this is only in my own name, and in the name of some of our Brethren now here upon the place, earnestly to desire you immediately upon receipt of this letter to come hither with what convenient speed you can, not taking notice of any, that you are sent for. Wishing you a prosperous journey and us all a happy meeting, I remain your very loving Brother, W.C.[60]

Dr. William Lloyd, Bishop of St. Asaph, responded at once to the archbishops summons, and traveling as quickly as possible, arrived the following Wednesday. He stayed with Lord Clarendon with whom he had long been on the friendliest terms.[61] The next day, Lloyd, accompanied by Turner of Ely, Tenison, and Patrick dined with Thomas Ken, Bishop of Bath and Wells, and Jonathan Trelawney of Bristol, and later conferred with Sancroft. In the evening of May 18, the final and fateful conference was held at Lambeth. Seven bishops were present besides the archbishop and six representatives of the London clergy. Of the remaining bishops who had been summoned, Peter Mewes, Bishop of Winchester, was prevented by illness, and Robert Frampton, Bishop of Gloucester, arrived just too late.[62]

Resistance could only be formidable if it were general. It is one of the severest tests of human sagacity to call for instantaneous judgment from a few leaders when they have not support enough to be assured of the majority of their adherents. Had the bishops taken a single step without concert, they would have been assailed by charges of a pretension to dictatorship. Strengthened by the resolution of the

[59] Singer (ed.), *Clarendon Correspondence*, II, 171.
[60] Gutch, *Collectanea Curiosa*, I, 329.
[61] Singer (ed.), *Clarendon Correspondence*, II, 168.
[62] Gutch, *Collectanea Curiosa*, I, 329-330.

London clergy, and the unanimous support of the bishops who attended, Sancroft drew up and wrote out a petition to the King in language as moderate and unprovocative as he deemed compatible with firmness and clarity.

One of the most foreboding comments at the time came from the Papal nuncio, Ferdinand d'Adda, who said, "This matter seems very serious and perhaps the most critical that has yet arisen in this realm. It could have more implications than are yet apparent." [63] Just how critical the next month would verify.

---

[63]   Mackintosh, *History of the Revolution*, 654-656.

CHAPTER VII

THE BISHOPS PETITION AND TRIAL

Among the prominent clergy who were present at the final discussion and approval of the petition were William Tillotson, Edward Stilling-fleet, Dean of St. Paul's Symon Patrick, Dean of Petersborough, William Sherlock, Master of the Temple, and Dr. Thomas Tenison.[1] It is said that Archbishop Sancroft urged the bishops to wait for the Bishop of Gloucester, a prelate for whom James had an especial affection, and showed them a letter in which Gloucester promised to be on time, but the six bishops were impatient to be on their way, and rather rejoiced in the fact that together with the archbishop they completed the sacred number of seven.[2]

The bishops who signed the petition were William Lloyd, Bishop of St. Asaph, Francis Turner, Bishop of Ely, Henry Mordaunt, Bishop of Peterborough, Jonathan Trelawney, Bishop of Bristol, Thomas Ken, Bishop of Bath and Wells, and Edward Lake, Bishop of Chichester. Sancroft as Archbishop signed first, but it is difficult to believe that he was more than nominally the leader. He was by nature retiring, and though he behaved on occasion with courage, it was a passive courage, and he always refrained from justifying himself in public. It is more likely that the moving spirit was Henry Compton, Bishop of London, whose suspension from episcopal functions by the Ecclesiastical Commission precluded him from signing the petition.

The bishops opened by stating that the petition did not result from any lack of duty or obedience to James, nor from the lack of tenderness to Dissenters.

That the great averseness they find in themselves to the distributing, and publishing in all their churches your Majesty's late Declaration for Liberty of Conscience proceedeth—neither from any want of duty and obedience

[1] Singer (ed.), *Clarendon Correspondence*, II, 171.
[2] *The Petition of William Sancroft, Archbishop of Canterbury and Six other Bishops to his Majesty touching their not distributing and publishing the Declaration of Conscience* (London, 1688).

to your Majesty; our Holy Mother, the Church of England, being, both in her principles and constant practice, unquestionably loyal, and having (to her great honor) been more than once publicly acknowledged to be so by your gracious Majesty:—nor yet from any want of due tenderness to Dissenters; in relation to whom they are willing to come to such a temper, as shall be thought fit, when that matter shall be considered and settled in Parliament and Convocation.[3]

The course of action became increasingly apparent.

Among many other considerations, from this especially, because that Declaration is founded upon such a dispensing power, as hath often been declared illegal in Parliament; and particularly in the years 1662, and 1672, and in the beginning of your Majesty's reign; and is a matter of so great moment and consequence to the whole Nation, both in Church and State, that your Petitioners cannot do it, as the distribution of it all over the Nation, and the solemn publication of it once, and again, even in God's house, and in the time of his divine service, must amount to in common and reasonable construction.

Your Petitioners, therefore most humbly and earnestly beseech your Majesty, that you will be graciously pleased not to insist upon their distributing and reading your Majesty's said Declaration.[4]

In the evening of the same day, the petition being finished, all the subscribers went over to Whitehall to deliver it to the King. The Bishop of St. Asaph went first to find the Earl of Middleton, the Principal Secretary, for he desired his assistance in introducing them to his Majesty, but Middleton, sick for a fortnight, was confined to his chamber.[5] Consequently the Bishop of St. Asaph made the same request of the Earl of Sunderland, asking him to read the petition and acquaint his Majesty with it, so that he might not be surprised at its contents; and further to beseech his Majesty to assign the time and place when and where they might all attend him and present their petition. Sunderland refused to look at it, but agreed to announce their arrival to the King. As the King was out and not due to return before nine that night, they were not able to see him until that evening.[6] About ten o'clock, when James did return, they were ushered into the royal presence and the King received them very graciously and "carried them into his closet".[7]

On being introduced into the royal closet, the bishops knelt and

[3] Ibid., 1.
[4] Ibid., 2.
[5] Gutch, Collectanea Curiosa, I, 338.
[6] Taylor (ed.), The Works of Symon Patrick, IX, 551.
[7] Ibid.

presented the petition. The King received it very graciously and looking at it, observed, "This is my Lord of Canterbury's handwriting." "Yes sir, it is his own hand", replied the bishops.[8] No doubt William Cartwright, the bishop of Chester, had warned James that something was afoot and that the bishops would probably seek some modification of the Declaration, but James did not dream for a moment of having any real trouble from them.[9] The secret had been very well kept, and the King had no idea of the dismay and indignation his Declaration had aroused among churchmen. He thought they had come merely to ask that the order for reading in churches should not be sent to them, but to the Chancellors of their dioceses, and James was quite willing to accommodate them in so small matter.[10] However, when he had glanced at the petition and realized its purpose, James completely lost his temper, and, as had happened at Oxford nine months earlier, he threw away all sense of royal dignity. "This is a great surprise to me; here are strange words. I did not expect this from you. This is a standard of rebellion." [11] The Bishop of St. Asaph replied that the bishops "would rather lose the last drop of their blood, than lift up a finger against the King".[12] James said that he had never seen such an address and that it was definitely a standard of rebellion. It was at this instant that Trelawney, Bishop of Bristol, fell upon his knees, saying:

For God's sake do not believe, we are, or can be guilty of a Rebellion. 'Tis impossible that for any of my family should be so. Our Majesty cannot but remember, that you sent me down into Cornwall to quell Monmouth's Rebellion; and I am as ready to do what I can to quell another, if there were occasion.[13]

"I will keep this paper", James continued, "Tis the strangest address which I ever saw: it tends to Rebellion. Do you question my dispensing Power?" [14] He went on to accuse them of printing and preaching for the dispensing power as long as it was for their purpose. The Bishop of Peterborough maintained that what the bishops stated in their petition essentially had been only those powers which had been declared in Parliament.[15] James answered him very abruptly that the

8   Singer (ed.), *Clarendon Correspondence*, II, 479.
9   Hart, *William Lloyd*, 98-99.
10 Burnet, *Own Times*, III, 216.
11 Gutch, *Collectanea Curiosa*, I, 339.
12 *Ibid.*, 338-339.
13 *Ibid.*, 339.
14 *Ibid.*
15 *Ibid.*

dispensing power was never questioned by the men of the Church of England. The Bishop of St. Asaph contradicted him by saying the dispensing power had been declared against in the first Parliament called by Charles II, and by that which was called by James.[16] Thomas Ken, the Bishop of Bath and Wells, then stated that they were bound to fear God, and honor the King, "We desire to do both: we will honour you; we must fear God." [17] The King then asked:

Is this what I have deserved, who have supported the Church of England, and will support it? I will remember you that have signed this paper. I will keep this paper; I will not part with it. I did not expect this from you: especially from some of you. I will be obeyed in publishing my Declaration.[18]

He went on to say that if he thought fit to change his mind, he would send for them. "God hath given me this dispensing power, and I will maintain it. I tell you there are seven thousand men, and of the Church of England too, that have not bowed the knee to Baal." [19] With this statement James dismissed them.

The bishops on their side were no less surprised. They had been aware that their action was bold, but they had not expected that they would incur so extreme a measure of the King's displeasure, and they were dismayed at being classed as rebels. It may also be said that they certainly did not anticipate the enormous results their petition would have on the course of events. If they had, it is unlikely that some of them would have concurred in the signing.

After the meeting with James the bishops returned by water to Lambeth only to find, to their great consternation, that the petition they had presented to the King was already on sale in the streets of London. The identity of the person who communicated to the press this very secret document is inconclusive. Sancroft's conscience most certainly would not have allowed him to do it; besides, he declared later that he knew of only one copy, and that was the one he himself had written for the King.[20] The facts seem to point to Henry Compton, Bishop of London. He was present with the bishops, and would have had no difficulty in making a secret copy and securing its immediate publication while the bishops were at the Palace. Also

[16]   *Ibid.*
[17]   *Ibid.*, 340.
[18]   *Ibid.*
[19]   *Ibid.*
[20]   Agnes Strickland, *The Lives of the Seven Bishops* (London, Bell and Daldy, 1866), 348.

such a deed fits in with Compton's hasty temperament, his occasional irresponsibility, his anxiety to be up and doing, and his great hatred for James. The biographer of Bishop Ken suggests that Compton took this step: he certainly had the opportunity and the motive.[21] This is also the view taken by Arthur Tindal Hart in *William Lloyd*;[22] H. M. Luckock, however, in *The Bishops in the Tower*, suggests that Lord Sunderland was the culprit.[23] According to Luckock, Sunderland did it to widen the breach between the King and the bishops because he was secretly in the service of William of Orange.[24]

It has been argued in James' favor that the manner and timing of the bishops' petition was such that he was practically forced into rejecting it, and then prosecuting the authors for the sake of asserting the dignity of his office, which had been so flouted:

The great mark of insincerity in this affair, was, that either designedly or indiscretely they had put it out of His Majesty's power to consult about, and by consequence to grant what they required; the Declaration of Conscience was no new thing, it had been published about a year before, and this reiteration of it had been since the 27th of April, which was time enough to have considered the matter; and yet the Bishops made no scrupple until the 18th of May, about ten o'clock at night (at which time they gave their Petition) and the 20th it was appointed to be read: they could not believe the King would depart from an opinion and resolution he was so settled in, without consultation, and what time was there for that? Much less for countermanding his orders in the compass of one day: this looked therefore as if they had been numbering the people, to see if they would stick by them, and finding it in their power to whistle up the winds were resolved to raise a storm, while they seemingly pretended to stay it; they found the people disposed to follow the cry they heard from the Altar; this made his Majesty give a worse interpretation to it, than that it was merely of conscience.[25]

Certainly this publication was not wise, for it could not but reflect on the bishops. The petition was not, as James had said in his closet, a standard of rebellion, but, dispersed in the streets, it became exactly that. The bishops had presented public opinion with an outlet for indignation and the clergy with popular support in their resistance to the royal decree. Without publication the text of the petition would have been a secret; there would have been a considerable body of

[21] Dean E. H. Plumptre, *The Life of Thomas Ken*, I (London, William Isbister Limited, 1890), 309.
[22] Hart, *William Lloyd*, 100.
[23] H. M. Luckock, *The Bishops in the Tower* (London, 1877), 153.
[24] *Ibid*.
[25] Clarke (ed.), *James II*, II 155-156.

rumor that the bishops had protested to the King, but the country was always full of rumors which had been proved baseless, and a great many of the populace could not have decided on any concerted form of action.

The following Sunday, May 20, the first day appointed for the reading of the Declaration in London, the order was generally disobeyed. "It was not read", wrote Patrick, "by any considerable person; but our Dean sent it to one of the petty canons to read it in the Abbey." [26] Apart from Thomas Sprat, Bishop of Rochester, the names of only four complying clergymen are presented: Adam Elliot, a Roman Catholic, John Martin, Chaplain to the Earl of Nottingham, Richard Thomson, another Catholic, and Timothy Hall, Rector of All Hallows, each of whom expected the vacant bishopric of Oxford as his reward. It fell to Timothy Hall, through the influence of the Duchess of Portsmouth.[27] Some distinguished clergy, nevertheless, adopted the policy that discretion was the better part of valor. "Neither Stillingfleet nor Tenison were at their churches," wrote Clarendon scornfully, "but as I am told, went yesterday to their country houses; so overwise are some sort of men". [28]

The bishops had no sooner taken their ground in direct opposition to James' measures, than pamphlets and briefs of every description were published against them with unreserved hostility under governmental authority. The King no longer resolved to keep terms with the Church of England but to publish the petition in his own way, and with his own comments. Accordingly in the following piece, which appears to have been printed by authority, the Crown cast the gauntlet to the Church. Henry Care, the author of this work, in his answer to the bishops' paper to his Majesty stated that he blamed the bishops, who had over a year to complain or petition the Declaration, for waiting until the King could do nothing about it. Once read, it was too late.

And if the Loyalty of the Church of England receive any blemish by it, what can she say, but that she was wounded in the House of Her Friends? The apostle says, submit yourselves to every ordinance of man for the Lords sake. And upon this, the Bishop of Hereford guards his judgment for the Reading this Declaration. And therefore, let us (as his Majesty by this declaration urges us) lay aside all private animosities, and ground-

26   Taylor (ed.), *The Works of Symon Patrick*, IX, 512.
27   Hart, *William Lloyd*, 101.
28   Singer (ed.), *Clarendon Correspondence*, II, 173.

less jealousies: Let us Fear God, and Honor the King, and not discover the falseness of our own Hearts, by distrusting our Princes.[29]

The next week an anonymous pamphlet supported this position.[30] The author scolded the bishops by saying that they knew how unexpected their address was to his Majesty, who had contributed so much to the placing of most of them in their Episcopal chairs, and would so willfully have believed they were of the same loyal temper as they were in Charles II's reign.

For where the judges have determined the Point of Law, it, at least in your Lordships case, seems to be Extrajudicial acting out of your Diocese, and to be the assuming a Power I never read that your Lordships predecessors challenged. To have declared it to have been against your Conscience or your Religion, had been something modest; but to arraign the Legality of the King's Proceedings, any respect, is something with the boldest.[31]

In answer to the Court-sponsored works, Jonas Proast, ex-chaplain of All Souls College, Oxford, set forth four reasons against reading the Declaration.[32] He argued that the intent of the Declaration itself was that men would use such a liberty, in matters of religion, as could not be used without violating the laws of God and the Kingdom, that the intent of the order would have the fuller effect, in the more general use of the unlawful liberty, that in the King's intention and according to the most natural construction of the thing itself, the clergy's reading the Declaration was a direct promoting the use of that unlawful liberty; and finally that the clergy could not lawfully obey the order for their reading the Declaration.[33]

Herbert Croft, Bishop of Hereford, an anti-papist, but still loyal to the monarchy, seconded this pamphlet by another concerning the reading of the Declaration in the churches. He claimed the bishops' petition was greatly upsetting to him. He quoted I Peter, II, 13, "Submit yourself to every ordinance of man for the Lord's sake." [34] Croft maintained that the fact that the bishops read the Declaration in no wise compelled their consent.

[29] Henry Care, An Answer to a Paper importing a Petition of the Archbishop of Canterbury and Six other Bishops to His Majesty (London, 1688), 31.
[30] An Address to His Grace the Lord Archbishop of Canterbury and the Right Reverend the Bishops Upon Account of their Late Petition (London, 1688).
[31] Ibid., 5.
[32] Jonas Proast, The Case of Reading the Declaration for Liberty of Conscience Briefly Stated in Four Propositions (London, 1688), 1-4.
[33] Ibid., 4.
[34] Herbert Croft, A Short Discourse Concerning the Reading His Majesty's Late Declaration in the Churches (London, 1688), 4.

But you ask me, why do I read this in the Church? and I answer because the King commands it, and I know nothing in Scripture that forbids it, and therefore I am bound to read it. There is no doctrine taught in the Declaration. . . for tis impossible a True Son of the Church of England should have any disloyal thoughts in his Heart.[35]

In another anonymous work concerning the refusal of the bishops to read the Declaration, the author after having traced the progress of the penal laws and the test, remarked:

Jealous as the founders of that test were (or pretended to be) of the danger of popery, they well knew the great church of England had two impregnable bulwarks, the two acts of Uniformity, that themselves sufficiently alone established, guarded and preserved the church of England in all points without any fortification from the test, nor indeed was the test wanted in the ecclesiastic administration, those very statutes being a greater and stronger test before: for by those statutes is the whole liturgy, and administration of the sacraments, and indeed all the canons and articles of the church supported. For by the sense of those laws first no Romanist can possibly be admitted into the clergy. . . . Secondly, no other divine service as the mass or the like can be introduced into our churches already constituted or assigned for the divine service of the Church of England.[36]

The author's memory must have failed him when he asked, "Where in and what have our churchmen or our non-dispensing churchmen suffered by all this toleration? Have they lost the least particle of their government, discipline, rights, privileges, or professions whatever?" [37]

It was too much to expect that all the oppressed Dissenters could be won by the reasoning of Halifax and Burnet. Daniel Whitby, preceptor of Salisbury cathedral, answered for the Dissenters. While Whitby's piety, learning, and extensive charity will not be disputed, his judgment, sagacity and reasoning powers do not appear to have matched his extensive acquirements. The author stated:

I challenge you (after all your exclaiming against the poor dissenters as factious and rebellious) to give an instance of their disobeying their princes command in any such matters; what they struck at was purely for conscience sake, which you have not to plead in this thing. How many scores of prisons were filled with dissenters not many ages past, and their families suffering at home, nor did your lordships, out of your great revenues, ever send a penny to relieve them; here would have been a notable proof of your tenderness, and to have been a testimony against

[35]   Ibid., 9-10.
[36]   The examination of the Bishops Upon their Refusal of Reading His Majesty's Most Gracious Declaration (London, 1688), 1-8.
[37]   Ibid., 10.

the horrible wrongs, oppressions, and abuses put upon them, even to the ruining of their families. Retract — Retract.[38]

On Sunday May 27, disobedience was equally widespread, and it became clear that the majority of the Church was behind its bishops. "The whole Church", wrote the papal nuncio to his master, "espouses the cause of the bishops. There is no reasonable expectation of a division among the Anglicans, and our hopes from the Nonconformists are vanished." [39] Nine days elapsed before the King took any decided step tending to demonstrate his displeasure with the bishops. At one time, as he has himself recorded, he had determined to pass the matter over in silence, but the Lord Chancellor, Lord Jeffreys, persuaded him that he should punish them for disobedience and contempt of his royal authority.[40]

The King consulted for some days with all that were now employed by him as to what he should do in this emergency and talked with people of all persuasions. Some of the popish nobility urged him to let the matter drop, for it appeared that many of the clergy were resolved not to read the Declaration. Only seven obeyed in the city of London, and not more than two hundred in all of England; and of these some read it the first Sunday, but changed their minds before the second.[41] Others declared in their sermons that though they obeyed the order, they did not approve of the Declaration and one, more pleasantly than gravely, told his people that, though he was obliged to read it, they were not obliged to listen to it. The members left and the Declaration was read to an empty church.[42] The clergy in the county of Cheshire, for example, so far as one observer could ascertain, generally agreed not to read the Declaration, notwithstanding the bishop's order; they preferred to follow the metropolitan example.[43]

Three courses were open to James. He could bring the bishops separately before the Commission; in that case he would be sure of their conviction. Secondly, he might go to the opposite extreme and, while oppressing his deep resentment at their behavior in disobeying the "Supreme Governor" of the Church and disputing the royal pre-

---

[38]   Daniel Whitby, A Treatise of Traditions (London, 1688), 2-3.
[39]   James Macpherson, Original Papers, I, 253.
[40]   Clarke (ed.), James II, II, 187.
[41]   Burnet, Own Times, III, 218.
[42]   Historical Manuscripts Commission, Manuscripts of the Earl of Charlesmont, I (London, Her Majesty's Stationary Office, 1891), 347.
[43]   Historical Manuscripts Commission, Manuscripts of the Duke of Portland, III (London, Her Majesty's Stationary Office, 1892), 365.

rogative, merely threaten to refer the matter to the next Parliament, unless in the meantime their conduct had secured his forgiveness. Or, finally, the bishops could be prosecuted collectively before the Court of the King's Bench for publishing a seditious libel. Lord Sunderland favored the second, and Jeffreys the third solution.[44] The latter was mistakenly adopted since in the King's Bench, unlike the Commission, the bishops might very well be acquitted.

The situation remained stable for some time; and though in the meanwhile many different methods of severity intended against the bishops were discussed in the talk of the town, nothing seems to have been decided. Between May 23 and 29, Henry Compton, Bishop of London, William Lloyd, Bishop of Norwich, and Robert Freyton, Bishop of Gloucester, had approved and subscribed the petition.[45] The King, regarding the manner in which this had been done and particularly the publication of the petition as an almost unjustifiable breach of confidence, was induced to summon the archbishop and subscribing prelates to appear before the council on June 8, to answer such matters of misdemeanor as should be objected against them. Late in the evening of May 27, one of his Majesty's messengers served the Archbishop of Canterbury with the following summons signed by Lord Sunderland.

These are in his Majesty's name to require William Lord Archbishop of Canterbury, to appear personally before his Majesty in Council upon the eight day of June next at five in the afternoon to answer to such matters of misdemeanor, as on his Majesty's behalf shall then and there be objected against him: and You are hereby required to appear accordingly: and so doing this shall be your warrant. Given at the Court of Whitehall the 27th day of May 1688.[46]

Several of the petitioners who were in town were served with summons by others of the King's messengers at the same time; and other summons were sent after those who had gone home to their dioceses.[47]

On Friday, June 8, at five in the afternoon, his Majesty came into the Privy Council. About half an hour later, the archbishop and six bishops who were waiting in the next room were called into the council chamber, and graciously received by his Majesty. The Lord Chancellor took a paper then lying on the table, and, showing it to the Archbishop, asked him in words to this effect: "Is this the petition

[44]   Hart, *William Lloyd*, 101.
[45]   Gutch, *Collectanea Curiosa*, I, 340.
[46]   *Ibid.*, 341.
[47]   *Ibid.*

that was written and signed by your Grace, and which these bishops presented to his Majesty?" [48] Sancroft replied:

Sir, I am called hither as a criminal, which I never was before in my life, and little thought I ever should be, especially before your majesty; but since it is my unhappiness to be so at this time, I hope of answering questions. No man is obliged to answer questions that may tend to the accusing of himself.[49]

Provoked by this implied distrust, James so far departed from his courtesy as to explain, "Why, this is downright chicanery. I hope you do not deny your own hand." [50] James went on to say that he would not command them to answer but if they denied their own hands, he did not know what to say to them.

The Lord Chancellor then desired them to withdraw. In a few minutes they were called in again, and after they had finally acknowledged their respective signatures, the Lord Cancellor informed them that it was his Majesty's pleasure to have them proceeded against for writing and publishing a seditious libel, but that it should be with all fairness, in Westminster Hall, and required them to enter into recognizances for their appearance.[51] Sancroft refused to do so, claiming their privileges as members of the House of Peers.[52] The Bishop of St. Asaph agreed and said:

Whatsover favour your Majesty vouchsafes to offer to any person, you are pleased to leave it to him whether he will accept it, or no; and you do not expect, he should accept it to his own prejudice. We conceive, that this entering into Recognizance may be prejudicial to us; and therefore we hope, your Majesty will not be offended at our Declining it.[53]

To this the Lord Chancellor replied that there were but three ways to proceed in matters of this kind; it must be by commitment, by Recognizance, or by *Subpoena* out of King's Bench. "His Majesty was not willing to take the common way in proceeding against you, but he would give you leave to enter into Recognizance." [54] The bishops still insisted that there was no precedent for it, that no member of the House of Peers should be bound in Recognizance for misdemeanor. The Lord Chancellor said there were precedents, but being asked to

[48]   Singer (ed.), *Clarendon Correspondence,* II, 481.
[49]   *Ibid.,* 487.
[50]   *Ibid.*
[51]   Gutch, *Collectanea Curiosa,* I, 348.
[52]   *Ibid.,* 349.
[53]   *Ibid.,* 351.
[54]   Singer (ed.), *Clarendon Correspondence,* II, 483.

name one, he could not. The bishops desired to be proceeded against the common way, but that was not allowed, and they were commanded to withdraw a third time.[55]

Soon they were called in a fourth time and asked whether they had changed their minds, and whether they would accept his Majesty's favor. The archbishop said he had the advice of the best counsel in town, and they had warned him of this, assuring him it would be to his prejudice; and therefore he desired that it might not be required, offering his promise again to appear and to answer, whenever he should be called.[56] But the King seemed to be displeased, and said, "you will believe others before you will believe me?"[57] James told them it was offered as a favor, and to save them from any imprisonment, for they might return peaceably to their respective places of abode if they would enter into recognizance and he would accept the very smallest amount, making them merely nominal. They were, however, firm in refusing to give them, and were again ordered to retire.

They were presently joined by the Earl of Berkeley, vice-admiral of the fleet, from the council chamber, who tried to persuade Sancroft and the others to enter into the recognizances, but finding them immovable, he returned to the Council, and in about half an hour a sergeant-at-arms, a Mr. Riley, came out with a warrant to arrest them and take them to the Tower; and with another warrant addressed to the lieutenant of the Tower commanding him to receive their persons into safe custody until they should be delivered by the course of law.[58]

The Council was very reluctant to commit them to the Tower, for they were aware that a great crowd had assembled outside the palace and that it would be impossible to convey them through the streets without a large armed escort, but there was no alternative. They succeeded in frustrating the mob, by sending the bishops to the Tower by water, but they could not prevent the people from crowding to the banks of the river and making a great anti-government demonstration.

The day they were being taken to the Tower, a soldier who had deserted his colors was on his way to be hanged. A priest tried to persuade him to change his religion, but he told him he was a Protestant and would die so; then he pulled his cap over his face and

[55] *Ibid.*
[56] Gutch, *Collectanea Curiosa*, I, 352.
[57] *Ibid.*
[58] *Ibid.*, 353.

fell to his prayers. Just in the nick of time, a pardon came, without the priests solicitation. The steadiness of the man gave the bishops great satisfaction.[59]

The right reverend prisoners were treated with the utmost respect by the lieutenant, and allowed the liberty of the Tower, and to see anyone they pleased. They were, of course, the heroes of the nation and their friends and supporters, including many prominent Noncon-formists and the diarist John Evelyn, flocked to visit them.[60]

The Tower imprisonment was hailed by James' enemies as the best chance the rashness of the King had given them. Such treatment they naturally concluded would excite a desire for revenge among the prelates. Though Sancroft had led the protest, he rebuked with great anger his chaplain for praying in Lambeth Palace chapel for William and Mary as King and Queen, saying that "as long as King James was alive no other person could be sovereign of the country".[61]

The imprisonment of the bishops lasted only seven days, for they were removed from the Tower on Friday, June 15 by a writ of *habeas corpus*, to the Court of King's Bench, being brought there by the lieutenant of the Tower. The bishops appeared before the four judges of the King's Bench, Chief Justice Sir Robert Wright, who had given an opinion for the dispensing power in the Sir Edward Hales Case, and Justices Sir Richard Allibone, a Roman Catholic, Sir John Powell, and Sir Richard Holloway. They were received with great respect by the bench, and immediately accommodated with chairs, a civility without precedent in cases where the Crown prosecuted.[62] The information against them charged William, Archbishop of Canterbury, and the other six with consulting and conspiring one with another to diminish the royal authority, prerogative, and power, by maliciously and scandalously fabricating and writing, under the pretense of petition, a pernicious and seditious libel, and causing it to be published, in manifest contempt of the King and against his peace.[63]

They again pleaded not guilty and this time they allowed the Court to take their recognizances to appear for their trial on June 29; the

[59] *Historical Manuscripts Commission, Manuscripts of Lord Kenyon*, (London, Her Majesty's Stationary Office, 1894), 14th Report, Appendix, Part IV, 192.
[60] De Beer (ed.), *Evelyn Diary*, IV, 587.
[61] W. H. Hutton, *A History of the English Church from the Accession of Charles I to the Death of Anne* (London, MacMillan and Co., Limited, 1903), 232.
[62] Howell, *State Trials*, XII, 183-184.
[63] *The Proceedings and Trial in the Case of the Most Reverend Father in God William Lord Archbishop of Canterbury* (London, 1689): or a complete account may be found in Howell's *State Trials*, XII, 183-431.

Archbishop for £200 and the bishops £100 each.[64] As they went home the people crowded around them, asked their blessing; and in Little Place Yard, for example, outside the House of Lords, William Lloyd suddenly found himself caught up in a great mob, seeking to touch his garments and kiss his hands.[65]

During the next fourteen days the bishops were very busy and "settled everything with their counsel".[66] They remained quietly confident of a successful verdict. The night before the trial began an attempt was made, through the agency of Lord Dartmouth, one of James' most trusted advisers, and Admiral of the navy, to get at William Turner, Bishop of Ely, and persuade him to make his submission to James, but the bishop remained constant.[67]

Typical of the feeling of the public was this poem issued at the time of the bishops' confinement.

> Where is there Faith and Justice to be found?
> Sure the World tremble, Nature's in a swound;
> To see her pious sons design'd to fall
> A victim to Religion; Truth, and all
> The charms of Piety are no defense
> Against the new-found power, that can dispense
> With Laws to murder Sacred Innocence.[68]

The bishops were charged with the purely secular crime of "publishing a seditious libel, under the pretence of presenting a humble petition to his Majesty";[69] and the trial opened with an attempt by the prosecution to prove that the petition had been written and delivered by the bishops. As handwriting experts were then unknown, the only way this could be done was by calling the Clerk of the Privy Council and revealing the confessions made in obedience to the King's command. Unfortunately, the Clerk also had to admit the bishops had confessed solely on the condition that no advantage would afterwards be taken against them.[70]

Another subtle question sprang from the principles of English law; having proved the authorship, the Crown then had to prove that the petition was published, that is, delivered to the King; for the defense

---

[64]   Gutch, *Collectanea Curiosa,* I, 357.
[65]   Singer (ed.), *Clarendon Correspondence,* I, 177.
[66]   *Ibid.,* 179.
[67]   Hart, *William Lloyd,* 109.
[68]   Miscellany Poems, *The Muses Farewell,* 28.
[69]   *Proceedings and Trial in the Case of the Most Reverend Father in God William Lord Archbishop of Canterbury* (London, 1689), 5.
[70]   *Ibid.,* 67-68.

claimed the alleged libel had been written by Sancroft at Lambeth in Surrey, and hence the offense could not be tried at Westminster hall in Middlesex.[71] In vain the prosecution strove to show the delivery; since, although the bishops had owned to their signatures before the Privy Council, they never admitted handing the petition to James. It looked as though the trial was over and the seven would escape on a technical point.

The bishops' lawyers decided to base the defense on the illegality of the dispensing power; that history showed Parliament had never sanctioned it, and "that the power to suspend was in effect a power to abrogate; that it was an assumption of the whole legislative authority, and laid the laws and liberties of the kingdom at the mercy of the King".[72] This bold move took the prosecution completely by surprise and they could only reply with bluster and abuse.

In the summing up, the Lord Chief Justice Wright properly ruled out of consideration the difficult problem of the dispensing power, and put two questions to the jury — was publication proved, and was the petition libelous, in the sense that it disturbed the government and made a stir among the people?[73] Judge Holloway spoke next and stated that if the intention of the bishops was only to make an innocent provision for their own security, the writing could not be a libel.[74] Judge Powell declared that they were innocent of sedition, or of any other crime saying, "If such a Dispensing Power be allowed, there will need no Parliament; all the legislature will be in the King. I leave the issue to God and to your consciences."[75] Lord Allibone went beyond many of the standards of prudence by affirming, "That no man can take upon himself to write against the actual exercise of the government, unless he have leave from the government, but he makes a libel, be what he writes true or false."[76]

The jury retired at seven p.m. and remained locked up all night. According to John Evelyn their decision was delayed owing to the violent opposition of Arnold, a member of the jury and the brewer of the King's house, but by six a.m. even his stubborn will had given way and the whole jury was agreed.[77] At nine o'clock in the morning

[71] *Ibid.*, 71-74.
[72] *Ibid.*, 103.
[73] *Ibid.*, 125-126.
[74] *Ibid.*, 137.
[75] *Ibid.*, 127-138.
[76] *Ibid.*, 138-139.
[77] *Ibid.*, 139.

of June 30, the foreman of the jury, Sir Robert Langle, gave their verdict "not guilty," upon which Clarendon writes "There was a most wonderful shout, that one would have thought the Hall had cracked." [78] Lord Halifax led an enormous burst of cheering, which was taken up outside, and the good news spread across the country from village to village. James was at the military camp at Hounslow Heath on that morning. He heard the man outside cheering, and send Lord Feversham, Lieutenant-General of his army, to inquire the cause: Feversham returned saying, "It is nothing, only the soldiers rejoicing at the acquital of the Bishops." "Nothing" said James; "you call that nothing" and he left the camp in violent agitation.[79]

That night there were illuminations and bonfires which James foolishly and in vain ordered the Lord Mayor to check. The national rejoicing could not have been greater at a great military or naval victory.[80] A large silver medal was designed and struck on the occasion, having a half-length portrait of Archbishop Sancroft in the center, and those of the six bishops grouped around him.[81] The Prince of Orange sent the most flattering congratulations to the Primate and the other six bishops through Compton, Bishop of London, with whom he was in correspondence. They returned a polite answer by the same prelate, but without in the slightest degree forgetting their duty to their sovereign.[82]

The bishops case is from a strictly legal point of view curiously unsatisfactory. A multiplicity of issues were raised, including the right of petition and the privilege of bishops as Lords of Parliament. The suspending power itself was not the main question. It arose incidentally to a charge of seditious libel. Counsel for the bishops had contended that their action in reminding the King, by a petition neither false in content nor malicious nor seditious in intention, that known laws existed in the ecclesiastical sphere among which the suspending power found no place, could not be punishable. For the King it was argued that the proper place for presenting a petition was Parliament: with more force, the only presumption against the suspending power was found in resolutions of the Commons which had no legal effect, while a proclamation was at least a legal instrument issued by virtue

[78]   Singer (ed.), *Clarendon Correspondence*, II, 193.
[79]   Campana di Cavelli, II, 234-235.
[80]   *Ibid.*
[81]   Strickland, *The Lives of the Seven Bishops*, 71.
[82]   *Ibid.*, 72.

of the prerogative; and that the imputation that the King was a law-breaker must be regarded as seditious. The court was weak, divided, and outweighed by the counsel arrayed for the bishops. Exceptionally, the question of motive was left to the jury; their verdict was unanimous for the bishops.

The importance of the trial lies in the grounds on which the bishops were acquitted, and for this reason it is fortunate that they were not acquitted or discharged on the technical pleas which were from time to time urged by their counsel — of the privilege of peerage, failure to prove fact or place of publication of the alleged seditious libel — for the Court was forced to pronounce judgment on one of the main points at issue between James and his political opponents: the legality of the dispensing power.

The popular pressure was brought home to both judges and jury by the presence in court of a large number of prominent peers, who made no secret of their support of the bishops. As an eye-witness said, "At this great trial were between thirty and forty lords, which indeed frightened the judges and jury for they fancied that every one brought a halter in his pocket." [83] Another indication of the amount of public opinion aroused by the trial are these lines of verse written about the Bishop of Bristol. The Cornishmen had identified themselves with Trelawney in his struggle with the King, and, according to a local tradition, they raised a song of which the refrain ran: "And shall Trelawney die? Then twenty thousand Cornishmen will know the reason why." [84]

The people would not have been so moved if it had not been for another event awaited with hope and fear, which happened two days after the bishops were sent to the Tower. All through the earlier months of the reign the friends of the existing order had one consolation which made them patient. The King had no heir. He had been married to Mary of Modena for fifteen years and they had had children but only to see them die in infancy, and it was believed that they would have no more. The heir presumptive, if not in law at least for all practical purposes, was, of course, William of Orange. True, he also was childless, but he was much younger than his uncle, a Protestant, and no one expected then that James would live to be sixty-eight. As early as the fall of 1687, rumors had circulated con-

[83] *Historical Manuscripts Commission, Manuscripts of the Duke of Portland*, III, 412-413.
[84] Burnet, *Own Times*, III, 217.

cerning the expected birth.[85] With the birth of the Prince on June 10, Mary and Anne, his Protestant half-sisters, were displaced from the direct line of succession. Jeffreys and Sunderland tried to persuade James that the birth of the Prince was an admirable opportunity for a general pardon, which would include the bishops; but James remained obstinate.[86]

In several respects the trial was ill-timed on James' part. He not only was disappointed in his attempts to project the dispensing power, but the trial deprived the birth of his son of the most important and unquestionable of witnesses, the Archbishop of Canterbury. If Sancroft had been present on that occasion, and deposed that he was in the chamber when the Prince was born, no one could have dared to impugn his testimony. As it was, the Orange faction took occasion to convert his enforced absence into presumptive evidence that a spurious child had been secretly introduced into the queen's bed in a warming pan and this story was industriously exploited by the King's enemies.

The publication of the petition was extremely important as making it necessary for James to take notice of what he considered to be an affront. There could be no doubt that the disobedience of the clergy during May to his decree had been encouraged by the bishops' petition; he naturally felt that his authority had been challenged, and it was impossible for a man of his temperament to refuse to take up this challenge. James had made a serious miscalculation, for the country clergy had followed the lead of their brethren in London. Most men, and certainly his brother, would have seen the red light, recognized the danger, and then retreated with whatever dignity such a situation allowed them to muster. But the King was thoroughly convinced that it was compromise which had led his father to the scaffold. This is seen in the words of James' biographer. "His prepossession against the yielded temper which had proved so dangerous to his brother and so fatal to his father." [87] James even thought of issuing a second Declaration and this was actually sent to the printers, though almost at once withdrawn.[88]

James was determined that the bishops should be punished. A man less angry or more politic would have realized into what an impasse

[85]   *Ibid.*, 233.
[86]   Singer (ed.), *Clarendon Correspondence*, II, 177.
[87]   Macpherson, *Original Papers*, I, 151.
[88]   Clarke (ed.), *James II*, II, 208.

he had fallen by his misjudgment of the amount of strain which the loyalty of the Church of England could bear. For if he entered into conflict with the bishops he was bound in the long run to be a loser. Even if he were successful and punished them, the nation would look on them as martyrs in a national cause and universal indignation would at the least put an end to all the hopes which he had nourished, in spite of persistent discouragement from the beginning of his reign, of getting the principles of the Declaration of Indulgence accepted by the nation and legalized by Parliament.

Perhaps the best solution from James' point of view would have been a conviction followed immediately by a royal pardon. It would have been better to have accepted defeat and humiliation at the outset either by ignoring the bishops or by administering to them a public reprimand and pardon in view of their previous loyal conduct. But, as always happens, popular indignation in favor of the bishops had aroused equal indignation at Court against them, and even the most moderate of James' counsellors could not advice too mild a solution, nor in fact could they have expected James to accept it. Sunderland's latest biographer claims that the Earl wanted James to overlook the affront,[89] but Sunderland was far too wary to oppose James openly on any subject on which he had made up his mind. If Father Petre had advised moderation before the decision was taken, he soon changed his opinion, and made no secret of his delight at the humiliation which the bishops were to undergo. Barillon also had the impression that both Sunderland and Petre opposed the prosecution.[90] James himself says that it was chiefly on the advice of Lord Jeffreys that the decision was taken,[91] but that again is unlikely, for Jeffreys, unscrupulous as he was, had a respect for law, at any rate in courts which he could not himself dominate, and he must have realized the extreme weakness of the charge against the bishops. However confusing the unusual case was, it was the first of the kind which had gone against the Crown since the days of Sir Edward Coke.

[89]   Kenyon, Earl of Sunderland, 197.
[90]   Ibid., 199.
[81]   Clarke (ed.), James II, II, 210.

CHAPTER VIII

INVITATION TO WILLIAM AND HIS INVASION

The night the bishops were acquitted, June 30, while the people triumphed in the streets, seven men sat down at the house of Lord Shrewsbury, leader of the Whigs, to take the decisive step to bring James' reign to an end.[1] Three of them were Whigs of the old Lord Shaftesbury faction: Lord Russell's cousin, Edward Russell, later Admiral and treasurer of William's navy; the Earl of Devonshire, and Henry Sidney, Algernon's brother. These were men who would have seized any chance at any time of destroying the Stuarts; powerful individually and in their family connections, they were not yet capable by themselves of commanding a majority of effective opinion. It was the other four who represented the decisive swing of the country interest, forced at last to choose between Church and King: Shrewsbury himself, and Richard Lumley, the Earl of Scarborough, a recent convert to Protestantism and later a Privy Councillor under William; Henry Compton, the Bishop of London whom the High Commission had suspended for opposing the repeal of the Test Act, and who sprang from a fine Cavalier tradition; and Thomas Osborne, the Earl of Danby, who had spent five years in the Tower for Church and King. These stood for all the men who had been clinging gloomily on, comforted by the thought that James was an aging man and that his heiress, Mary, Princess of Orange would quickly reverse all the chaos of the last two years. All such hopes had been dashed three weeks before by the birth to James of a son who would certainly be brought up a Catholic. This event coupled with the decision in the Bishops Case ended all hope of a peaceful solution. Behind these seven, too, stood a great deal of opinion thrust automatically into opposition by such previous incidents as the dismissal of the Hydes and the dispossession of the Lord Lieutenants.

The invitation to William which they drafted is remarkable not only

[1] Dalrymple, *Memoirs*, III, Part I, Appendix, Book V, 229.

for its results but equally for its manner — cool, business-like, and unemotional, as carefully phrased as a lawyer's conveyance. After a survey of the situation, the signatories stated:

The people are so generally dissatisfied with the present conduct of the government, in relation to their religion, liberties, and properties (all which have been greatly invaded) and they are in such expectation of their prospects being daily worse, that your Highness may be assured there are nineteen parts of twenty of the people throughout the Kingdom, who are desirous of a change; and who, we believe, would willingly contribute to it. That your compliment upon the birth of the child (which not one in a thousand here believe to be the Queen's) hath done you some injury.[2]

The signers went on to say that they would attend William when he landed in England and do all within their power to prepare others to be in as much readiness as possible.

If, upon a due consideration of all these circumstances, your Highness shall think fit to venture upon the attempt, or at least, to make such preparations for it as are necessary (which we wish you may) there must be no more time lost, in letting us know your resolution concerning it, and in what time we may depend that all the preparations can be so managed as not to give them warning here, both to make them increase their force, and to secure those they shall suspect would join with you.[3]

When, by whom, and in what terms the suggestion of an armed descent first emanated from Englishmen is not known. It can be traced to the spring of 1687 when Dykvelt came to England on his mission from the States General, but in all probability the idea had not occurred to individuals before this time. The inclusion of Dykvelt in that commission to negotiate renewal of a treaty was another indication of the close watch which William kept over his interests in England at the same time that he was striving to give James the impression of friendliness. In addition to being a highly trained diplomat, Dykvelt was as much in William's confidence as any of his countrymen with the exception of William Bentinck, William's adviser, confidant, and ambassador-at-large. To assume that this man spent more than three months in London without consulting those of Orangist sympathies is to assume that he lived in a mental and social vacuum. The letters which Dykvelt carried home, however, showed that the Tories, at least, had no concerted plan. Both Hydes were noncommittal and Rochester lamented his lack of power; Lord Churchill, whose wife was all-powerful with the Princess Anne, declaimed at large upon

[2]   *Ibid.*
[3]   *Ibid.*, 229-230.

her Protestant staunchness, and, of course, upon his own. The Earl of Nottingham abounded in like laudable generalities.[4] Only Danby went further. Between him and the King there could be no real truce; his unabated Tory zeal could expect no employment under this Catholic monarch, and he looked with unconcealed longing for a new era. From the first. Danby seems to have pushed on faster than the caution of such conservatives as Lord Halifax could approve. He had tried the previous summer to go abroad, but the King refused him leave,[5] and his chief lament was this lack of personal contact; it obliged him he said, in deference to Halifax, not to tell Dykvelt several things which he could wish the Prince were informed on.

I confess, that could there be a convenient opportunity for some of us to have a personal conference with your Highness, it is not only my opinion, but the opinion of others, that some overtures might be made which would be of use to your service, and I hope from these hands your Highness is well informed of their thoughts who are devoted to your service.[6]

It was against this tense relationship between Whitehall and The Hague that the Bishop of London sent the following letter to the Prince on October 27, 1687.

The terms by which you were pleased to express yourself in preference to the Church of England were everyway so obliging and satisfactory that I look upon myself as bound in duty to acknowledge the deep sense I and every true member to the same Church ought to have of so great a blessing. And though you are at present at a distance from us, and not so well able to partake of the fruits of so good intentions, yet when we shall have served this King with all fidelity, so long as it shall please God to continue him amongst us; as none that you know will question the sincerity of your performance, so I make no doubt, but you will soon find the benefit of the sincerity having taken up so wise resolutions. For Sir, you that see all the great motions of the world; and can so well judge of them, know there is no reliance upon anything that is not steady in principles, and profess not the common good before private interest. I pray God to continue to be gracious to you, and to direct and prosper all your consummation of all happiness.[7]

In these letters a modern eye would find nothing treasonable; in particular there is not a vestige of a hint that William's interest in

4   *Ibid.*, 202-212.
5   Andrew Browning (ed.), *Earl of Danby*, II, 186.
6   Dalrymple, *Memoirs*, III, Appendix, Book VI, 195.
7   Dalrymple, *Memoirs*, II, 87.

England went beyond his legitimate desire that, when by right of his wife he should in due course have a direct part in the government, the Kingdom should be in eternal peace and predominantly Protestant. But no doubt the writers put no trust in the royal courts for there is evidence that the letters were not sent by the ordinary post but by the hand of someone making the journey to Holland.

Among these travelers the one of greatest consequence was Edward Russell who arrived at The Hague sometime in April, 1688. He proposed to find out for himself and for the principal members of the conspiracy in England, when the Prince would act, and what he could be expected to do.[8] The time had come when some cards had to be laid on the table, for there was rising apprehension that a few still undecided might yield to the King, thus starting a stampede over to the royal cause unless specific word of action came from the prince. The situation reveals some of the complications created by the necessity of drawing together several factions essentially different from one another and hence, in a crisis, likely to respond more to mutual jealousies than to common grievances, and, also by William's hesitation to take his English backers completely into his confidence. He had been wise in not doing so, for until these men were so deeply involved that only he could save them, he could not be sure of their unqualified support. Therefore, his answer to Russell was cautious. He warned his English supporters that they could expect no intervention on his part unless he received a written invitation signed by a considerable number of men who might be supposed to understand the sense of the nation.[9]

From many of the contemporary letters it is easy to infer the reasons which deterred eminent and clear-sighted noblemen from taking an active part in the Revolution. One such letter reflecting the confusion is Halifax's written late in April.

The men at the helm are certainly divided amongst themselves, which will produce great effects if men will let it work and not prevent the advantages that may be expected by being too unquiet or doing things out of season; the great thing to be done now is to do nothing but wait for the good consequences of their divisions and mistakes. Unseasonable stirrings or anything that looketh like the Protestants being the aggressors will tend to unite them, and by that means will be disappointing to those hopes which otherwise can hardly fail. Nothing therefore in the present conjuncture can be more dangerous than unskillful agitators, warm

---

8   Burnet, *Own Times*, III, 229-230.
9   *Ibid.*, 230.

men who would be active at a wrong time and want patience to keep their zeal from running away with them.[10]

The Earl of Nottingham wrote two months later.

The birth of the Prince of Wales and the designs of a further prosecution of the bishops, and of new modelling the army and calling of a Parliament are matters that afford various reflections. But I cannot apprehend from them such ill-consequences to our religion or the just interests of Your Highness that a little time will not effectively remedy, nor can I imagine that the Papists are able to make any further considerable progress.[11]

Other factors confronted William of Orange as he picked his way among the conflicting opinions about English affairs. Intervention might take various forms, but one thing he would not do was to repeat the mistakes of Monmouth. He had made it known that he could not come at all unless he received a written invitation from responsible men. William wanted the various groups of opposition in England to form a coalition strong enough so that James would be without reliable support at home.[12] Until this time it was not feasible or sage to make any definite moves. He was now a potential usurper who stood an excellent chance of becoming a *de facto* king. The significance of his position derived from the strength of his military preparations and from his refusal to make an appreciable compromise with his own followers or any compromise whatsoever with James. He was going to invade England and not once did he offer to call off or even delay the invasion in order to give the English time to solve their own problems.

Between the acquittal of the bishops and the realization by James that William's military and naval preparations were directed against himself, twelve weeks passed; this period was marked by no diminution of James's hopes for the ultimate success of his plans and no slackening in his activities, but among his intimate advisers two parties were forming. Lord Sunderland and Jeffreys were beginning to see that if James were to regain what he had lost by the prosecution of the bishops he would have to moderate his methods and recover the support of a larger section of influential men;[13] Petre and the Jesuits, on the other hand, shared their master's optimism and were for pushing home the victory which they thought was in their grasp.[14] In

10 Foxcroft, *Character of a Trimmer*, 252.
11 Dalrymple, Part I, Book V, Appendix, 118.
12 Lucile Pinkham, *William III and the Respectable Revolution*, 61.
13 Kenyon, Earl of Sunderland, 218-219.
14 *Ibid.*, 220.

every sense the moment was decisive; the Prince's refusal to concur in the Catholic policy, even for the hope of succeeding to the throne, threw James back upon his Popish advisers.

Among the signs of relaxation of the fear of the power of the King to bring retribution on anyone who opposed him was the action of the University of Oxford on receipt of the news of the death of their Chancellor, the Duke of Ormonde, on July 21. The graduates of the University, anticipating a mandate for the appointment of one of James favorites, met on Monday, July 23, and elected the late Duke's grandson, the second Duke, as Chancellor; only two hours later a royal mandate arrived to elect Jeffreys.[15] The Vice-Chancellor wrote Jeffreys a letter excusing in very submissive terms the action of the University, but it is obvious that their rapid action had no other object than to defeat James' intentions.[16]

Another symptom was the great disrespect with which the Judges on circuit were treated by the local gentry. This disrespect was in part due to the contempt into which the Bench had fallen as exponents of the Law; men no longer felt that the judges even pretended to act impartially and according to law, for at all stages in the struggle between the royal prerogative and the people, judges were dismissed who could not find law to justify the King's demands. Judges Holloway and Powell, for instance were dismissed during the first few days of July after their refusal to sanction the dispensing power in the Seven Bishops Case.[17] But it was also due to the conduct of the judges themselves, acting on instructions originating with James. James issued these instructions to the itinerant judges in the summer of 1688:

That all his Majesty's subjects of what degree, quality or condition soever (especially such as would be esteemed truly loyal and well affected to the Government) should give their utmost assistance for the supporting of his Majesty's late gracious Declaration of Conscience. And to let them know, that his Majesty intended very speedily to call a Parliament, and to use his utmost endeavors that the same may be passed into a law.[18]

Consequently the judges spoke for the King, made election speeches against the penal laws and test, and condemned the verdict in the Bishops Trial.[19]

The most serious trouble, however, occurred in the army. Early in

15   *Ellis Correspondence*, II, 180.
16   *Ibid.*
17   Luttrell, *Brief Relations*, I, 449.
18   Gutch, *Collectanea Curiosa*, I, 391.
19   Howell, *State Trials*, XII, 503-504.

his reign James had selected Hounslow Heath as the camp for training on account of its proximity to London: partly, no doubt, because James wanted to be able to pay frequent visits himself, both from Whitehall and from Windsor, to supervise the organisation and drill and to gratify his own taste for military display; but he also may have had a stronger motive, namely, to overawe the city of London. The strength of this army has often been overestimated, however. The army raised to subdue Monmouth was estimated in August, 1685, immediately after the rebellion, to number about 30,000 men.[20] Contrary to rumor this army was not substantially increased during the next three years. In October, 1688, a month before William invaded, the armed forces of the Crown consisted of 34,320 English, 2981 Scots, and 2816 Irish.[21]

Rumors of the military preparation by William had, by the close of August, reached a peak; Orange manifestoes circulated, and a sudden recall of officers of the Plymouth garrison from London leave seemed a first small symptom that the Government might be awakening from its complacence.[22] Until September the royal policy showed no sign of fundamental change, for William had, up to the middle of October, taken every precaution to conceal the real purpose of his preparations. Vessels hired, or bought, in different parts, and under pretense of different adventures in trade, were continuously ordered to shift their stations.[23]

James turned first to the bishops, whom so lately he had persecuted. During the months following their acquittal, Archbishop Sancroft had earnestly and carefully avoided entangling himself with politics, and employed all his thoughts and energies in the maintenance of order in the Church and the extension of education. He also desired to effect a bond of union with the more moderate Protestant Dissenters, by making such concessions as would remove some of their objections to join in the worship of the Church of England.[24] On September 24, James invited the bishops to an interview. Sancroft could not attend, but the bishops of Winchester, Ely, Chichester, Bath and Wells, Peterborough, and Rochester were received very graciously.[25] The King expressed in general terms his goodwill toward the Church; and

[20]   Luttrell, *Brief Relations*, I, 386.
[21]   *Historical Manuscripts Commission, Manuscripts of the Earl of Dartmouth,* Report XI (London, Her Majesty's Stationary Office, 1887), 198-199.
[22]   Edward M. Thompson (ed.), *Hatton Correspondence*, II, 90.
[23]   Dalrymple, *Memoirs*, I, Part I, Book V, 199.
[24]   Carpenter, *The Protestant Bishop*, 131-132.
[25]   Gutch, *Collectanea Curiosa*, I, 409-413.

as an earnest token of his future intentions, removed the Bishop of
London's suspension.[26]

A second and more important Conference, with Sancroft present,
took place on October 3 when the bishops presented to James a
written petition, which called for various reforms, including the abolition of the Ecclesiastical Commission and the restoration of the Fellows
of Magdalen College; the calling of a free and regular Parliament, and
the humble suggestion that the King himself should return to the
communion of the Church of England.[27] These points struck at the
very heart of the King's dispensing powers.

That your Majesty will be graciously pleased that no Dispensation may
be granted, or continued, by virtue whereof any person, not duly qualified
by Law, hath been or may be put into any Place, Office, or Preferment
in Church, or State, or in the Universities, or continued in the same;
especially such, as have cure of souls annexed to them.[28]

Eight other topics were touched upon and then they concluded with
the following:

And we heartily beseech Almighty God, in whose hand the heart of all
Kings are, so to dispose, and govern yours, that in all your thoughts, words,
and works you may ever seek his honour and glory, and study to preserve
the people committed to your charge in wealthy peace and godliness, to
your own both temporal, and eternal happiness.[29]

The signature of William Lloyd, Bishop of St. Asaph is attached to this
document, but, according to Clarendon, he was not present in person
at this interview.[30]

On October 10 the Prince of Orange published his Declaration
showing the reasons why he was about to invade England.[31] In this
Declaration one can see most clearly how William made certain concessions to the Whigs at the same time that he was bidding for the
continued support of the Tory Anglicans with whom he had first
entered into negotiations. This document, drawn up by Heer Fagel
and translated into English by Burnet,[32] protected the royal dignity

---

[26]   Howell, *State Trials*, XII, 489-490.
[27]   Gutch, *Collectanea Curiosa*, II, 193.
[28]   Gutch, *Collectanea Curiosa*, I, 411.
[29]   *Ibid.*, 413.
[30]   Singer (ed.), *Clarendon Correspondence*, II, 193.
[31]   Gilbert Burnet, *The Prince of Orange His Declaration Showing the Reason
Why he invades England with a Short Preface and Some Modest Remarks on It*
(London, 1688).
[32]   *Ibid.*, 3.

from direct attack by the old device of blaming evil counsellors for arbitrary acts.

Upon these grounds it is, that we cannot any longer forbear, to Declare that to our great regret, we see that those Counsellers, who have now the chief credit with the King, have overturned the Religion, Laws, and Liberties of those Realms: and subjected them in all things relating to their Consciences, Liberties, and Properties, to Arbitrary Government: and that not only by secret and Indirect ways, but in an open and undisguised manner.[33]

The Prince goes on to accuse the counsellors of, "having invented and setting on foot the King's dispensing power, by virtue of which they pretend that according to law he can suspend and dispense with the execution of laws." [34] They did this partly through a judges' decision, "as if it were in the power of the twelve judges, to offer up the laws, rights and liberties, of the whole nation, to the king, to be disposed of by him arbitrarily and at his pleasure." [35] Much was made of the sufferings of the Church of England, very little of freedom of religious worship. Other grievances were the use of the power to suspend the operation of laws the dismissal of judges, the efforts to pack Parliament and to admit into it members who should be disqualified by the Tests.[36] One of the chief criticisms, however, was the accusation and attack upon Mary's heritage by the setting up of an imposter as Prince of Wales.[37] On most of these points both Whig and Tory could agree, although the Whigs were not particularly disturbed about the rights of the Anglican Church and emphasis upon royal electioneering must have been a little embarrassing to them. The most important concession to the Whigs came toward the end, and this was the promise to submit all problems to a freely elected Parliament.

Therefore it is, that we have thought fit to go over to England, and to carry over with us a force, sufficient by the blessing of God, to defend us from the Violence of those Evil Counsellors. . . . and that the Writs for the Members of Parliament shall be addressed to the Proper Officers, according to law and Custom. That also none be suffered to choose or to be chosen Members of Parliament but such as are qualified by Law: And that the Members of Parliament being thus Lawfully chosen they shall meet and sit in Full Freedom.[38]

[33] *Ibid.,* 5.
[34] *Ibid.,* 6.
[35] *Ibid.*
[36] *Ibid.,* 8.
[37] *Ibid.,* 12.
[38] *Ibid.,* 13.

William concluded this declaration by calling on all the peers of the realm, both spiritual and temporal, to come and assist him in order that his designs might be carried out.[39]

From the Crown's standpoint there were several objections to calling a Parliament and several problems which would be raised. In the first place, the converts to Romanism were very few, and the attempts to make converts and to persuade members of Parliament to change their views had had the effect of hardening the rest in their opposition. But the second objection to calling Parliament was still stronger. There was no likelihood that the members would confine their discussions to the subjects on which they had been called together to legislate, and that in addition to the negative danger of a disappointment to the royal hopes there was a danger, amounting almost to a certainty, that questions would be raised which James was averse to submitting to public discussion.

A Parliament can never be an indifferent thing, and therefore it is a very weak argument to say that it will be tried and if doth not comply it shall be dissolved. Things of this kind are not so handled: the consequences may be too great to make the experiment without better grounds to expect success than at present appear.[40]

We may form a safe conjecture of the apprehension with which the assembly of Parliament was viewed by these about the King. Sunderland, Jeffreys, the Catholic Lords, the judges; not one of them was safe from impeachment: Sunderland and Jeffreys for having, among other things, given unconstitutional advice to the King and for having sat on the Ecclesiastical Commission; the judges for their verdict in the case of *Godden vs. Hales*; and the Catholic lords for having acted on that verdict and continued in office without taking the oaths.

Since early June a common rumor circulated throughout Europe and especially in England and Holland that the Prince of Wales was not born of the body of Mary Beatrice, the Queen. What ought the King to have done? About fifty people were present in the room when the child was born, including many peers and members of the Privy Council, several of them Protestants. William's Declaration and reference to the birth of the Prince of Wales convinced James at last to take serious notice of the calumny, and to allow an official inquiry to be held and witnesses to be called. A shameful scene took place at Whitehall on Monday, October 22, 1688. Depositions were taken

[39] *Ibid.*
[40] Clarke (ed.), *James II*, II, 208.

upon oath from over forty men and women, including Lord Sunderland, Lord Godolphin, and the Queen Dowager. After the witnesses had been heard, James concluded his own statement with a noble restraint:

And there is none of You but will easily believe Me, who have suffered so much for Conscience-sake, uncapable of so great a Villany, to the Prejudice of My Own Children, and I thank God, that those that know Me, know well that it is My Principle to do as I would be done by, for that is the law and the Prophets: And I would rather die a Thousand Deaths, than do the least Wrong to any of My Children.[41]

The truth apparently came out when after the Revolution Mrs. Dawson, one of the Queen's midwives, was sent for by the Princess of Denmark to come to her when she was dressing to go to her sister's coronation. She asked Mrs. Dawson if the child which was called her brother was really the Queen's child. Mrs. Dawson answered her that it was, "As much as she could answer that she, the Princess, was the late duchess, having seen them both born"; and added that Mary of Modena made Anne feel her belly, and she said that "she believed that the Queen would be brought to bed before her return from Bath".[42]

The lie had done its work, for the accusation that the child was suppositious was one of the biggest talking points used to win the masses of the people over to William at the time of his landing, and the extent to which it took root among them is testified by its growth into folk legend through the famous folk song:

> Rock-a-bye baby, in the tree top.
> When the wind blows the cradle will rock.
> When the bough breaks the cradle will fall,
> and down will come baby, cradle, and all.

When the "Protestant Wind" blew William of Orange to England, the cradle would rock, and if it blew strongly enough to break the parent bough, the cradle and the baby would go down with it.

The special inquiry was of grave consequence, but the chief event of October was the dismissal on the 26th of Lord Sunderland from his posts of Lord President of the Council and Secretary of State.[43] There had been a number of rumors, particularly that he had been in treasonable correspondence with William and had sent him a very

---

[41]   Great Britain, Privy Council, At The Council Chamber in Whitehall, Monday October 22, 1688 (London, 1688), 36-37.
[42]   Macpherson, *Original Papers*, I, 157.
[43]   Bramston (ed.), *Autobiography*, 327-328.

secret letter which Louis had written to James.[44] James in council said he had dismissed him for private reasons best known to himself, and he was in no sense disgraced, but after two vain attempts to reestablish his influence, Sunderland six weeks after his fall fled, strange to say, to Amsterdam.[45] Two letters which he addressed to his brother-in-law Halifax, one before and one after his flight, are among the most abject exhibitions of grovelling servility which it is possible to conceive.[46]

During the second half of the month the first copies of William's declaration had been filtered into the country, and several copies were sent to the King. He was again angered at the reference to his son, but what occupied his immediate attention was William's statement that he had been invited to England by a number of Lords spiritual and temporal. So on November 2, James again sent for Sancroft and the bishops to show them the passage. "I am fully satisfied of the innocence of my bishops", said the King, "yet I think it only proper to acquaint you with this statement".[47] Sancroft after thanking the King for his good opinion so graciously expressed, protested that the assertions, as regarding himself, were utterly false, for he had never held the slightest communication with the Prince of Orange nor could he believe that any of his episcopal brethren had given him any such invitation. "For my part", he continued, "I have but one King, him to whom my allegiance is naturally due, and which I have voluntarily renewed in oaths of homage and supremacy".[48] The King on this point pressed Sancroft and the other bishops to draw up and sign a paper expressing their abhorrence of the Prince of Orange and his designs.[49] This they declined to do though all verbally protested their innocence of having invited him, with the exception of Compton, who had really done so, and evasively observed, "I have given his Majesty my answer yesterday". It was couched in these prevaricating words, "I am confident that the rest of the bishops will as readily answer in the negative as myself".[50] In conclusion, the bishops said they were ready to serve his Majesty either in Parliament or with their prayers. James then dismissed them by saying, "This is the last time; I will urge you

---

[44] *Ibid.*
[45] De Beer (ed.), *Evelyn Diary*, IV, 610.
[46] Helen C. Foxcroft, *George Savile, Marquis of Halifax*, II (London, 1898), 60-61.
[47] Gutch, *Collectanea Curiosa*, I, 427.
[48] *Ibid.*, 427-428.
[49] *Ibid.*
[50] *Ibid.*, 428.

no further; if you will not assist me as I desire I must stand upon my own legs, and trust to myself and my own arms." [51]

It was impossible for James any longer to be unaware of his danger. Rumors of the sailing of the Dutch fleet reached James at Whitehall, and finally a dispatch from d'Albeville, his envoy at The Hague, confirmed his worst fears.[52] Day by day William had been preparing his group; the stores collected, put aboard and the army brought down in a multitude of small craft.

The Prince was ready to sail on his mission of "pacification". The troops who accompanied the Prince were to be "solely for the protection of his person".[53] The succession to the throne was in no way his concern, but, as a Prince on whose actions the future of European peace so largely depended, he could not but be interested in the civil dissention that threatened England. The English King was, it is true, a Catholic, and one of the main causes of the discontent that the Prince desired to heal was the King's religion and his determination that it should not in England involve civil death for those who professed it. But here too, for his part, the Prince could claim for his aim the same disinterest that marked his efforts in the cause of international peace, and to these Catholic allies he pledged himself to employ all his credit and authority to secure to the English Catholics liberty of conscience and freedom from persecution.[54]

Three days before he sailed, in a solemn audience of farewell, the States General bade him Godspeed as the deliverer and protector of the Protestant faith. It is reported that William's speech on October 13 to the States General moved even the Amsterdamers to tears.

My Lords, I am going to the navy to embark. I hope you do not take it ill that I do not make it known to you all where I am going. I will assure your Lordships, that what I am designing is for the good of the Protestant Religion in general, and of your State in particular, as is not unknown to some among you. I will either succeed in it, or spend my blood to the last drop. My Lords, your trust in me, and kindness to me at this time, is unbounded; if I live, and make it not the business of my life to make your Lordships suitable returns for it, may God blast all my designs, and let me pass for the most ungrateful wretch that ever lived.[55]

A solemn fast was proclaimed for the day of departure. Services con-

[51] Singer (ed.), *Clarendon Correspondence*, II, 498.
[52] *Ellis Correspondence*, II, 131.
[53] Philip Hughes, *The Catholic Question, 1688-1829* (New York, Benziger Brothers, 1929), 1.
[54] *Ibid.*, 2.
[55] *Ellis Correspondence*, IV, 140.

tinued through the day and until nightfall. Long prayers filled all the churches of The Hague, while, in the chapel of the Spanish ambassador, a solemn high mass was sung for the success of the expedition.[56]

The general feeling of the English people seemed to be reflected in a letter from the Earl of Dunmore, Mary Beatrice's master of the horse, to Danby.

Every post brings us news of the great preparations that are made in Holland for the invasion, but the wind has been contrary, which has hindered them from coming out, if they were ready, which I hear they are not. Our forces are in so good order and so much increased, that I believe they will find it very difficult, if not impossible, to compasse their designs, especially since there is a fleet out, which my Lord Dartmouth goes tomorrow to command.[57]

Dartmouth's instructions from James are significant and interesting.

We (out of Our entire reliance upon your approved Loyalty, Valour, Circumspection, and Experience) do hereby Authorize and Empower you to lead, and by your Orders to direct and dispose of at all such Times, and in all Emergencies, as you in your Discretion shall judge most conducing to Our Honour, and the Security of Our Dominions, and particularly in the preventing the approach of any Fleet or Number of Ships of War from Holland upon any of our Coasts, or their making any Descent upon the same.[58]

Obviously, by the time the instructions were issued, the Dutch preparations could no longer be misunderstood.

An outbreak of fighting was, indeed, what William had most to fear. If he allowed his fleet to become embroiled with Lord Dartmouth's in the Channel, James' sailors might well forget their Protestantism and remember the Dutch only as the bitter enemies of three hard-fought wars. If he dodged James' fleet and got ashore he faced a double danger. He was bringing with him 11,000 foot and 4,000 horse; and though he would strive always to thrust into the limelight the English and Scottish regiments which had been serving with him and such volunteers as joined him, the fact remained that three-quarters of his landing force was Dutch, and that, if England once

[56] John Davenport (ed.), *Memoirs of the Court of France,* I (London, Henry Colburn, 1825), 132-133.

[57] *Historical Manuscripts Commission, Manuscripts of Lord Kenyon,* 197.

[58] *Historical Manuscripts Commission, Manuscripts of the Earl of Dartmouth,* 198; An excellent discussion of the complete naval preparations and maneuverings is found in Edward B. Powley, *The English Navy in the Revolution of 1688* (London, Cambridge at The University Press, 1928).

began to think of his expedition as a foreign invasion, he was doomed.

On November 5, 1688, William landed at Torbay, on the West coast of England, after a series of fortunate accidents which he may have taken as confirmation of his belief in predestination. A strong easterly wind on the morning of November 3, together with the vagaries of the Channel winds and breezes in the next three days, land-locked the English fleet and made impossible a meeting between the antagonists, and assured the Dutch success as far as the disembarkation was concerned. Lord Dartmouth cannot be blamed for preventing the landing for nothing short of miraculous foreknowledge of the winds and tides or the knowledge of the landing place would have helped the royal navy. James did not blame Dartmouth for letting the Dutch past him for he was wise enough in the ways of the sea to know that the prevailing winds were all important.[59]

The Prince had landed where he had been least expected; but the land design, at least, at first moved much less rapidly than he had anticipated. Two or three ships were still expected with arms and money,[60] but for nine days little happened and William began to think that he had been betrayed; then events moved rapidly. On Saturday, November 17, James set forth from his capital to face the invader, and by the time he reached his headquarters at Salisbury on the 19th, the defections had commenced. The two pillars of the royal cause, the army and the country gentlemen, were slipping away. It was on Friday night, November 23, however, that John Churchill, the Commander-in-chief of James' forces, accompanied by the late King's natural son, the Duke of Grafton, and followed by a troop of horses fled to the invader.[61] As early as August 4 we have the first indication of the treachery of Lord Churchill. At this time he wrote a letter to the Prince of Orange in which he stated:

Mr. Sidney will let you know how I intend to behave myself: I think it is what I owe to God and my country. My honor I take leave to put into your Royal Highness's hands, in which I think it safe. If you think there is anything else that I ought to do, you have but to command me, and I shall pass an entire obedience to it, being resolved to die in that religion that it hath pleased God to give you both the will and power to protect.[62]

[59]   *Historical Manuscripts Commission, Manuscripts of the Earl of Dartmouth,* 204.
[60]   Browning (ed.), *Earl of Danby,* II, 139.
[61]   Macpherson, *Original Papers,* I, 162.
[62]   Dalrymple, *Memoirs,* III, Appendix, Book V, 239.

Churchill was convinced that the military effort was failing and that there was no prospect of negotiating a peace between James and William. He therefore wrote the following message to James the night before he left.

Since men are seldom suspected of sincerity, when they act contrary to their interest, and though my dutiful behaviour to Your Majesty in the worst of times may not be sufficient to incline you to a charitable interpretation of my actions, yet I hope the great advantage I enjoy under your Majesty, which I own I can never expect in any other change of government, may reasonably convince your Majesty and the world that I am actuated by a higher principle, when I offer that violence to my inclination and interest as to desert your Majesty at a time when your affairs seem to challenge the strictest obedience from all your subjects. This, sir, could proceed from nothing but the inviolable dictates of my conscience, and a necessary concern for my religion... and with which I am instructed nothing can come in competition.[63]

Winston Churchill, in an attempt to justify this desertion, maintained "All he could give the King was the faithful declaration of his opinion, and this on many occasions he made abundantly clear. If James, knowing his mind, employed him, it was at his own risk." [64]

Being extremely discouraged by these defections and incapacitated somewhat by a bleeding nose, [65] James was retreating back to London when he was mortified to find that Princess Anne had secretly left the capital the previous day under the escort of the Bishop of London. "God help me!" exclaimed the unhappy father, "my own children have forsaken me".[66] James was now desperate, so the next day the King called a long session with his Council and he summoned all the temporal and spiritual peers who were in London to attend a meeting the following day. On November 27, some thirty or forty who were in town attended.[67] The King asked their advice and there was much plain speaking, particularly from Clarendon, who ironically enough, deserted four days later to the Prince. The counsellors seemed to be divided into two groups. The moderates including Halifax, Godolphin, the two Secretary's of State, Lord Richard Preston, and Lord Middleton, together with Lord Belayse, and other moderate Catholic peers,

[63] *A Collection of Papers Relating to the Present Juncture of Affairs in England* (London, 1688), 27.
[64] Winston S. Churchill, *Marlborough His Life and Times* (New York, Charles Scribner's Sons, 1950), I, 251.
[65] Thompson (ed.), *Hatton Correspondence*, II, 111.
[66] *Historical Manuscripts Commission, Manuscripts of Le Fleming*, 220-223.
[67] Clarke (ed.), *James II*, II, 226.

urged James that he must on no account think of leaving the country. He must satisfy his subjects as to the security of the law and of the Protestant religion, and he must call a Parliament. They furthermore assured James that, if he would act thus, he would gain widespread support and would suffer no personal risk. Led by Clarendon, they demanded the sending of commissioners to treat with the Prince, then on his way from the west.[68] To James this attitude of his ministers must have been indeed humiliating, and he may well have felt that his worst enemies were of his own household. On the other hand, the other party, headed by Lord Melford, protege of Sunderland, and other violent Catholics, urged James to escape. In their view, the Prince would find it difficult to form a government, and to satisfy the ambitions and the jealousies of his supporters.[69]

On November 28, while the King was still meeting with the peers, a third declaration, supposedly written by the Prince of Orange, was published but the Prince claimed he knew nothing about it.[70] This pamphlet obviously doomed all James' counsellors to the scaffold. It was penned with great spirit and had great effect. The proclamation set forth the desperate designs of the papists, and the extreme danger the nation was in by their means, and required all persons immediately to fall on such papists as were in any employments, and to turn them out, and to secure all strong places, and to do everything else that was in their power to execute the laws.

So we are resolved and do declare that all Papists, who shall be found in open Arms, or with Arms in their Houses or about their Persons, or in any Office or Employment Civil or Military, upon any pretence whatsoever, contrary to the known Laws of the Land, shall be treated by Us and our Forces not as Soldiers and Gentlemen, but as Robbers, Free-Booters and Bandits. . . . And that for those Magistrates and others, of what condition soever they be, who shall refuse to assist us, and in Obedience to the Laws, to Execute vigorously what We have required to them, and suffer themselves at this Juncture to be cajoled or terrified out of their Duty, We will esteem them the most Criminal and Infamous of all Men, Betrayers of their Religion, the Laws and their Native Country.[71]

This Declaration alarmed the entire populace for it was believed that

---

[68]   Singer (ed.), *Clarendon Correspondence*, II, 203-205; Foxcroft, *Character of a Trimmer*, 263.
[69]   *Ibid.*
[70]   Hugh Speke, *The Prince of Orange His Declaration of November 28, 1688* (London, 1688).
[71]   *Ibid.*, 2-3.

it was truly the Prince's. James was so disturbed by it that on November 29 he put out a proclamation, forbidding and admonishing all persons not to publish, dispense, or repeat any of the papers or declarations of the Prince of Orange, nor to read, receive, conceal, or keep the same. Several men who were caught doing so were imprisoned for high treason.[72]

For the time being the bewildered King gave way to his advisers. He ordered writs to be issued for a meeting of Parliament on January 15, 1689, and agreed that Halifax, Nottingham, and Godolphin should act as his intermediaries with the Prince; so on December 7, the Prince met with the three ambassadors.[73] Their mission was a delicate one. They had to announce that James had summoned a Parliament: to remind him that this had been one of the avowed objects of his mission; and they were empowered to assure the Prince that James was willing to enter into a treaty guaranteeing that the elections would be free. But the mission had little success. William announced that these conditions were not enough, and it was obvious that the march of his army would not be delayed by negotiations.[74]

Meanwhile James had been making plans for the escape of the Queen, who by this time was thoroughly frightened and was eager to leave the country. On the night of December 19 the Queen and the Prince of Wales slipped out of London and were sent to France.[75] On the 11th at three in the morning, attended by Sir Edward Hales, and two servants, James withdrew by a private passage from Whitehall, and crossed the river in a barge after giving orders to the Duke of Northumberland, who was Lord in Waiting, not to mention until the morning what he had seen.[76] Sometime before he had destroyed the writs for a new Parliament, and new threw the great seal into the river. The seal was afterwards found by a fisherman and brought to London.[77]

When the king's party was on board they found the boat had no ballast; the master easily persuaded the King to let them take some in. It was half ebb before they ran ashore, planning to sail as soon as afloat. When they were nearly afloat three fishing boats from Faversham stopped them, seized the King and the others. Supposing them

---

[72] Luttrell, *Brief Relations*, I, 472-473; *Ellis Correspondence* IV, 130.
[73] *Royal Tracts. In Two Parts* (London, 1692), 56-58.
[74] *Ibid.*, 58-60.
[75] Powys (ed.), *Life and Times of Antony Wood*, 270.
[76] *Ibid.*, 270-272.
[77] Burnet, *Own Times*, III, 326.

papists endeavoring to escape, they were taken up to Faversham. The King was still not known, however. Sir Edward Hales whispered to the Captain, and privately gave him fifty guineas with a promise of more, if he would let him go before they would put ashore. The captain promised, but did not keep his word. "They were carried prisoners to their town, where as they were marching along the street, a brewer first discovered the King; whose opinion at length was confirmed by others." [78]

The finality of James' flight filled Lord Dartmouth with horror; "Oh God, what could make our master desert his kingdoms and his friends." [79] For a month Dartmouth had swung at anchor between loyalty to the King and the feeling for his country. He had seriously hoped to meet the Dutch fleet, but on the other hand he refused to convey the Prince of Wales to France "The most I can apprehend", he bluntly wrote, "Your highness may be jealous of, is his being brought up in the religion of the Church of England, that ought to be the prayer of every local honest subject." [80] Dartmouth's son-in-law, Philip Musgrave, warned him from London not to throw away the fleet, as Faversham had the army, but actually Dartmouth had spontaneously resolved to offer it to the Prince and the Peers for the national safety.[81] But still, especially after hearing of the King's enforced halt, he hoped for a compromise, and told Rochester, "We must put all our hands to the reestablishing him in the government, and resettlement of our holy religion, laws, and properties." [82] On the 12th, however, Dartmouth surrendered the fleet. His protest is too long for full quotation but he stated that he did so with the greatest dread and grief of heart.

Out of duty to my country and the Reformed religion of the Church of England, (of which as I am, I have always professed myself a true son,) I embrace readily the invitation given me by your Highnesses particular letter, of the 29th of November, (come just now to my hands,) to dispose the fleet under my command to join with your Highnesses, towards supporting our religion, laws, liberties and properties, not doubting, according to your Highnesses declarations, but you will prosecute the same with utmost regard and tenderness.[83]

[78] Powys (ed.), *Life and Times of Antony Wood*, 270-271.
[79] *Historical Manuscripts Commission, Manuscripts of the Earl of Dartmouth*, 231-232.
[80] *Ibid.*
[81] *Ibid.*, 231.
[82] *Ibid.*, 235.
[83] Powley, *English Navy in the Revolution of 1688*, 143-144.

James returned to London on Sunday, December 16, but the remainder of his short stay was one of fitful hope and bitter despair. He had now thoroughly lost his nerve, just when he most needed it, and set his mind only on escape. The Lords, assembled at Westminster, now intervened between the contestants, suggested that the King should take up his residence at Ham near Richmond, once the house of Lauderdale. Here he might have improved his situation by negotiation, for so long as he was in England he was the sovereign. But James decided to go to Rochester instead.[84] It was obvious to almost everyone that William wanted him to go, and local evidence of this desire was furnished by the absence of guards at the rear of the house.[85] James himself said that the only matter on which he and William were in agreement was that he should leave the country. He saw that as long as he remained in England he could claim to be King *de facto* and could demand the right to be heard in any proposals for settlement, and that the high Tories who had disapproved of his policy would nevertheless, as their declaration of December 11th had shown, refuse to countenance his deposition; but if once he left the realm he might retain the academic rights of a king *de jure*, but would virtually have abdicated.[86] James had apparently made up his mind, however, and on the morning of the 23rd, he left the city in which he had reigned so short a time by a barge at Whitehall stairs: He was never to return. On Christmas Day, in company with the Duke of Berwick, his personal bodyguard, he stepped ashore at Ambleteuse on the soil of France. It was not only the fall of a monarch, and the collapse of a royal house — it was the end of an age.

[84]   Singer (ed.), *Clarendon Correspondence*, II, 230.
[85]   Campana di Cavelli, II, 401.
[86]   Clarke (ed.), *James II*, II, 248.

CHAPTER IX

CONCLUSION

James' flight inaugurated a monarchy as different as the essential
continuity of English constitutional development permitted. In December of 1688 sovereignity, for all practical purposes, was grasped
by the nation. No Parliament existed nor was there any valid means
of convoking one, since James had destroyed the writs prepared for
the Parliament which was contemplated, and had removed the Great
Seal. William, still merely Prince of Orange and therefore an alien
without any constitutional standing, had been invited by an informal
assembly of peers to send out writs summoning a Convention. This
equally irregular assembly condemned in a Declaration of Right the
alleged illegalities of James, and asserted that his flight was equivalent
to abdication, thereby reconciling Whig and Tory views of that event.

Resolved, That King James the second, having endeavoured to subvert
the constitution of the Kingdom, by breaking the original contract between
King and People; and, by the advice of Jesuits, and other wicked persons,
having violated the fundamental laws, and withdrawn himself out of the
Kingdom, hath abdicated the government, and that the throne is thereby
vacant.[1]

Many members preferred "deserted" to "abdicated", but the Commons
would not accept the substitution. Pamphlets *pro* and *con* circulated
in London during the first few months of 1689.[2] The attempts to prove

---

[1] *Parliamentary Debates,* II, 183-184.
[2] Edmund Bohun, *The History of the Desertion, or an account of all the Publick
Affairs in England From the Beginning of September 1688 to the 12th of February
Following* (London, 1689); Gilbert Burnet, *An Enquiry into the Present State of
Affairs* (London, 1689); Gilbert Burnet, *Reflections on a Paper Entitled His
Majesties Reasons For Withdrawing Himself from Rochester* (London, 1689);
Jeremy Collier, *The Desertion Discussed in a Letter to a Country Gentleman* (Lon-
don, 1689); *A Remonstrance and Protestation of All the Good Protestants of this
Kingdom, against Deposing their Lawful Sovereign King James II with Reflections
Thereupon* (London, 1689); John Somers, *A Vindication of the Proceedings of the
Late Parliament of England* (London, 1690); Edward Stephens, *Important Ques-*

that James had abdicated the throne seemed more persuasive as the Commons rejected "deserted". Legally, the assembly's resolution that the throne was vacant, even if it had come from a legal Parliament, was devoid of substance for strictly the throne can never be vacant. Passing by all legitimist claims, the Convention though its Tory members vainly tried to save the principle of legitimacy by attempting an offer of the throne to Mary alone, finally asked William and Mary to accept it jointly. The offer was accepted.

The acts of the Convention, which were not acknowledged by James, were from the narrow standpoint of the constitutional lawyers, acts of treason. In the event of a counter revolution its members would have lain at the mercy of James; nor could they under a regency have appealed to the well-known statute of Henry VII under which obedience to a King *de facto* cannot be punished as rebellion.[3]

As a practical measure the offer of the throne to William and Mary was necessary in order to bar the claim of James' son, and practical necessity triumphed over law. James' second flight killed any prospect of a regency for his son, though such a regency in the middle of December would have seemed the ideal solution to most Englishmen. The bishops clung to the idea, and those in London were still in favor of it as late as January 15, 1689,[4] but the practical objections to such a course increased and took a firmer hold on moderate men. The attitude of many was probably determined more by ecclesiastical than by political considerations.

During the winter of 1688, the quality of political pamphleteering dropped to an extremely low level, and the victory of the Prince of Orange was greeted in print with a vulgarity and a grossness which no comment can exaggerate. One of the most popular specimens, which was issued a few days after Christmas and obtained a wide circulation among the soldiers and peasants of England, purported to be a letter addressed by Pope Innocent XI to William of Orange. A short paragraph from the text will illustrate the kind of propaganda which helped to drive King James out of England.

---

tions of State, Law, Justice, Prudence, Both Civil and Religious, Upon the Late Revolutions and Present State of these Nations (London, 1689); Edward Stephens, *Reflections Upon the Occasioners of the Last Year from 5 November 1688 to 5 November 1689* (London, 1689).

[3] 2 Henry VII, c. 1, Reprinted in Carl Stephenson and Frederick G. Marcham (ed.), *Sources of English Constitutional History* (New York, Harper and Brothers Publishers, 1937), 301-302.

[4] Singer (ed.), *Clarendon Correspondence*, II, 247-248.

To ingratiate myself further in the Kingdom of England's favour, I will licentiate your ladies of pleasure, in London, and all females in general there, to whore, pick pockets, and for a Julio or Sixpence a week, which is no more than my own Order of Harlots pay at Rome, and all Italy over. And to all men within the Walls of London, and Westminster, I will freely give Liberty to be as intimate with their neighbours wives, as ever Pope Hildebrand was with Mathilda.... and in one word, I will let the inhabitants of the Whole Isle of Britain fulfill their hearts desire, in all kinds of villanies and Abominations, without sinning.[5]

As the anti-Catholic propaganda increased, rumors of preparations by the papists to murder all Protestants in their beds circulated throughout London.[6] On November 11, for instance, a mob assembled outside a Popish monastery on a report that gridirons, spits, and great caldrons were inside. At the end of the month another story went around that a French ship had been captured with several chests on board in which were found a strange sort of knife, "about two feet long, with the back to chop and the point turning inward to rip; reported by some to be for the destruction of Protestants".[7] A further story circulating was the one concerning an instrument called "Protestant Bridles". These were to lead the heretics of England about the streets of London and Westminster.

They are made of iron work in the nature of a crown to wear on the head, within the inside there is an iron to put into the mouth, edg'd on both sides like a knife, and sharp pointed like a lance, which are to prick and cut the tongue as they are led or pulled along.[8]

To throw a veil of romance over the credulity, the obscenity, and the profanity of the English populace during those days is perhaps to make pleasant but scarcely truthful reading. The King was driven out of his realm by an appeal to the lowest instincts of the rabble. In late December and early January anti-Catholic pamphlets and ballads flowed from the presses of London. Portions of two of the strongest ballads are the following:

> Here's a piece of the Bag,
> By Age turn'd to a Rag,
> In which Judas the money did bear;

[5] *A Letter from His Holiness the Pope of Rome, to his Highness the Prince of Orange* (London, 1689), 2-3.
[6] Luttrell, *Brief Relations*, I, 474-481.
[7] *Ibid.*
[8] *Revolution Politics: Being a Compleat Collection of All the Reports, Lyes, and Stories Which were the Fore-runners of the Great Revolution in 1688* (London, 1783), 60-62.

With a part of his Rope,
Bequeath's to the Pope,
As an antidote against all Despair.

But by the Faith of a Priest,
This is no time to jest,
Since we baulk'd in our great Expectations;
Before I will swing,
Like a Dog on a string,
I'll renounce the Transubstantiation.[9]

and this last two stanzas of the *Last Will and Testament of Father Petre*.

For if there's a Hell,
I deserve it so well
I need not despair of the Place,
And none but an ass
Will believe that the Mass,
Can ever restore him to Grace.

I would have Enlarged,
But my Conscience discharg'd,
I'll here make an end of my Sermon,
And wish all this throng
May be damn'd, Old and Young,
And so drive away, Honest Carman.[10]

The attempts of James through his two Declarations of Indulgence to repeal the Penal Laws and the Test Act point to an epoch in the history of England of the greatest possible interest. To the present age, both burdens in every sense belong to the past, and now that their repeal and the toleration of all sects are accomplished facts, one can scarcely regard the matter properly from our present altered position. We can either penetrate the feelings of the seventeenth century Englishmen with regard to the injustice, nor sufficiently appreciate the hardships which they pressed upon the Roman Catholic and Dissenting community. On the other hand, we cannot adequately value the stubbornness and inflexible tenacity of those who persisted in maintaining them as the chief anchor of their religious liberties. Too near to the Reformation, and nearer still to the subsequent return to popery, it seemed necessary to impose a barrier to the possible reestablishment of the Romish Church.

[9] *Religious Relicks: Or, the Sale at the Savoy, Upon the Jesuits Breaking Up Their School and Chappel* (London, 1689), 42-47.
[10] The Muses Farewell, *Last Will and Testament of Father Petre* (London, 1689), 29.

In regard to the Revolution, James might be accused of acting too late. A pertinent question might be: too late for what? It was not within his power to call off the invasion. He could only try to unite his people. One of the truest of Halifax's aphorisms is: "The people can seldom agree to move together against a Government, but they can to sit still and let it be undone." [11] Such was the case in the Fall of 1688. With a united country to back him the prospect of an invasion need not have crushed James. He could not achieve that unity; on the contrary, he faced a divided people and a strong opposition. Any concession that James might make was called either insufficient or insincere, and attempts to make up for insufficiency merely heightened the charge of insincerity. It is easy to assert that a man does not intend to keep his promises if he is never given a chance to prove otherwise. The time has long gone by when anyone can say whether James would or would not have stood by his word, but one does not have to be a sentimental Jacobite to point out that he had never been notorious for duplicity. On the contrary, he had been all too forthright in stating his aims. True, he issued writs for Parliamentary elections and then recalled them when he became certain of William's intentions. That might indeed be called a broken promise, but it should be noted that the breaking, not the making, was caused by the threat of rebellion. Even so, the rescinding of these writs was probably James' most serious mistake. Had he gone through with the plans he would have deprived his enemies of one of their greatest talking points against him, and he actually had less to fear from Parliament than they did. But it was a strategic rather than a moral error, and it is not difficult to see why it was made. Throughout the autumn James insisted on the impossibility of holding Parliament during a state of civil war. Much may be said for his contention. At the time the writs were being recalled the invasion was expected within a few days and it would actually have occurred much earlier had not unforeseeable circumstances and weather caused delay.

James should not be condemned too harshly for his views and certainly least of all on the ground that they were out of keeping with his time. The trend of later developments has led to over-emphasis on certain aspects of the seventeenth century. Republicanism and the more moderate Parliamentarism were indeed popular with some people of England, but for a great many of the inhabitants of the country they evoked uncomfortable memories of the Commonwealth

[11]   Foxcroft, *Halifax*, II, 501.

and later disturbances. Good government meant strong government, one that could keep the peace at home and maintain or improve England's position abroad. Political thought had as yet discovered no means more effective to achieve that desired end than absolute monarchy. Thus many of his subjects believed as firmly as James in the principles of Divine Right, and accepted obedience to their King as a moral obligation. Had James been able to understand that popular belief in the Divine Right of Kings was first produced by and nourished in the national church, and that any attack on the parent growth would inevitably weaken and ultimately destroy the product, he might have proceeded with less interference in ecclesiastical affairs or at least with a show of legality and caution. Nevertheless, powerful as the beliefs just mentioned were, equally powerful was the conviction that England must be kept Protestant and Episcopalian, and it was against this conviction that James had to fight when he tried to introduce religious toleration.

James failed less from tactlessness than haste, though the two were closely connected. His motives, nevertheless, are intelligible. Fifty-one years of age when he ascended the throne, he had no reason to expect a long reign. His heirs were his daughters, and their Protestant husbands who would do little or nothing for his co-religionists. His desire for toleration probably surpassed his desire freely to exercise his kingly power, but he attempted to realize the one through use of the other, thus posing for the modern evaluator of his reign the problem of how to condemn the one objective, which the twentieth century rejects, without disapproving of the other, which it claims to uphold. The solution would be easier if one could accept the claim, so often made, that James was trying to force the people of England to become Roman Catholic. That accusation, however, can be validated only on the assumption that every one of his own assertions to the contrary was a deliberate lie, for he himself said that his aim was religious toleration for those of all faiths, including Protestant Dissenters no less than Roman Catholics. Although his followers included Jesuit zealots who may have hoped for the exclusive victory of their own church, at no point can one find unquestionable proof that James agreed with them. Like most people of his own time and a good many of our own, he believed in the theory of the Ecumenical Church and hoped that the schisms of the Reformation might be healed, but he wanted this to come about through conviction or conversion rather than through force. Only two subsidiary fictions enabled the bulk of the Tories to accept the settlement at all. The first was the doctrine that James, by his flight and by throwing the Great Seal into the Thames, had abdicated *de facto* and left the throne vacant; the second was the warming pan myth.

Because Archbishop Sancroft, six of his bishops, and four hundred of the lower clergy could not take a second oath of loyalty and obedience when their lawful King was still alive, they forfeited their benefices to go out into the wilderness as a standing reproach to those who had compromised with the Revolution. The tormenting difficulties with which James had faced his own most loyal supporters can best be realized from the fact that among these non-juror bishops were five who had stood their trial among the famous seven for opposing the second Declaration of Indulgence. King James was not the first prince who loved justice, hated iniquity, and died in exile; yet there never was, perhaps, any ruler of any country who in his lifetime suffered so much from the disloyalty of his own family and the ingratitude of his friends, and, after his death from the opprobrium of posterity.

BIBLIOGRAPHY

BOOKS

Aitken, George, *Later Stuart Tracts*, Vol. III (New York, E. P. Dutton and Co., 1856).

Akerman, John Y. (ed.), *Moneys Received and Paid for Secret Services of Charles II and James II* (London, Printed for the Camden Society, J. B. Nichols and Son, 1851).

Barbour, Violet, *Henry Bennet, Earl of Arlington* (Washington, American Historical Association, 1914).

Bastide, Charles, *The Anglo-French Entente in the Seventeenth Century* (London, John Lane, n.d.).

Bate, Frank, *The Declaration of Indulgence 1672* (London, University of Liverpool Press, 1908).

Bathurst, A. Benjamin, *Letters of Two Queens* (London, Robert Holden and Company, Ltd., 1924).

Baxter, Stephen B., *The Development of the Treasury 1660-1702* (Cambridge, Harvard University Press, 1957).

Berthier, Joachim Joseph (ed.), *Innocentii P. P. XI Epistolae AD Principes*, Vol. II (Rome, Apud Spithover Bibliopolam, 1895).

Birch, Thomas, *The Life of the Most Reverend Dr. John Tillotson, Lord Archbishop of Canterbury, compiled chiefly from His Original Papers and Letters*, (London, 1752).

Blencowe, R. W. (ed.), *Diary of the Times of Charles the Second*, Vol. II (London, Henry Colburn, 1843).

Bloxam, J. R. (ed.), *Magdalen College and King James II, 1686-1688*, 2 vols. (Oxford, Printed for the Oxford Historical Society at the Clarendon Press, 1886).

Bramston, Thomas W. (ed.), *The Autobiography of Sir John Bramston* (London, Printed for the Camden Society, John B. Nichols and Son, 1845).

Braybrooke, Richard, *Diary and Correspondence of Samuel Pepys*, Vol. IV (London, George Bell and Sons, 1890).

Browning, Andrew (ed.), *English Historical Documents, 1660-1714* (New York, Oxford University Press, 1953).

——, *Thomas Osborne, Earl of Danby and Duke of Leeds*, Vol. II (Glasgow, Jackson, Son and Co., 1944).

Buckley, W. F. (ed.), *Memoirs of Lord Ailesbury*, Vol. II (Roxburghe Club, London, 1890).

Burnet, Gilbert *Bishop Burnet's History of The Reign of King James The Second* (Oxford, At The Clarendon Press, 1852).

Cardigan, Earl of, Chandos Sydney Cedric Brudenell-Bruce, *The Life and Loyalties of Thomas Bruce* (London, Routledge and Kegan Paul, Ltd., 1951).

Cardwell, Edward, *Documentary Annals of the Reformed Church of England*, Vol. II (Oxford, At The University Press, 1844).

Carpenter, Edward, *The Protestant Bishop* (London, Longmans, Green and Co., 1956).

Carrel, Armand, *History of the Counter Revolution in England for the Re-establishment of Popery Under Charles II and James II* (London, H. G. Bohn, 1857).

Cavelli, Campana di, *Les Deniers Stuarts a Saint Germain en Laye,* Vol. II (Hamburg, 1871).

Churchill, Winston S., *Marlborough His Life and Times,* Vol. I (New York, Charles Scribner's Sons, 1950).

Clark, Henry W., *History of English Non-conformity, Vol. II* (London, Chapman and Hall, Ltd., 1913).

Clarke, T. S. (ed.), *Life of James II By Himself,* Vol. II (London, Longman, 1816).

Clarkson, Thomas, *Memoirs of the Public and Private Life of William Penn* (London, Bradshaw and Blacklock, 1849).

Conder, G. B., *Bishop Burnet and The Times of the English Revolution and Protestant Settlement* (London, James Nisket and Co., 1863).

Costin, William C., and J. Stephen Watson, *The Law and Working of the Constitution: Documents 1660-1914,* Vol. I (London, Adam and Charles Black, 1952).

Cragg, G., *From Puritanism to The Age of Reason* (Cambridge, Harvard University Press, 1950).

Dalrymple, John (ed.), *Memoirs of Great Britain and Ireland,* Vol. III (London, Strahan and Cadell, 1773).

Davenport, John (ed.), *Memoirs of the Court of France, From the year 1684 to 1720,* Translated from the Diary of Marquis De Dangeau. Vol. I (London, Henry Colburn, 1825).

De Beer, E. S. (ed.), *The Diary of John Evelyn,* Vol. IV (Oxford, At The Clarendon Press, 1955).

Doebner, Richard (ed.), *Memoirs of Mary, Queen of England* (Leipzig, Veit and Company, 1886).

Douglas, David C., *English Scholars 1660-1730* (London, Eyre and Spottiswoode, 1939).

Drysdale, A. H., *History of the Presbyterians in England* (London, Publication Committee of the Presbyterian Church of England, 1889).

Duckett, George (ed.), *Penal Laws and Test Act, Questions Touching their Repeal, Propounded in 1687-8 by James II,* Vol. I (London, 1882).

Ellis, Henry, *Ellis Original Letters Illustrative of English History* (London, Harding and Lepard, 1827).

Every, George, *The High Church Party, 1688-1718* (London, S.P.C.K., 1956).

Feiling Keith, *A History of The Tory Party, 1640-1714* (London, Oxford At The Clarendon Press, 1924).

Firth, C. H., *Stuart Tracts, 1603-1693* (London, Archibald Constable and Co., Ltd., 1903).

Fox, Charles James, *A History of the Early Part of the Reign of James The Second;* Appendix (London, William Miller, 1808).

Foxcroft, Helen C., *A Character of the Trimmer* (London, Cambridge University Press, 1945).

——, *The Life and Letters of Sir George Savile,* 2 Vols. (London, Longmans, Green and Co., 1898).

Foxcroft, Helen C., and T. E. S. Clarke, *A Life of Gilbert Burnet* (London, Cambridge at The University Press, 1907).

Garbett, Cyril, *Church and State in England* (London, Hodder and Stoughton, 1950).

Graf, Ernest (ed.), *History of the Popes by Ludwig Pastor,* Vol. XXXII (St. Louis, B. Herder Book Co., 1940).

Grew, Marion E., *William Bentinck and William III* (London, John Murray, 1924).

Gutch, John, *Collectanea Curiosa; or Miscellaneous Tracts*, Vol. I (Oxford, At The Clarendon Press, 1781).

Gwatkin, Henry M., *Church and State in England to the Death of Queen Anne* (London, Longmans, Green and Co., 1917).

Hart, Arthur Tindal, *William Lloyd, 1627-1717* (London, Published for the Church Historical Society, 1952).

Hawkins, L. M., *Allegiance in Church and State* (London, G. Routledge and Sons, Ltd., 1928).

Hay, Malcolm V., *The Enigma of James II* (London, Sands and Co., 1938).

Hills, Henry, *The Catholic Almanac For The Year 1687 Containing Both the Roman and English Calendar* (London, 1687).

The History of King James Ecclesiastical Commission (London, 1711).

Hogan, James (ed.), *Negociations de M. Le Comte D'Avaux en Irelande, 1689-1690* Dublin, Published by the Stationary Office, 1934).

Howe, P. P. (ed.), *The Complete Works of William Hazlitt in Twenty One Volumes*, Vol. XVI (London, T. M. Dent and Sons, Ltd., 1932).

Howell, Bayly T.] *State Trials*, Vol. XII (London, T. C. Hansard, 1810).

Hughes, Philip, *The Catholic Question, 1688-1829* (New York, Benziger Brothers, 1929).

Hunter, Joseph (ed.), *The Diary of Dr. Thomas Cartwright, Bishop of Chester* (London, Printed for the Camden Society, Nichols and Sons, 1843).

Hutton, W. H., *A History of the English Church from the Accession of Charles I to the Death of Anne* (London, Macmillan and Co., Limited, 1903).

Inderwick, F. A., *Side Lights on The Stuarts* (London, Sampson Low, Marston, and Rivington, 1888).

James II., *Royal Tracts, In Two Parts* (Paris, Lucas Imprinter, 1692).

Jessup, Augustus (ed.), *The Lives of the Norths*, 3 Vols. (London, George Bell and Sons, 1890).

Jones, David, *A Continuation of the Secret History of Whitehall From the Abdication of the late King James in 1688 to the Year 1696* (London, 1697).

Jones, David, *The Secret History of Whitehall, from the Restoration of Charles II, Down to the Abdication of the Late King James* (London, 1689).

Jones, Thomas (ed.), *A Catalogue of the Collection of Tracts for and Against Popery*, 2 Vols. (London, Printed for the Chetham Society, 1859, 1864).

Keir, David Lindsay, *The Constitutional History of Modern Britain, 1485-1937* (London, Adam and Charles Black, 1947).

Kenyon, John P., *Robert Spencer, Earl of Sunderland, 1641-1702* (London, Longmans, Green and Co., 1959).

Kerr, Russell J., and Ida Coffin Duncan, *The Portledge Papers being Extracts from the letters of Richard Lapthorne, Gent., of Hatton Garden London, to Richard Coffin* (London, Jonathan Cape, 1928).

Leslie, Stephen, and Sidney Lee, *The Dictionary of National Biography*, Vol. VI (London, Oxford University Press, 1922).

Letters of Eminent Men Addressed to Ralph Thoresby, Vol. I (London, Henry Colburn and Richard Bentley, 1832).

Life of Reverend Richard Baxter (New York, American Tract Society, n.d.).

The Life of William III Late King of England, and Prince of Orange (S. and J. Sprint, 1703).

Lister, T. H., *Life and Administration of Edward, first Earl of Clarendon*, Vol. III (London, Longman, Orme, Brown, Green and Longmans, 1838).

Lomas, Sophie, *Diplomatic Relations of England and France* (Oxford, B. H. Blackwell, 1906).

Luckock, H. M., *The Bishops in the Tower* (London, 1877).

Luttrell, Narcissus, *A Brief Historical Relation of State Affairs from 1678 to 1714*, Vol. I & II (London, Oxford At The University Press, 1852).

Macaulay, Thomas Babington, *The History of England From the Accession of James II*, 2 vols. (New York, Harper and Brothers, 1849).

Mackintosh, James, *History of the Revolution in England in 1688* (London, Longman, Rees, Orme, Brown, Green and Longmans, 1834).

Macpherson, James, *Original Papers; containing the Secret History of Great Britain, From the Restoration To the Accession of the House of Hanover*, Vol. II (London, W. Strahan and T. Cadell, 1774).

Mazure, A. J., *Histoire de la Revolution de 1688 en Angleterre* (Paris, 1825).

Miscellany Poems: The Muses Farewell to Popery (London, 1690).

Negociations De Monsieur Le Comte D'Avaux en Hollande 1685-1688, Vol. VI (Paris, 1753).

Nicholson, Thomas C. and A. S. Turberville, *Charles Talbot, Duke of Shrewsbury* (London, Cambridge at The University Press, 1930).

Ogg, David, *England in the Reigns of James II and William III* (Oxford At The Clarendon Press, 1953).

——, *William III* (London, Collins, 1956).

Orwell, George and Reginald Reynolds (eds.), *British Pamphleteers*, Vol. I (London, Allan Wingate, 1948).

Osborne, Thomas (ed.), *The Harleian Miscellany: or a Collection of Scarce, Curious and Entertaining Pamphlets and Tracts*, Vol. I (London, T. Osborne, 1744).

Petrie, Charles, *The Jacobite Movement* (London, Eyre and Spottiswoode, 1958).

Petty, William (ed.), *The Petty-Southwell Correspondence 1676-1687* (London, Constable and Company, Ltd., 1928).

Pinkham, Lucile, *William III and the Respectable Revolution* (Cambridge, Harvard University Press, 1954).

Plumptre, E. H., *The Life of Thomas Ken*, 2 vols. (London, William Isbister Limited, 1890).

Pollock, John, *The Popish Plot* (London, Duckworth and Company, 1903).

Portus, Garnet, *Caritas Anglicana* (London, A. R. Mowbray and Company, Ltd., 1912).

Powicke, Frederick J., *A Life of The Reverend Richard Baxter. 1615-1691* (Boston, Houghton Mifflin Company, 1924).

Powley, Edward B., *The English Navy in the Revolution of 1688* (London, Cambridge at The University Press, 1928).

Powys, Llewelyn (ed.), *The Life and Times of Anthony Wood* (London, Wishart and Company, 1932).

Quadriennium, Jacobi, *Of the History of the Reign of King James II* (London, James Knapten, 1689).

Raleigh, Walter, *The Complete Works of George Savile First Marquess of Halifax* (Oxford, At The Clarendon Press, 1912).

Reresby, John (ed.), *The Memoirs of the Honorable Sir John Reresby* (London, 1734).

Revolution Politicks: Being a Compleat Collection of All the Reports, Lyes, and Satires which were the Fore-runners of the Great Revolution in 1688 (London, 1783).

Robertson, C. Grant (ed.), *Select Statutes Cases and Documents To Illustrate English Constitutional History 1660-1832* (London, Methuen and Co., 1904).

Rosenfeld, Sybil (ed.), *The Letterbook of Sir George Etherage* (London, Oxford University Press, 1928).

Schlatler, Richard, *Richard Baxter and Puritan Politics* (New Brunswick, New Jersey, Rutgers University Press, 1957).

Scott, Walter, *A Collection of Scarce and Valuable Tracts of the Most Interesting and Entertaining Subjects*, Vol. I (London, T. Cadell and W. Davies, 1809).

The Secret History of The Happy Revolution in 1688 (London, 1715).

Shelmerdine, J. M., *The Secret History of Henrietta, Princess of England Together with Memoirs of the Court of France for One Year, 1688-1689* (London, George Routledge and Sand, Ltd., 1929).

Singer, Samuel W. (ed.), *The Correspondence of Henry Hyde, Earl of Clarendon and of His Brother, Laurence Hyde, Earl of Rochester*, 2 vols. (London, Henry Colburn, 1828).

Stephenson, Carl and Frederick G. Marcham (eds.), *Sources of English Constitutional History* (New York, Harper and Brothers Publishers, 1937).

Stoughton, John, *History of Religion in England*, Vols. IV, V (New York, A. C. Armstrong and Son, 1882).

Strickland, Agnes, *The Lives of the Seven Bishops Committed to The Tower in 1688* (London, Bell and Daldy, 1866).

Sykes, Norman, *William Wake, Archbishop of Canterbury, 1657-1737*, Vol. I (London, Cambridge at The University Press, 1957).

Taylor, Andrew (ed.), *The Works of Symon Patrick*, Vol. IX (London, 1858).

Thompson, Edward Maunde (ed.), *Correspondence of the Family of Hatton* (London, Printed for The Camden Society, Nichols and Sons, 1878).

Thoresby, Ralph, *Letters of Eminent Men Addressed to Ralph Thoresby* (London, Henry Colburn and Richard Bentley, 1832).

Turner, Edward, Raymond, *The Cabinet Council, 1622-1784*, Vol. I (Baltimore, The Johns Hopkins Press, 1930).

Turner, F. C., *James II* (New York, The Macmillan Company, 1948).

Ward, R. Plumer, *An Historical Essay on the Real Character and Amount of the Precedent of the Revolution of 1688*, 2 vols. (London, John Murray, 1838).

Welwood, James, *Memoirs of the Last Hundred Years Preceding the Revolution of 1688* (London, 1736).

PAMPHLETS

An addres to his Grace the Lord Archbishop of Canterbury and the Right Reverend the Bishops Upon Account of their Late Petition (London, 1688).

Adramite, Adam, *A Pastoral Letter from the Four Catholick Bishops to the Lay Catholicks of England* (London, 1688).

Aldrich, Henry, *A Reply to two Discourses Lately Printed at Oxford Concerning the Adoration of our Blessed Saviour in the Holy Eucharist* (Oxford, 1687).

Allen, William, *Killing No Murder: Briefly Discussed in Three Questions* (London, 1689).

Allix, Peter, *A Discourse Concerning Penance Showing How the Doctrine of It in the Church of Rome Makes Void True Repentance* (London, 1688).

——, *An Historical Discourse Concerning the Necessity of the Ministers Intentions in Administering the Sacraments* (London, 1688).

Altham, Michael, *The Creed of Pope Pius IVth, or a Prospect of Popery, Taken from that Authentick Record. With Short Notes* (London, 1687).

——, *Some Queries to Protestants Answered, And an Explanation of the Roman Catholic Beliefs in Four Great Points Considered* (London, 1686).

——, *A Vindication of the Church of England from the foul Aspersions of Schism and Heresie unjustly cast upon her By the Church of Rome,* Part I (London, 1687).

An Answer to the Bishop of Rochester's First Letter to the Earl of Dorset Concerning the Late Ecclesiastical Commission (London, 1689).

An Answer to Two Papers Called a Lords Speech without Doors, and a Commoners Speech Wherein the Objections Against the Present Management of Affairs are Dissolved (London, 1689).

Anglesey, Arthur, *The Kings Right of Indulgence in Spiritual Matters with the Equity thereof, Asserted* (London, 1688).

Atterbury, Lewis, *The Grant Charter of Christian Feasts with the Right Way of Keeping them in a Sermon Preach'd At a Meeting of Several of the Natives and Inhabitants of the County of Buckingham* (London, 1686).

Attlebury, Francis, *An Answer to some Considerations on the Spirit of Martin Luther and the Original of the Reformation* (Oxford, 1687)

Barlow, Thomas, *A Few Plain Reasons why a Protestant of the Church of England Should not Turn Roman Catholic* (London, 1688).

Bent, James, *The Bloody Assizes: or a Compleat History of Life of George Jeffries From His Birth to this Present Time* (London, 1689).

Beverley, Thomas, *The Command of God to His People to Come out of Babylon Demonstrated to Mean the Coming out of the Present Papal Rome* (London, 1688).

Birt, John, *The History of the Persecution of the Valley of Piedmont Containing An Account of What Hath Passed in the Dissipation of the Church and the Inhabitants of the Valleys, which Happened in the Year 1686* (London, 1688).

Bohun, Edmund, *The History of the Desertion, or an Account of all the Publick Affairs in England from the Beginning of September 1688 to the Twelfth of February Following* (London, 1689).

Bossuet, Jacques, *An Exposition of the Doctrine of the Catholick Church in Matters of Controversie: Done into English from the Fifth Edition in French* (London, 1685).

——. *A Pastoral Letter from the Lord Bishop of Meaux to the New Catholics of the Diocese Exhorting them to Keep their Easter* (London, 1686).

——, *A Brief Vindication of the Parliamentary Proceedings Against the Late King James II* (London, 1689).

Brown, Thomas, *Heraclitus Ridens Redivivus: Or a Dialogue Between Harry and Roger Concerning the Times* (Oxford, 1688).

Burnet, Gilbert, *An Answer to a Letter to Dr. Burnet, occasioned by His Letter to Mr. Lowth* (London, 1685).

——, *An Answer to a Paper Printed with Allowance entitled a New Test of the Church of Englands loyalty* (The Hague, 1687).

——, *A Discourse Concerning Transubstantiation and Idolatery. Being an Answer to the Bishop of Oxford's Plea Relating to Those Two Points* (The Hague, 1689.)

——, *A Discourse Wherein is Held Forth the Opposition of the Doctrine, Worship and Practices of the Roman Church, To the Nature, Design, and Character of the Christian Faith* (London, 1689).

——, *An Enquiry into the Measures of Submission to the Supreme Authority* (London, 1687).

——, *An Enquiry into the Present State of Affairs* (The Hague, 1688).

——, *An Enquiry into the Reasons for Abrogating the Test Imposed on All Members of Parliament* (London, 1689).

——, *Fourteen Papers* (The Hague, 1688).

——, *Their Hignesses the Prince and Princess of Orange's Opinions About a*

General Liberty of Conscience Being a Collection of Four Select Papers (The Hague, 1688).

——, The ill Effects of Animosities Among Protestants in England Detected (London, 1689).

——, A Letter from Gilbert Burnet to Mr. Simon Lowth, Vicar of Cosmublene in the Diocese of Canterbury (London, 1685).

——, A Letter Occasioned by the Second Letter to Dr. Gilbert Burnet (London, 1685).

——, The Prince of Orange, His Declaration Showing the Reason Why he Invades England With a Short Preface and Some modest Remarks on It (London, 1688).

——, Reflections on a Paper Entituled His Majesties Reasons For Withdrawing himself from Rochester (London, 1688).

——, Reflections on the Relation of the English Reformation Lately Printed at Oxford, Part I (Amsterdam, 1689).

——, Six Papers Containing Reasons Against Repealing the Acts of Parliament Concerning the Test (The Hague, 1687).

Care, Henry, Animadversions on a Later Paper, entitled a letter to a Dissenter Upon Occasion of his Majesties late Gracious Declaration of Indulgence (London, 1687).

——, Answer to a Paper importing a Petition of the Archbishop of Canterbury and Six other Bishops to His Majesty (London, 1689).

——, The History of Popery; or Pacquet of Advice from Rome, Vol. IV, Containing the Lives of Eighteen Popes (London, 1685).

——, A Modest Enquiry Whether St. Peter were Ever At Rome and Bishop of that Church? (London, 1687).

——, A Reply to the Answer of the Man of No Name to His Grace the Duke of Buckingham's Paper of Religion, and Liberty of Conscience (London, 1685).

Carrington, Henry, An Answer to a Late Pamphlet entitled the Judgment and Doctrine of the Clergy of the Church of England, Concerning one Special Branch of the King's Prerogative; viz in Dispensing with the Penal Laws (London, 1687).

Cartwright, Thomas, A Sermon preached upon the Anniversary solemnity of the Happy Inauguration of our Dread Sovereign Lord King James II in the Collegiate Church of Ripon (London, 1686).

Charles II, Copies of Two Papers Written by the Late Charles II Together with a Copy of a Paper Written by the Late Duchess of York (London, 1686).

——, Declaration of Breda (London, 1660).

——, His Majesty's Declaration to All His Loving Subjects, December 6, 1662 (London, 1662).

——, His Majesty's Declaration to All His Loving Subjects, March 15, 1672 (London, 1672).

——, His Majesty's Declaration to all His Loving Subjects, listing the Causes and Reasons that moved him to dissolve the last two Parliaments (London, 1681).

Claggett, Nicholas, A Persuasive to an Ingenuous Tryal of Opinions In Religion (London, 1685).

Claggett, William, A Discourse Concerning the Worship of the Blessed Virgin and the Saints With an Account of the Beginnings of the Rise of it amongst Christians in Answer to M. de Meaux's Appeal to the Faith Age, in his Exposition and Pastoral Letter (London, 1686).

——, The Queries offered by T. W. to the Protestants Concerning The English Reformation Reprinted and Answered (London, 1689).

——, Several Captious Queries Concerning the English Reformation First Proposed by Dean Manby in Latin, and Afterwards by T. W. in English (London, 1689).

——, A View of the Whole Controversy between the representer and the Answerer with an Answer to the representers last reply. In which are laid open some of the methods by which Protestants are Misrepresented by Papists (London, 1687).

A Collection of Papers relating to the Present Juncture of Affairs in England. The Third Edition (London, 1688).

Collier, Jeremy, The Desertion Discussed, in a Letter to a Country Gentleman (London, 1688).

Corker, James, Roman Catholic Principles, in Reference to God and the King (London, 1687).

Croft, Herbert, A Short Discourse Concerning the Reading His Majesties Late Declaration in the Churches, Set Forth by the Right Reverend Father in God Herbert Lord Bishop of Hereford (London, 1689).

Darrell, William, A Letter to the Author of the Reply to the Author of the Late Paper called a full Answer to Dr. Tenons Concerning the Eucharist (London, 1687).

A Discourse for taking off the Tests and Penal Laws about Religion (London, 1687).

Ellis, Thomas, The Protestant Resolved: or a Discourse Shewing the Unreasonableness of his Turning Roman Catholic for Salvation (London, 1689).

Evans, John, The Case of Kneeling at the Holy Sacrament Stated and Resolved, Part II (London, 1685).

An Exact Account of the Whole Proceedings Against the Right Reverend Father in God, Henry Lord Bishop of London, Before the Lord Chancellor, and the other Ecclesiastical Commissioners (London, 1689).

Fagel, Mijn Heer Gasper, The Highnesses the Prince and Princes of Orange's Opinion about a General Liberty of Conscience (The Hague, 1688).

——, A Letter writ by Mijn Heer Fagel Pensioner to the Great and Mighty Lords, the States of Holland and Westfriedland, Writ in French on the 9th of April, 1688 (The Hague, 1689).

——, A Letter Writ to Mr. James Stewart (The Hague, 1689).

Fairfax, James, An Impartial Relation of the Whole Proceedings Against St. Mary Magdalen College in Oxon, In the Year 1687 of our Lord, Containing Only Matters of Fact, As they Occurrred (London, 1689).

Ferguson, Robert, A Brief Justification of the Prince of Orange's Descent into England and of the Kingdoms Late Recourse to Arms With a Modest Disquisition of What May Become the Wisdom and Justice of the Ensuing Convention in Their Disposal of the Crown (London, 1688).

——, The Design of Enslaving England discouraged in the Incroachments upon the Power and Privileges of Parliament by King Charles II (London 1688).

——, A Representation of the Threatening Dangers Impending over Protestants in Great Britain Before the Coming of His Highness the Prince of Orange (London, 1688).

A Fifth Collection of Papers Relating to the Present Juncture of Affairs in England (London, 1689).

Fleetwood, William, The Life and Death of the Blessed Virgin Giving an account of the Miracles Ascrib'd to Her by Romish Writers With the Grounds of the Worship Paid to Her (London, 1689).

A Form of Prayer and Thankgiving to Almighty God, for having made his Highness the Prince of Orange The Glorious Instrument of the Great Deliverance of the Kingdom from Popery and Ambitious Power (London, 1689).

A Fourth Collection of Papers relating to the Present Juncture of Affairs in England (London, 1689).

Free Thoughts of the Penal Laws, Tests, and some Late Printed Papers Touching Both (London, 1689).

Frezer, Augustus, *The Divine Original and the Supreme Dignity of Kings, No Defensative against Death* (Oxford, 1685).

A Friendly Letter to Father Petre Concerning his Part in the Late King's Government (London, 1690).

Gee, Edward, *An Answer to the Compiler of the Nubes Testium* (London, 1689).

——, *The Primitive Fathers no Papists: In Answer to the Vindicator of the Nubes Testium* (London, 1689).

——, *A Vindication of the Principles of the Author of the Answer to the Compiler of the Nubes Testium from the Charge of Popery* (London, 1689).

Giles, William, *A Defence of Dr. Sherlock's Preservative against Popery in Reply to a Jesuit's Answer Wherein the Reverend Father's Reasonings are fully Confuted* (London, 1689).

Goodwin, Thomas, *Examination of the New Articles of the Roman Creed by Catholic Tradition* (London, 1688).

——, *Transubstantiation, a Peculiar article of the Roman Catholick Faith Which was never own'd by the Ancient Church or Any of the Reform'd Churches, In Answer to a Late Discourse Call'd, Reasons for abrogating the Test* (London, 1689).

Gother, John, *An Amicable Accomodation of the Difference between the Representer and the Answerer in Return to the Last Reply Amongst the Papists Protesting against Protestant Popery* (London, 1686).

——, *A Discourse of the Use of Images: In Relation to the Church of England and the Church of Rome, in Vindication of Nubes Testium* (London, 1687).

——, *Good Advice to the Pulpits Delivered in a few Cautions for Keeping up the Reputation of those Chairs, and Preserving the Nation in Peace* (London, 1687).

——, *Nubes Testium: or A Collection of The Primitive Fathers* (London, 1687).

——, *A Papist Misrepresented and Presented: Or a Twofold Character of Popery* (London, 1685).

——, *A Papist Misrepresented and Represented: Or a Twofold Character of Popery* (London, 1685).

——, *Papist Protesting against Protestant Popery in Answer to a Discourse Entitled A Papist not Mis-represented by Protestants. Being a Vindication of the Papist Mis-Represented and Represented, And the Reflections upon the Answer* (London, 1685).

——, *The Pope's Supremacy Asserted From the Considerations of Some Protestants And the Practice of the Primitive Church in A Dialogue Between a Church-Divine and a Seeker: In Vindication of Nubes Testium* (London, 1689).

——, *Transubstantiation defended, and Proved from the Scripture, in Answer to the first Part of a Treatise, Intitled a Discourse Against Transubstantiation* (London, 1687).

Grove, Robert, *An Answer to Mr. Lowth's Letter to Dr. Stillingfleet, In Another Letter to a Friend* (London, 1687).

——, *Seasonable Advice to the Citizens, Burgesses and Freeholders of England Concerning Parliaments, and the Present Elections* (London, 1685).

Hartcliffe, John, *A Discourse Against Purgatory* (London, 1685).

Hascard, Gregory, *A Discourse About the Charge of Novelty upon the Reformed Church of England, made by the Papist, Asking of us the Question, Where was our Religion before Luther* (London, 1685).

Herbert, Edward, *A Short Account of The Authorities in Law, Upon Which Judgment Was given in Sir Edward Hales His Case* (London, 1689).

Hickes, George, *Speculum Beatae Virginis: A Discourse of the Due Praise and Honour of the Virgin Mary* (London, 1686).

An Historical Relation of Several Great and Learned Romanists Who did embrace the Protestant Religion, With Their Reasons for their Change, deliver'd in their Own Words (London, 1689).

Hodges, Thomas, *The Necessity dignity and duty of Gospel Ministers Discoursed of before the University of Cambridge* (London, 1685).

Howell, John, *A Discourse on persecution, or suffering for Christ's sake, Clearing the Notion of It* (London, 1685).

James, Elinor, Mrs. *James Vindication of the Church of England, in an Answer to a Pamphlet Entitled A New Test of the Church of England's Loyalty* (London, 1686).

James II, *Copies of Two Papers written by the late King Charles of Blessed memory; as also a copy of a Paper written by the Late Duchess of York* (London, 1686).

——, *Directions Concerning Preachers* (London, 1685).

——, *His Majesties Gracious Declaration to All His Loving Subjects for Liberty of Conscience* (London, 1687).

——, *His Majesties Gracious Declaration to All His Loving Subjects For Liberty of Conscience* (London, 1688).

——, *Instructions to Ministers, To the Most Reverend Fathers in God, William Lord Archbishop of Canterbury, Primate of all England and Metropolis, and John Archbishop of York* (London, 1685).

——, *A Proclamation for a Toleration in Scotland, February 12, 1687* (London, 1687).

Johnson, Samuel, *The Absolute Impossibility of Transubstantiation Demonstrated* (London, 1689).

——, *A Humble and Hearty Address to all English Protestants in the Army* (London, 1686).

——, *Remarks Upon Dr. Sherlock's Book, entitled the Case of the Allegiance due to Sovereign Princes Stated and Resolved* (London, 1690).

Johnston, Joseph, *A Vindication of the Bishop of Condoms Exposition of the Doctrine of the Catholic Church in Answer to a Book Entitled An Exposition of the Doctrine of the Church of England, etc., with a Letter from the said Bishop* (London, 1686).

The Judgment and Doctrine of the Clergy of the Church of England Concerning one special Branch of the King's Prerogative, viz, Reverend Father in God (London, 1687).

A Justification of the Whole Proceedings of his Majestic King William and Mary of their Royal Highnesses Prince George and Princess Anne, of the Convention, Army, Minister of State, and Others, in this Great Revolution (London, 1688).

Kidder, Richard, *The Judgment of Private Discretion in Matters of Religion* (London, 1687).

——, *A Second Dialogue between a New Catholick Convert and a Protestant, Showing Why he cannot believe the Doctrine of Transubstantiation Though he do firmly believe the Doctrine of the Trinity* (London, 1687).

L'Estrange, Roger, *An Answer to a Letter to a Dissenter Upon Occasion of His Majesties Late Gracious Declaration of Indulgence* (London, 1687).

——, *The Observator defended, by the Author of the Observator* (London, 1685).

A Letter in Answer to Two Main Questions of the First Letter To A Dissenter (London, 1687).

Leyburn, John, *A Reply to the Answer Made Upon the Three Royal Papers* (London, 1686).

Lloyd, William, *An Answer to The Bishop of Oxford's Reasons For Abrogating The Test Imposed on All Members of Parliament* (London, 1689).

Maimbourg, Louis, *A Peaceable Method for the Remitting Protestant and Catholics in matters of Faith: Principally on the Subject of the Holy Eucharist* (London, 1686).

Manningham, Thomas, *A Short View of the Most Gracious Providence of God in the Restoration: In A Full Answer to Several Scandals Cast Upon him in Matters of Religion, Government, and Succession* (London, 1685).

——, *A Solemn Humiliation for the Murder of Charles I, With Some Remarks on Those Popular Mistakes, Concerning Popery, Zeal, and the extent of Subjection, which had a fatal Influence in our Civil Wars* (London, 1686).

Marvell, Andrew, *A Short Historical Essay Touching General Councils, Creeds, and Impositions in Matters of Religion. Very Seasonable At This Time* (London 1687).

Maurice, Henry, *The Antithelemite, or An Answer to Certain Queries by the Duke of Buckingham, Concerning toleration, and to the Consideration of an Unknown Author* (London, 1685).

——, *Doubts Concerning the Roman Infallibility* (London, 1689).

——, *The Ministers Reasons for his Not Reading the Kings Declaration Friendly Debated* (1689).

A Memorial from the English Protestants for Their Hignesses the Prince and Princess of Orange (1688).

A Modest Censure of the Immodest Letter to a Dissenter Upon Occasion of His Majesty's late Gracious Declaration for Liberty of Conscience (London, 1688).

Nalson, John, *The Present Interest of England: or a Confutation of the Whiggish conspirators Anti-Monyan principle* (London, 1685).

——, *Transubstantiation Contrary to Scripture: Or, The Protestants Answer To The Seekers Request* (London, 1689).

The New Test of the Church of England's Loyalty, Examined by the Old Test of Truth and Honesty (London, 1688).

Northleigh, John, *Parliamentum Pacificum: Or, The Happy Union of King and People in an Healing Parliament* (London, 1689).

Parker, Samuel, *Reasons for Abrogating the Test, Imposed Upon All Members of Parliament* (London, 1689).

Patrick, Symon, *The Virgin Mary Misrepresented by the Roman Church, In the traditions of that Church, Covering her Life*, Part I (London, 1689).

Pelling, Edward, *The Antiquity of the Protestant Religion: With An Answer to Mr. Sclater's Reasons, and the Collections Made by the Author of the Pamphlet Entitled Nubes Testium, the First Part* (London, 1688).

——, *A Fourth Letter to a Person of Quality Being an Historical account of the Doctrine of the Sacrament* (London, 1689).

——, *The Apostate Protestant, A Letter to A Friend Occasioned by the Late Reprinting of a Jesuits Book About Succession To the Crown of England* (London, 1685).

——, *The True Mark of the Beast: or the Present Degeneracy of the Church of Rome* (London, 1685).

Penn, William, *An Answer to a Dissenter Upon Occasion of his Majesties Late Gracious Declaration of Indulgence* (London, 1687).

——, *Good Advice to the Church of England, Roman Catholick and Protestant Dissenter* (London, 1687).

——, *The Great and Popular Objection against the Repeal of the Penal Laws and Tests Briefly stated and Considered* (London, 1689).

——, *The Reasonableness of Toleration and the Unreasonableness of Penal Laws* (London, 1688).

——, *Three Letters Tending to demonstrate How the Security of this Nation Against All future persecution for Religion Lies in the Abolishment of the*

Present Penal Laws and Tests, and in the Establishment of a New Law for Universal Liberty of Conscience (London, 1689).

Popple, William, *A letter to Mr. Penn: With His Answer* (London, 1689).

The Proceedings and Trial in The Case of the Most Reverend Father in God William Lord Archbishop of Canterbury (London, 1689).

Proast, Jonas, *The Case of Reading the Declaration for Liberty of Conscience Briefly Stated in Four Propositions* (London, 1688).

Pulton, Andrew, *An Answer to a Letter From a Clergyman in the City, to His Friend in the Country, Containing his reasons for Not Reading the Declaration* (London, 1689).

——, *Remarks of Andrew Pulton Master in the Savoy upon Dr. Thomas Tenison's Late Narrative with a Confutation of the Doctor's Rule of Faith, and a Reply to A. Chresners Pretended Vindication* (London, 1688).

——, *A True and Full Account of a Conference Held About Religion Between Dr. Tenison and Andrew Pulton One of the Masters in the Savoy* (London, 1688).

Rawlett, John, *A Dialogue betwixt two Protestants, In Answer to A Popish Catechism Called A Short Catechism against all Factions* (London, 1686).

Reflections upon the Late Great Revolution (London, 1688).

Reflections Upon the New Test, and the Reply Thereto With A Letter of Sir Francis Walsingham's Concerning the Penal Laws Made in the Reign of Queen Elizabeth (London, 1688).

Reflections Upon Our Late and Present Proceedings in England (London, 1688).

Remonstrance and Protestation of All the Good Protestants of this Kingdom, against Deposing their Lawful Sovereign King James II with Reflections Thereupon (London, 1688).

Roberts, Richard, *A Sermon Preached at St. Thomas' Church in Bristol, September 3, 1685* (London, 1685).

Sabran, Lewis, *Dr. Sherlock's Preservative Considered. The First Part and its defence Proved to Contain Principles Which destroy All right use of Reason, Fathers, Counsels, undermined Divine Faith, and Abuse* (London, 1689).

Savile, George, *The Anatomy of an Equivalent* (London, 1688).

——, *A Letter from a Clergyman in the City, To his Friend in the Country Containing his Reasons For not Reading the Declaration,* (London, 1689).

——, *A Letter to a Dissenter upon Occasion of His Majesties Late Gracious Declaration of Indulgence* (London, 1688).

——, *Remarks Upon a Pamphlet Stiled a Letter To a Dissenter* (London, 1687).

——, *A Second Letter to a Dissenter Upon Occasion of His Majesties Late Gracious Declaration of Indulgence* (London, 1688).

Sclater, Edward, *The Reasons of Edward Sclater, Minister of Putney, for his Conversion to the Catholic Faith and Communion* (London, 1687).

A Seasonable Discourse Shewing the Necessity of Union Amongst Protestants in Opposition to Popery, As the only Means 'Under God' to preserve the Reformed Religion (London, 1689).

See, Thomas, *Seek and you will Find: or a Search into the Grounds of Religion* (London, 1685).

Sergeant, John, *A Letter to Edward Stillingfleet in Answer to the Arguing Part of his First Letter to Mr. Thomas Godden* (London, 1687).

——, *The Schism of the Church of England Demonstrated in Four Arguments* Oxford, 1688).

Seven Papers, viz, the Grounds and Reasons of the Laws against Popery (London, 1688).

Seventh Collection of Papers relating to the present Juncture of Affairs in England (London, 1688).

Sharp, John, *A Discourse Concerning Conscience, Concerning a Doubting Conscience, The Second Part* (London, 1685).

Sheldon, Gilbert, *Fair Warning or XXV Reasons Against Toleration and Indulgence of Popery* (London, 1663).

Sherlock, William, *An Answer to the amicable accomodation of the Difference Between the Representer and the Answerer* (London, 1686).

——, *An Answer to a discourse intituled Papists Protesting Against Protestant Popery* (London, 1686).

——, *An Answer to the Request to Protestants, to Produce Plain Scripture directly Authorizing These tenets* (London, 1688).

——, *A Letter from a Gentleman in the City to a Friend in the Country* (London, 1688).

——, *A Letter to a Member of the Convention* (London, 1688).

——, *A Letter to Anonymous In Answer to his Three Letters to Dr. Sherlock about Church Communion* (London, 1686).

——, *A Papist Not Misrepresented by Protestants, Being a Reply to the Reflections Upon the Answer to a Papist Misrepresented and Represented* (London, 1686).

——, *A Preservative against Popery: Being some Plain Directions to Unlearned Protestants, How to Dispute with Romish Priests* (London, 1688).

——, *A Short Summary of the Principal Controversies Between the Church of England and the Church of Rome* (London, 1688).

——, *A Vindication of both Parts of the Preservative against Popery in Answer to the Cavils of Lewis Sabran, Jesuit* (London, 1688).

Shute, Giles, *A New Test in lieu of the Old One, by way of Supposition* (London, 1688).

Sixth Collection of Papers Relating to the Present Juncture of Affairs in England London, 1689).

Smith, Thomas, *A Pacifist Discourse of the Causes and Remedies of the Differences About Religion, Which distract the Peace of Christendom* (London, 1688).

Speke, Hugh, *The Prince of Orange His Declaration of November 28, 1688* (London, 1688).

Sprat, Thomas, *A Letter from the Bishop of Rochester, To the Right Honorable The Earl of Dorset and Middlesex, Lord-Chancellor of His Majesties Household Concerning his Sitting in the Late Ecclesiastical Commission* (London, 1688).

Stanley, William, *A Discourse Concerning the Devotions of the Church of Rome. Especially, as compared with those of the Church of England* (London, 1685).

Stephens, Edward, *Important Questions of State, Law, Justice, Prudence, Both Civil and Religious, Upon the Late Revolutions and Present State of these Nations* (London, 1689).

——, *Reflections Upon the Occasioners of the last Year From 5 November 1688 to 5 November 1689* (London, 1689).

——, *The True English Government, and Misgovernment of the last Four Kings, With the ill-Consequences Thereof, Briefly noted in Two Little Tracts* (London, 1689).

Steward, Richard, *A Brief But Full Vindication of the Church of England from the Romanists Charge of Schism* (London, 1688).

Stewart, James, *J. S. Answer to a Letter writ by Mijn Heer Fagel Pensioner to the States of Holland and Westfrieland Concerning the Repeal of the Penal Laws and Test* (London, 1688).

Stillingfleet, Edward, *An Answer to some Papers lately printed Concerning the Authority of the Catholic Church in Matters of Faith, and the Reformation of the Church of England truly Represented* (London, 1686).

——, *The Doctrine and Practice of the Church of Rome, In Answer to a Book Intituled, A Papist Misrepresented, and Represented, etc.* (London, 1686).

——, *The Doctrine of the Trinity and Transubstantiation Compared As To Scripture, Reason, and Tradition in A New Dialogue Between a Protestant and a Papist* (London, 1688).

——, *A Vindication of the Answer to some Late Papers Concerning the Unity and Authority of the Catholic Church and the Reformation of the Church of England* (London, 1688).

Stratford, Nicholas, *A Discourse Concerning the Necessity of Reformation,* 1st Part London, 1685).

——, *The Necessity of Reformation with Respect to the Errors and Corruptions of the Church of Rome,* 2nd Part (London, 1686).

——, *The People's Right to Read the Holy Scriptures Asserted* (London, 1688).

——, *The Lay Christians Obligation to Read the Scripture* (London, 1688).

Tenison, Thomas, *A Defence Between the Protestant and Socinian Methods In Answer to a Book Written by a Romanist, and Intitled, The Protestant Plea for a Socinian* (London, 1687).

——, *A Friendly Debate Between a Roman Catholick and A Protestant Concerning the Doctrine of Transubstantiation* (London, 1688).

A Third Collection of Papers Relating to the Present Juncture of Affairs in England (London, 1688).

Thurlin, Thomas, *The Necessity of Obedience to Spiritual Governors, Asserted in a Sermon, May 10, 1686* (London, 1686).

Tillotson, John, *A Discourse Against Transubstantiation* (London, 1687).

To the King's Most Excellent Majesty the Humble Address of the Atheists, or the Sect of the Epicureans (London, 1687).

The True Spirit of Popery or The Treachery and Cruelty of the Papists Exercised against the Protestants in All Ages and Countries Where Popery has had the Upper-hand (London, 1688).

The True Test of the Jesuits: Or, The Spirit of that Society Disloyal to God, Their King, and Neighbors (Amsterdam, 1688).

Villiers, George, *Considerations Moving to a toleration, and Liberty of Conscience with Arguments Inducing to a Cessation of the Penal Statutes against all Dissenters* (London, 1685).

——, *A Short Discourse Upon the Reasonableness of Mens having a Religion, or Worship of God* (London, 1685).

Wake, William, *A Continuation of the Present State of the Controversy* (London, 1688).

——, *A Discourse Concerning the Nature of Idolatry: In which a Late Author's True and Only Notion of Idolatry is Considered and Confuted* (London, 1688).

——, *A Second Defence of the Exposition of the Doctrine of the Church of England: Against the New Exception of M. de Meaux and His Vindicator* (London, 1688).

Ward, Thomas, *Monomachia: or a duel Between Dr. Thomas Tenison Pastor of St. Martins, and a Catholick Soldier* (London, 1687).

Warren, Erasmus, *Religious Loyalty or old Allegiance to the New King* (London, 1685).

Watts, Thomas, *Dialogues Between Philerene and Philalethe, A Lover of Peace, and a Lover of Truth Concerning the Pope's Supremacy, Part II* (London, 1688).

Welwood, James, *An Answer to the Late King James Declaration to All his Subjects in the Kingdom of England* (London, 1689).

——, *Reasons Why the Parliament of Scotland cannot Comply With the Late King James* (London, 1689).

Wharton, Henry, *The Speculum Ecclesiasticum, considered, or An Ecclesiastical Prospective-Class, Considered In Its False Reasonings and Quotations* (London, 1688).

Whitby, Daniel, *A Demonstration that the Church of Rome and Her Councils Have Erred* (London, 1688).

——, *A Treatise of Traditions* (London, 1688).

Whittie, John, *An exact Diary of the late Expedition of His Illustrious Highness the Prince of Orange, (Now King of Great Britain) From his Palace at The Hague, To His Landing at Torbay* (London, 1689).

Wild, Robert, *The Happy Union of England and Holland: Or, The Advantageous Consequences of the Alliance of the Crown of Great Britain With the States General of the United Provinces* (London, 1689).

Williams, John, *A Discourse Concerning the Celebration of Divine Service In An Unknown Tongue* (London, 1685).

——, *An Address to the Address Presented to the Ministers of the Church of England* (London, 1688).

——, *The Difference Between the Church of England and the Church of Rome in Opposition to a Late Book, Intitled An Argument Between the Catholics of England, and Catholics of Rome* (London, 1687).

——, *The Protestants Answer to the Catholic Letter to the Seeker, Or a Vindication of the Protestants Answer, to the Seekers Request* (London, 1688).

William III, *The Prince of Orange His Declaration Shewing the Reasons of the Present Invasion, For the Defence of the Protestant Religion, and for the Re Establishment of the Laws and Liberty of the Kingdom of Scotlund* (London, 1688).

——, *The Prince of Orange's Third Declaration* (London, 1688).

Witt, Cornelius, *A Letter from Holland touching Liberty of Conscience* (Amsterdam, 1088).

Woodhead, Abraham, *The Protestants Plea for a Socinian: Justifying His Doctrine from being opposite to Scripture or Church-Authority; And His from being Guilty of Heresie or Schism. In Five Conferences* (London, 1686).

——, *Two Discourses Concerning the Adoration of our Blessed Saviour in the Holy Eucharist* (London, 1687).

GOVERNMENT DOCUMENTS

Cobbett, William, *Parliamentary History of England from the Norman Conquest in 1066 to the Year 1803*, Vol. IV (London, 1806).

A Collection of the Parliamentary Debates in England, From the Year 1668 to the Present Times, Vol. II (London, 1741).

Great Britain, Public Record Office, *Calendar of State Papers Domestic, 1663-4* (London, His Majesty's Stationary Office, 1906).

Great Britain, Public Record Office, *Calendar of State Papers Domestic, 1670* (London, His Majesty's Stationary Office, 1908).

Great Britain, Public Record Office, *Calendar of State Papers Domestic, 1671-2* (London, His Majesty's Stationary Office, 1912).

Great Britain, Public Record Office, *Calendar of State Papers Domestic, 1673* (London, His Majesty's Stationary Office, 1914).

Great Britain, Public Record Office, *Calendar of State Papers Domestic, 1673-5* London, His Majesty's Stationary Office, 1914).

Great Britain, Historical Manuscripts Commission, *Manuscripts of the Duke of Portland*, Vol. III (London, Her Majesty's Stationary Office, 1892).

Great Britain, Historical Manuscripts Commission, *Manuscripts of the Duke of Hamilton,* Appendix, Part VI (London, Her Majesty's Stationary Office, 1887).

Great Britain, Historical Manuscripts Commission, *Manuscripts of the Duke of Rutland,* Vol. II (London, Her Majesty's Stationary Office, 1888-89).

Great Britain, Historical Manuscripts Commission, *Manuscripts of the Earl of Charlemont,* Vol. I (London, Her Majesty's Stationary Office, 1891).

Great Britain, Historical Manuscripts Commission, *Manuscripts of the Earl of Dartmouth,* Report XI, Appendix V (London, Her Majesty's Stationary Office, 1887).

Great Britain, Historical Manuscripts Commission, *Manuscripts of the Earl of Downshire,* Vol. I (London, His Majesty's Stationary Office, 1924).

Great Britain, Historical Manuscripts Commission, *Manuscripts of the Earl of Lindsey* (London, Her Majesty's Stationary Office, 1895).

Great Britain, Historical Manuscripts Commission, 8th Report (London, George Eyre and William Spottiswoode, 1881).

Great Britain, Historical Manuscripts Commission, *Le Fleming Manuscripts,* Vol. XII, Appendix Seven (London, Her Majesty's Stationary Office, 1890).

Great Britain, Historical Manuscripts Commission, *Manuscripts of Lord Kenyon,* 14th Report, Appendix, Part IV (London, Her Majesty's Stationary Office, 1894).

Grey, Anchitell, *Debates of The House of Commons From the Year 1667 to the Year 1694* (London, Herry and Cave, 1763).

The History and Proceedings of the House of Commons From the Restoration to the Present Time, Vol. II (London, Richard Chandler, 1742).

Journals of The House of Commons, Vols. VIII-IX (London, Printed by Order of the House of Commons).

Journals of The House of Lords, Beginning Anno Primo Jacobi Secundi, Vol. IV (London).

MAGAZINE ARTICLES

Abernathy, George R., Jr., "Clarendon and the Declaration of Indulgence", *The Journal of Ecclesiastical History,* XI (April, 1960), 55-73.

Marsh, J. B., "The Indulgence of 1672", *The Congregationalist,* I (1872), 460-467.

Mullett, Charles F., "A Case of Allegiance: William Sherlock and the Revolution of 1688", *The Huntington Library Quarterly,* X (November, 1946), 83-103.

——, "Protestant Dissent As Crime, 1660-1828", *The Review of Religion,* (May, 1949), 339-353.

——, "Religion, Politics and Oaths in the Glorious Revolution', *The Review of Politics,* X (October, 1948), 462-474.

——, "Toleration and Persecution in England, 1660-89", *Church History,* XVIII (March, 1949), 3-28.

NEWSPAPER

London Gazette, March 21, 1687.

INDEX